Sun Tzu and the Project Battleground

SUN TZU AND THE PROJECT BATTLEGROUND

CREATING PROJECT STRATEGY FROM 'THE ART OF WAR'

David E. Hawkins

and

Shan Rajagopal

First published 2005 by
PALGRAVE MACMILLAN
Houndmills, Basingstoke, Hampshire RG21 6XS and
175 Fifth Avenue, New York, N.Y. 10010
Companies and representatives throughout the world

PALGRAVE MACMILLAN is the global academic imprint of the Palgrave
Macmillan division of St. Martin's Press, LLC and of Palgrave Macmillan Ltd.
Macmillan® is a registered trademark in the United States, United Kingdom
and other countries. Palgrave is a registered trademark in the European
Union and other countries.

ISBN 1–4039–4321–4

This book is printed on paper suitable for recycling and made from fully
managed and sustained forest sources.

A catalogue record for this book is available from the British Library.

Library of Congress Cataloging-in-Publication Data
Hawkins, David E., 1947–
    Sun Tzu and the project battleground: creating project stratgegy from 'The Art of
    War' by Sun Tzu / by David E. Hawkins and Shan Rajagopal.
        p. cm.
    Includes bibliographical references and index.
    ISBN 1–4039–4321–4 (cloth)
        1. Strategic planning. 2. Business planning. 3. Project management. 4. Sunzi,
    6th cent. B.C. Sunzi bing fa. I. Rajagopal, Shan. II. Title.
    HD30.28.H387 2004
    658.4'04—dc22   2004051638

10   9   8   7   6   5   4   3   2   1
14   13   12   11   10   09   08   07   06   05

Printed and bound in Great Britain by
Creative Print & Design (Wales), Ebbw Vale

The one who figures on victory at headquarters before even doing battle is the one who has the most strategic factors on his side. The one who figures on inability to prevail at headquarters before doing battle is the one with the least strategic factors on his side. The one with many strategic factors in his favour wins, the one with few strategic factors loses – how much more so for one with no strategic factors in his favour. Observing the matter in this way, I can see who will win and who will lose.

Sun Tzu, 'The Art of War', circa 500 BC

Dedicated

to

the 'project warriors' of modern time

'May the Supreme Force, however one conceives it to be, guide the indwelling spirit of the warriors.'

Contents

Preface

The business world of major projects has always, to those involved, been referred to as a battlefield. This is perhaps less reflective of the participants and more to encapsulate the stresses and frustrations that are encountered when considering the complexity of such ventures. From our backgrounds in the construction world, we have both had to confess that many times we have felt as if waging war would be a lot simpler than some of the challenges we faced.

Despite having the firm view that most business activities prosper when based on collaboration rather than conflict, we have often felt that, at certain stages of various developments, recourse to a military perspective will help to focus one's attention.

Many years ago, we both read Sun Tzu's 'The Art of War', and since then have both repeatedly taken the book from the shelf to refresh our thinking. Interestingly, as we have matured, so we have found more value each time. We also formed the view that while the focus of Sun Tzu was as a military strategist, the underlying influence was to exploit power strategy rather than to rely on force in battle. In many cases there is a clear view that winning is better achieved without a battle, and that the development of alliances makes one stronger and aids success.

We have spent many hours studying the writings of Sun Tzu and the many interpretations that have been done. Each has its merit and opens up the thinking processes. We would strongly recommend that the writings of Master Sun be studied by anyone venturing into the business world. From the viewpoint of this book, we want to take Sun Tzu's original concepts and address them in terms of our own experiences in the execution of projects.

Many times we have found others who revert to military analogies when considering different and difficult situations. We all start by wanting to 'take the high ground' and we are sure readers have considered the cavalry maxim 'attack is the best means of defence'. The more we read the original text of 'The Art of War', the more we appreciate its value in terms of the application of strategy to our day-to-day activities.

The development of commercial organizations should always start from the perspective of establishing a business strategy, and devolve into planning, tactics and implementation. This is not new; every business guru or consultant will give you a similar message. In an ever more complex global market, the task becomes more difficult and the business landscape or terrain more inherently perilous to navigate. It therefore occurred to us that to try to utilize the original writings and translate these into modern guidelines might be helpful.

As devotees of Sun Tzu's writing, we wanted in any event to challenge our own thinking and try to elaborate within an environment of which we had some understanding. As with any ancient text, the words and similarities are not always clear-cut. Therefore we have leaned on earlier, more academic, authors for their help – in particular, the work done by Lionel Giles, whose translation and research we have found most helpful.

There was a certain dilemma when considering this project. In military terms it is not usually difficult to identify the opposition, which may be a single entity or an alliance, or even possibly disparate groups. In the global business world such identification of opponents is more complex. As an example, in initial negotiations it may be customer and contractor in opposition, but after contract it may be that most issues are related to external organizations and thus customer and contractor then work in alliance. We also felt that while the strategy implications of Sun Tzu are valid, using such terms as 'the enemy' would not be constructive. We have therefore chosen to refer to 'opponents' in all cases and leave the individual reader to assess the application of the writings in their own case.

What may also be a little confusing to the reader, at least initially, is that the original writings are not totally segregated by subject and content. Sun Tzu will address a specific stage in the strategy development but then interject comments which the reader may think should have been covered elsewhere. Our view is that this reflects the integrated nature of his approach. All martial arts specialist writings and applications are viewed around the harmony of many issues, influences and skills. Thus complete separation of subjects is neither possible nor desirable.

We would suggest that this philosophy is also true in the global market, since seldom is there a single cause and effect. Most problems are combinations of interrelated issues and more often than not so are the solutions. Therefore, in many ways, the approach taken 2,500 years ago in a military context is a good training medium for today's business world.

We have taken the key segments of the writings and assigned to these our view of their applicability within the project and business world. To aid those who may want to read further we have outlined these so there is a baseline against which to read, and we hope also to enjoy and to value, the interpretation.

Laying plans

In an increasingly complex global business world, the development of a clear strategy is essential to the success of any venture. The value of Sun Tzu's work and its applicability will, we hope, reinforce this view for the reader. In a project environment it is crucial that the organization is able to align the necessary strategy of the project with the overall business perspective. As projects generally cross corporate, functional and geographical boundaries, a uniform understanding of the overall goals and objectives is crucial.

Sun Tzu delineates his approach using five key factors: 'the moral law', which we would interpret as the overall business vision and mission combined with the objectives of the specific project; 'Heaven', which is in our view a correlation with the business economic environment; 'Earth', from an operational viewpoint reflects the political as well as the physical landscape; 'the Commander', which we hope is clear to all; and 'Method and Discipline', which we would consider to be the organizational structure, skills and business processes.

Waging war

Any battle is likely to require a large commitment of resources and its outcome is very dependent on the approach and skills deployed. Sun Tzu talks about establishing plans of attack and the deployment of resources. In a global project, the use of integrated planning and effective processes is linked inextricably to skills, resources and tools. It is also clear that, as related by Sun Tzu, the longer a battle lasts, the greater the depletion of resources and the less effective the troops. It is also a certain fact that the longer the battle is enacted the more dependence there is on adequate supply lines.

Attack by stratagem

In ancient times the laying of a siege was both costly and, in most cases, ineffective. The true art of any war is to win without fighting the battle. We would surmise that there are few, if any, direct correlations of a siege in the modern business world. But if you look at the project world, we confess that extended projects with a difficult customer have sometimes formed the opinion that the siege approach was still common.

Sun Tzu also addresses the benefits of splitting alliances of opponents and establishing alliances of one's own as an effective approach. We strongly believe that, in the world market and in particular the development of major projects, sound alliance partners can provide an invaluable route to success.

Tactical disposition

In this section the emphasis is on the effective deployment of resources, but more so on the analysis of what is needed to win. Those who have the strategy to win will in the main be successful. What Sun Tzu relates to is the five steps of Measurement, Assessment, Calculation, Comparison and Victory. In our terms this is risk management, a key part of establishing any sound project venture. Assessing the appropriate resources and skills and ensuring that they are available. Establishing what is needed, against the background of the opposition's capabilities, leads to a successful strategy.

Energy

Success in any venture is a factor of understanding one's strengths and weaknesses, and ensuring that energy is deployed effectively. This has to be done with a good understanding of the landscape of the business environment. It is essential to understand the use of both orthodox and unorthodox approaches. Sun Tzu clearly identifies the need to be cautious about relying simply on power and size, which may in fact being counter-productive.

Weak points and strong

The tactics involved in any battle, game or business venture are a crucial part of the route to success. As with any negotiation strategy, the position is often enhanced by establishing a reverse perspective of one's stance. Therefore, if you are strong, you appear weak; if you are organized, you appear disorganized. At the same time you need to understand the relative position of your opponents in order to exploit their weaknesses, then ensure that you do not create a consistent picture, which can be predictable, and maintain adaptability to react to change.

Manoeuvring

The essence of any successful campaign is not simply having the best-trained, and best-equipped, troops; it relies on strong leadership and clear, effective communications. In any project, time is usually the biggest problem. Extended projects will always create the need to change tactics, and maintaining a clear focus for all is crucial. To ensure success, it is important to support and encourage those who need to maintain enthusiasm.

Variation in tactics

Sun Tzu outlines the principle need for any military action to be successful – the organization must be responsive and adaptable. He links this firmly to the style of leadership which, if fixed in a certain style, will eventually create conflict with the events at hand. In any project, both external influences and the need for innovation will inevitably lead to change. Change is the curse of all projects, and the analysis of those projects that fail frequently highlights the cause originating with weak change management and a lack of adaptability.

The army on the march

Understanding one's relative position in the marketplace and those of one's opponents is fundamental in ensuring that one anticipates and reacts appropriately. The fulcrum of most business ventures is successful negotiations. This activity is perhaps the most likely to evoke conflict and, if not managed strategically and with forethought, will result in failure. It is the arena where the total focus of the project team will need to work in unison.

Terrain

In Sun Tzu's terms, any general must have a clear view of the terrain and the obstacles or advantages that this may provide. In any project, these challenges will vary over time and many will arise not from any planned approach but rather by chance and the actions of others. For the project, maintaining a close view of these impacts and counter-actions through critical analysis is crucial, because what may have been obvious at the start can be lost over time. In the same vein, the successful conclusion of a project will seldom reflect the original plan, and therefore all actions must be balanced against the eventual close-out programme.

The nine situations

Understanding the different marketplaces can also be seen in Sun Tzu's approach to defining the challenges and opportunities of opposing terrains. Considering these nine grounds, or battlefields, is perhaps a good analogy to use when considering an approach and tactics against the background of the business environment and landscape. In the world of global projects, the impact of influences external to the direct participants can be significant. A marsh or a mountain become difficult arenas in which to operate; similarly, in the business landscape some external influences, such as political/ cultural divides, can be equally challenging. In some cases, business success can be so risky that taking to the field may be totally wrong.

The attack by fire

The mastery of fire was the catalyst for human development and the creation of industry. In ancient times, the use of fire as a weapon was common. It is, however, very unpredictable and was often found to flash back on those who created it. In the business world, the catalyst is profit or money and in a similar way, the mismanagement of financial issues can have equally serious effects. Certainly in the global project world, financial management and currency swings can have a major impact on success or failure. All actions must therefore be considered against their cause and possible effect.

The use of spies

Almost 2,000 years after Sun Tzu's the Duke of Wellington initiated the foundation of the modern British military intelligence organization. Both men understood that most wars were in effect won not on the day of the battle but through superior intelligence regarding the strength and tactics to be faced. In the business world, while we may be concerned at the ethical dilemma of the term 'spies', market intelligence is crucial. Often the smallest piece of concrete information can set the seal on a complete strategy.

Sun Tzu has, in our view, as much to offer to today's business world as his advice was able to aid success 2,500 years ago in military conflicts in China. In the global project environment, we believe Sun Tzu's writings can contribute many ideas and reinforce the acknowledgement that successful projects are supported by sound strategy development and implementation. We hope that by the end of this book you will have gained some insight and shared a little of our admiration of Sun Tzu's foresight and perhaps gain an edge in business by adopting some of his basic thinking into your activities.

DAVID E. HAWKINS
SHAN RAJAGOPAL

Acknowledgements

The authors would like to acknowledge the work of Lionel Giles, whose original translation in 1910 was the first to be comprehensively translated in English, it has been the foundation of many subsequent translations. The authors have used Giles's translation as the firm basis for the sake of application and interpretation. Furthermore, the authors very much like to acknowledge Graham Bash Pte Ltd., based in Singapore, for very kindly giving us permission to use Lionel Giles translation.

In addition there are many experts in this field who have provided insight and encouragement. The authors would like to acknowledge and extend their appreciation to Peter Makin, Brian Flintoff, Mark Hunt, Mark Wilson, Phil Bircham, Alex Carter-Silk, Charles MacFarlane, James A. Merchant and Michael Mobley.

Finally, the authors would like to thank Stephen Rutt, Palgrave Macmillan's publishing director, for making the publication of the book a reality.

DAVID E. HAWKINS
SHAN RAJAGOPAL

Background on Sun Tzu

Sun Tzu was both a general and a philosopher in the period of Chinese history known as the Warring States. This was around 400 BC, at a time when the Chou dynasty had come to an end. At this time across China, the local warlords were seeking to build up their own territories from the remains of the collapsed empire.

Prior to this time there had been a long period of stability during which the ancient philosopher Confucius had developed his life, working towards the acceptance of human values, and with the collapse had seen the upsurge of conflict. It was natural, therefore, that the new voice to be heard was that of a warrior. The paradox in terms of Sun Tzu was that, while being a recognized strategist, his teachings reflected an anti-war background, the principle being that, in battle, the true skill was to win without a fight. Thus victory results not from pure strength but rather from an acute knowledge of ones opponents' methods and weaknesses.

He reflects the Taoist viewpoint that to be successful in any conflict, there had to be a merging of one's physical and spiritual elements. This is the essence of all martial arts, and the true focus of any great warrior. Since to win one had to be convinced of one's ability to win, so to develop this conviction it was necessary to understand *how* to win. If one established the strategy correctly, winning was a certainty, thus often avoiding a fight, since one's opponent could see the battle lost and therefore not pursue the battle.

This interaction of mind and body can be seen in many modern exponents of the martial arts. The ability to withstand pain, as exhibited by many exponents, leads to the understanding that inflicting pain is of little benefit in a conflict. The Zen philosophy mirrors this approach and therefore promotes the viewpoint that there has to be a more effective route to success, and it is this approach that underpins all the writings of Sun Tzu and the many commentators who produced similar teachings in the 1,500 years that followed 'The Art of War'. All of them recognized that the battle was fought in the mind of the opponents before taking to the field of conflict, the true skill being selecting the right strategy.

Sun Tzu shows how the route to success is in the objective analysis of the situation and through the exploitation of emotion rather than the use of sheer power. If an opponent believes he can only lose, then he will lose. Understanding this is crucial to winning, while at the same time it is necessary to remain flexible, and a good strategy must be intuitive. Thus having sound plans, well-trained warriors and the ability to react quickly will render the opponent's moves ineffective. Having sound knowledge and projecting a stance that reflected this knowledge leads to confusion in the opponent and thus success. Appearing weak when one is strong, or confused when one is clear encourages over-confidence in the opponents, thus opening up opportunities for success.

These philosophies have been the cornerstone of both military and business success through out Asia over 2,500 years. Sun Tzu thus paved the way for many who followed to create an approach that can be adapted to most environments.

CHAPTER 1

The battleground

Over the centuries there have been many volumes written recording the attributes of great armies and generals. A large number of these renowned and notable ventures took their basic success from strategies that have supported clever generals, going back to the days of Sun Tzu and beyond. What is common from all these case studies is the adaptability of the leaders in taking advantage of, and capitalizing on, the development of a detailed knowledge of the battlegrounds on which they fought.

The business environment, and in particular the global arena, offer both a challenge and great opportunity. In many ways, the pressures and drivers of business can be likened to a battleground and in the same way that Sun Tzu established his philosophy that winning was based on sound strategies, so successful business ventures need robust strategies to succeed. In the specific area of developing and executing projects, large or small, the creation of effective strategies is crucial in order to recognize the vulnerabilities and opportunities that may be presented.

The significant challenge for most projects is the activities that are created specifically from a single objective. Whether they are internal development programmes or major infrastructure developments, their unique structure and challenges are never repeated with exactly the same constituents. As such, there is no established winning pattern that can accommodate every variation to be found. There is a general framework that can be applied, but it will be the development of an effective strategy that will largely define the outcome.

Strategy is a term that is often used in discussion but seldom fully understood, frequently being confused with methodology and tactics. What Sun Tzu maintained, and we have set out to support, and link to his writings, is that projects need effective strategies which, if properly applied, will define a successful outcome before resources have been released on to the modern field of combat.

The key element of any strategy is to understand the terrain, the opponents and any potential allies that may help to shift the balance. In a military sense, opposing armies would seek to outmanoeuvre each other, to ensure that they enjoyed the best advantage from time and the layout of the land. Deciding when, and where, to fight was often more important than ensuring superior strength and capability. Some of the more notable battles in history, have been won, not by power, but with adaptability and stealth. Sun Tzu goes even further in his teachings to suggest that winning takes place at the development stage of a superior strategy.

Certainly, it is doubtful that any business venture is set on course before considering both the market and the competition. However, this often happens at a very high level and is seldom cascaded down to front-line execution. A truly successful strategic approach has to be developed that can be communicated down through the command and control structure of the operation. It is not necessary for everybody to understand every detail, but a good general will ensure that local commanders know where they fit into the big picture.

The business leaders of today often forget the basics of military organization, and while it is not our view that rigid military structures are the most effective, they do provide sound guidance for project managers to build upon – remembering, of course, that in many ways the modern project operation is far more fragmented than the armies of old.

It is perhaps worth considering the similarities between the government–army relationship alongside that of the board and operational sides of the business. CEOs will often see their role as being the implementer of shareholder policy, though perhaps in more general terms they spend their time trying to keep the shareholders satisfied, as do most governments. The general, or project manager, is there to implement the direction from above and to develop the organization to deliver the required results. The more successful managers are, the less interference they suffer, and vice versa.

At the commander level, clear direction and guidance is sought, structured to stretch but not to expose their divisions. In the same way, the task leaders within project organizations must understand their role and be able to direct their teams. At the working level, or front line, clear instructions and the tools to do the job effectively must be provided.

So when developing a strategic approach there is not much difference between the military leader and the project manager. It was this similarity and the common-sense ideas in 'The Art of War' that prompted this book and encouraged us to look at how it may help others in the very complex world of projects.

We should be clear that, when considering the world of projects, it is not simply the mega projects that need a strategic approach. Every project, large or small, has similar challenges in that they bring together diverse teams for a common objective. Thus, when reading this book we hope it will bring assistance to any project or venture that is creating a team which may be crossing organizational or geographical boundaries.

Building a virtual organization requires special leadership capabilities. In fact, projects are true virtual organizations, incorporating not only many different skills but also many diverse organizations. Developing projects today is very much along the lines of the old commanders who sought multiple alliances in order to field an army able to defeat its opponent, but often these alliances were formed purely to ensure that other players did not ally themselves with the opposition. If they were able to create an army that was so large that it looked unbeatable, then often there was no battle at all.

Today's business leaders can learn much from traditional military organization, which is perhaps why Sun Tzu is considered important reading in Far East business schools. What is most interesting in the Sun Tzu approach is that, rather than building armies to win battles, he prefers to utilize strategy to make the battles themselves unnecessary. This is, of course, the essence of all the martial arts – using the opponent's strengths and weaknesses against themselves.

When considering the organizational issues involved, it should not be difficult to find the similarities in developing a command and control structure. The challenge, however, is that in the business world, and in particular the area of projects, the various constituents of the project team will not, as in the military sense, simply be absorbed into one structure. They may be seconded from internal functional groups or from external organizations. Therefore the project manager has the challenge of building a common ethos that will bind the many players together and focus them on a single objective.

This does not mean that within a project group or team there are no command structures providing linkages between the project manager and the 'troops' in the front line undertaking specific tasks. The more global the project, the more important it is to have a sound communications network ensuring that all actions are planned and implemented in accordance with the overall strategy. Every member of the team must understand his/her individual role and function, both independently within their designated task and to maintain the links to the overall plan.

The challenge for business operations in this project world is the development of project managers who can both maintain interdependence across, often, geographical boundaries and at the same time encourage innovative thinking and attitudes. Considerable investment has gone into the creation of systems and technology to support global integration, but perhaps less towards exploiting the fundamental need to manage relationships, both internally and externally. The good military commander not only accepts the directions of the general but also translate them to his men, while also ensuring that his subordinates had the best possible support. In this situation, his men would trust the commander's direction and leadership.

Developing any strategy must also consider the tools and resources at hand. It may not be practical to implement certain actions because of certain constraints, but too often the leadership ignores impediments that may exist, with the result that failure is obvious to all and thus the efforts to achieve success are reduced. Failure is then inevitable and resources are wasted. Establishing the way forward must be balanced and focused, using the skills and resources that exist or by finding the additional necessary resources. It is often not simply a question of increased numbers of people either, but more to do with the specialists that will make the difference.

Developing the right combination of resources must be reflective of the capabilities of the opposition, whether in the business world this is the competition or the ultimate customer. While projects may have specific technical skill requirements, the greater challenge – as for the generals of old – is specialized capabilities to work effectively in certain environments. Thus one would not normally ask a sailor to operate in a jungle. It is the configuration of skill and experience that provides the most suitable players for any given objective.

The business landscape can be very varied, and in a global context the multiple variances and volatility can be dramatic. Therefore, as with the generals' predicament, the project manager has to consider the approach to be taken against a background of the capabilities at hand and the environment within which the work must take place. Building a strategic profile of the landscape is as important to the success of a project it has been for the military leader through the ages.

Once the terrain has been mapped and understood, then the leader looks to find the advantages or competitive edge that can be exploited. The general will structure the strategic approach to make take maximum use of the resources to hand, whether these are troops or equipment. The same profiling must be undertaken and directed by the effective project manager. In this respect we are not considering the technical challenges of the project, which may have its own physical obstacles, but rather referring to the economic, political and cultural environment, or terrain, within which the project must be undertaken. The specific approach to a project and its success will depend very much on the ability of the project team to focus on the job in hand at the same time as contending with the external influences that may create brakes on progress.

The challenges of a project that operates outside the traditional business culture brings to bear pressures that many project managers have not experienced previously, and therefore, when developing a strategic approach, they lean heavily on tried and tested methods. These may have been successful in more stable environments but falter when faced with the complexities of other national and business cultures. Developing alliance partners has been shown to provide extended capabilities without necessitating and major expansion of direct resources, which may limit competitiveness.

Throughout military history it has generally been the linking of allies that has built the most successful armies, particularly when these allies have specialist skills that offer expertise in certain terrains. Certainly the significant empires that have at various stages controlled the known world have been able to extend their reach through the development of strategic allies. In the modern business world these concepts are just as valid and, as every experienced project manager will attest, ensuring that you have alliances even for internal development projects is essential to success.

Relationship management is not a new idea but it is one that in today's business world is receiving greater consideration. The ability to field the right skills and appropriate resources is only part of the picture: to blend them into the most effective team takes a considerable amount of skill on the part of the leadership. Keeping the team focused over the extended duration of projects is crucial to success but this is not a talent that everyone has.

So, as we proceed to look at the writings of Sun Tzu and the development of project strategy, it is not difficult to appreciate the business environment in terms of a military battlefield. The challenges of today's business world have many common features with the strategic approach of great military leaders. It is this notion that first prompted our idea of working with Sun Tzu's writings, and we hope that our readers will also come to appreciate this.

Before we move on, there is one aspect we felt should be developed a little more, and that is to define in our minds the integration of Sun Tzu's work in terms of the project life cycle. In order to clarify the correlation between the various aspects of the military strategist and the fundamental building blocks of project management, we have outlined in Figure 1.1 the flow through the Sun Tzu writings and the linkage with the common elements of project strategy development. However, while this is developed in a linear format, readers should consider every aspect of strategy development in a more holistic perspective. Since what Sun Tzu recognized, and we support, is the view that each element interacts with all the others, so to have an effective strategy one must integrate ones thinking and test the outcomes before launching a project programme.

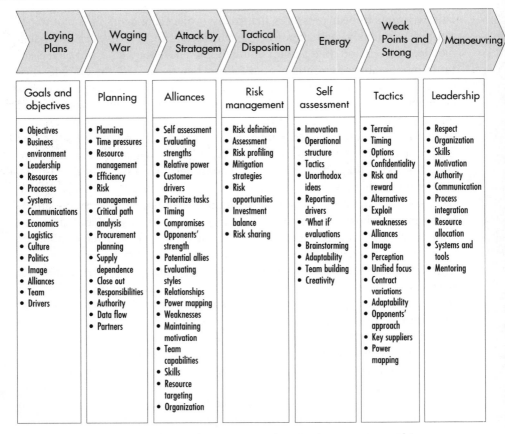

Laying Plans	Waging War	Attack by Stratagem	Tactical Disposition	Energy	Weak Points and Strong	Manoeuvring
Goals and objectives	**Planning**	**Alliances**	**Risk management**	**Self assessment**	**Tactics**	**Leadership**
• Objectives • Business environment • Leadership • Resources • Processes • Systems • Communications • Economics • Logistics • Culture • Politics • Image • Alliances • Team • Drivers	• Planning • Time pressures • Resource management • Efficiency • Risk management • Critical path analysis • Procurement planning • Supply dependence • Close out • Responsibilities • Authority • Data flow • Partners	• Self assessment • Evaluating strengths • Relative power • Customer drivers • Prioritize tasks • Timing • Compromises • Opponents' strength • Potential allies • Evaluating styles • Relationships • Power mapping • Weaknesses • Maintaining motivation • Team capabilities • Skills • Resource targeting • Organization	• Risk definition • Assessment • Risk profiling • Mitigation strategies • Risk opportunities • Investment balance • Risk sharing	• Innovation • Operational structure • Tactics • Unorthodox ideas • Reporting drivers • 'What if' evaluations • Brainstorming • Adaptability • Team building • Creativity	• Terrain • Timing • Options • Confidentiality • Risk and reward • Alternatives • Exploit weaknesses • Alliances • Image • Perception • Unified focus • Contract variations • Adaptability • Opponents' approach • Key suppliers • Power mapping	• Respect • Organization • Skills • Motivation • Authority • Communication • Process integration • Resource allocation • Systems and tools • Mentoring

Figure 1.1   Framework integrating Sun Tzu's strategies within a project life cycle context

Variations in Tactics	The Army on the March	Terrain	The Nine Situations	The Attack by Fire	The Use of Spies
Change management	**Negotiations**	**Business environment**	**Business landscape**	**Financial management**	**Market intelligence**
• Opportunities • Improvements • Visibility • Management • Impact assessment	• Goals and targets • Skills • Knowledge • Experience • Structure • Application • Teams • Authority • Process • Timing	• Economics • Politics • Regulation • Culture • Ethics • Volatility • Adaptability	• Culture • Change • Relationships • Demand • Market values • Bureaucracy • Knowledge transfer • Technology • Sustainability • Partners • Custom and practice	• Funding • Budgets • Cash flow • Currency • Taxes • Reporting • Planning	• Agents • Representatives • Market information • Customer profiles • Competitor profiles • Networking

CHAPTER 2

Laying plans

The art of war is of vital importance to the State. It is a matter of life and death, a road either to safety or to ruin. Hence it is a subject of inquiry, which can on no account be neglected.

The world of projects, whether internal developments or, as in our careers within the engineering and construction environment, often seems like a battle zone. It is certainly clear that effective project management is a crucial part of the business arena. We can also empathize with the need for those currently in that arena, or thinking of entering it, to have a clear understanding of the basic approaches that are necessary to be successful.

Over the years we have been involved with many organizations, either executing projects or working with contractors who have been undertaking projects on behalf of an organization we represented. What has surprised us on many occasions is the common use of the term 'project' and 'project manager', but the skills, processes and expertise required has varied from masters degree level to one perhaps below just paying lip service to the concept.

It is also not surprising to those who have worked in different industries that each assumes itself to be the true practitioner and there is little recognition of the commonality between industries. In fact, from our experiences in banking, chemical plants, aerospace, oil and gas, manufacturing, power generation, electronics and mining, the failure to look over the wall based on traditional thinking is very apparent. A truth not often recognized is that much of modern thinking with regard to projects takes its due from the aerospace industry.

So to readers we make one request: that you accept this offering with an open mind. You may not see yourself as an ancient Chinese warrior but we think you will find that much of what Sun Tzu has to say is very pertinent to your own challenges.

The first step towards gaining a new perspective is the recognition that there may be something to learn; not only from Sun Tzu but also from others in similar roles. If you want to have successful projects you need to examine what you do and how you do it.

> The art of war, then, is governed by five constant factors, to be taken into account in one's deliberations, when seeking to determine the conditions obtaining in the field. These are the Moral Law, Heaven, Earth, the Commander, Method and Discipline.

As with any campaign, the first stage must be to develop a strategy that is consistent with the goals and objectives of the individual organization. In order to do this, one must start by making an assessment of the business environment and your skills and attributes with which to address the market.

The most critical part of any project is to establish 'the moral law' or in modern-day terms, the target aims. We are constantly surprised that when we ask the question 'When does a project start?' seldom, if ever, is the initial idea identified. Whether this is an internal development or an opportunity in the market, the activity is started before any consideration of the true conditions and possibilities for success.

In today's global business world, the economic conditions can change overnight, and what seemed like valid objectives are left floundering. If one considered 'the heaven' as this economic uncertainty it is easy to see the value of developing a strategy that has some flexibility. There may also be good reason to establish early firebreaks in the commitments taken.

Equally difficult in this new global marketplace is the impact of political and cultural differences. 'The world can often be very confusing and unpredictable to those venturing out for the first time. Most of our careers have been spent working on projects in strange parts of the world, and only those who were knowledgeable were successful.

The role of the project manager is not necessarily seen as being a critical one, particularly in well-established functional organizations, and the title is assigned without true consideration of the skills needed to achieve success. 'The commander' in any business is perhaps the most significant factor in achieving the desired outcome.

Then one has to consider 'the method and discipline', or the processes and tools needed to understand and measure progress, and identify obstacles, while executing individual and team functions. Success does not come from individual talents but rather from the right combination of skills and a common focus of the project group.

> The Moral Law causes people to be in complete accord with their ruler, so that they will follow him regardless of their lives, undismayed by any danger.

Projects by their very nature tend to create virtual operations, bringing together appropriate combinations of resources. Their success, and perhaps more importantly their failure, is often dictated more by external influences than by the efforts and skills of the participants involved. Therefore any project must have clear goals and guidelines that are supported by the organization. This support must be both vertical and horizontal.

Internal development initiatives are generally sponsored by individuals for a variety of reasons, to underpin their own positions or those of a group within the organization, or to promote a position with external stakeholders. These programmes can develop their own life cycles and become disconnected from the main drivers of the organization – or worse, they can be doomed to failure by lack of support. Having worked with many corporations and seen research and development (R&D) or organizational initiatives become a goal into themselves, one soon recognizes that failure is assured.

In a global world of commercial projects which are both complex and risk-inherent, the failure rate is high. When these cases are analysed, the principle reasons for failure are lack of clear objectives, insufficient resources or over-enthusiastic expectations. All these in turn can be traced back to the lack of proper definition, poor communication and more often than not lack of commitment from across the necessary spectrum of functional support.

Within the project the players need to understand their individual roles and the overall objectives these are focused towards. They also need to see their roles as being consistent with the organization at large, and be able to receive support when needed. The linkage between corporate strategy, functional or divisional strategy, project objectives and individual targets is crucial for success. Any break in this chain will generate pressures and risks for the outcome of the programme.

> Heaven signifies night and day, cold and heat, times and seasons.

Most people would not consider taking a walk outside without first judging the weather. We say 'most', because there will always be the more cavalier among us who venture forth without planning. In the same vein, it would not be realistic to pursue any business opportunity without understanding the economic environment.

Many internal projects get started based on assumptions that are untested, and as a result invite failure, or simply fade away. The waste of resources and effort come not from the failure of the concept, but are more related to the inappropriate timing of the project. The hardest thing in the project world is to gamble on which projects to chase and which to turn away, yet in most cases the selection process can be assisted greatly by a more detailed analysis of the economic indicators that can govern the eventual outcome. Not necessarily those of one's own organization but more importantly those of the potential customer.

We have been involved over the years in the development stage of many projects, that we absolutely knew would never go ahead but still we carried on regardless of this. In other cases, projects have gone to contract and beyond when it was clear, at least to some, that the economics would eventually dictate failure, and in most cases this came about.

Market development and analysis is a key tool in the project world. Those who fly in the face of the weather and succeed are very few, and they are often heralded as being intuitive. In real terms they are a small percentage and perhaps just lucky, if there is such a thing as luck. At least if you understand the economic conditions that prevail you can prepare for the storms and thus develop an execution strategy that will provide some flexibility of approach. All business thrives on risk management, and mitigation of the risks is a fundamental aspect of project management.

Earth comprises distances, great and small; danger and security; open ground and narrow passes; the chances of life and death.

You would consider it crazy if some suggested taking a boat across a desert or riding a bicycle across a lake. Clearly, these tools or resources would be inappropriate. When considering some of the projects we have looked at, these suggestions would, in comparison, perhaps seem sensible. The question of logistics is only one aspect of global development projects and certainly it can be an important factor. The terrain, though, can be more dangerous when it cannot be seen.

Globalization has brought to the business arena far more difficulties than those experienced by the early pioneers; their challenges were largely physical, and success came from strength and endurance. Today's business ventures face a hidden terrain that is even more risky in terms of political and cultural issues. Endurance may ultimately be a factor, but against the bureaucracy and culture of a new country it is never enough.

We have seen experts in their field, with established successes behind them, fail because of their assumption that business was the same the world over. In the various industrial sectors we have been involved in, the life of a project can extend for years. This can be particularly true in countries where time has less significance than is perhaps appreciated in the industrialized world. It is also apparent that when governments are involved, the normal economic drivers of business may be secondary.

There is also a significant impact, which comes from the cultural divide, not simply of language but of the whole essence of life in certain parts of the world. Therefore, in understanding the terrain one should consider both the geography and the cultural/political landscape. The hill and river may be constant, but the government and regulations can change overnight.

> The Commander stands for the virtues of wisdom, sincerity, benevolence, courage and strictness.

The nature of leadership has been the subject of many books over the years. We doubt there is anyone in the industrialized world who at some point in their career has not been subjected to some form of leadership appreciation. In the world of projects, we consider this role to be one of the key elements of success.

The creation of a virtual team as it occurs within projects is part of the normal process. In fact, the essence of a project is building in the right combination of skills and resources for the objective. Thus by its very nature a project brings together many disparate parties. These may not only be from within a single organization, but may incorporate players from several. It is thus crucial that not only is there a clear focus on the way ahead but also a leader who can hold the team together, focused and motivated.

The role of the project manager is one that is often undervalued by organizations, with the title frequently being allotted by structure rather than capability. In some cases it is even totally inappropriate for the role undertaken. Thus, for example, a co-ordination function may be dubbed 'project management'.

The primary role of the project manager is to manage and direct a team. In this function, the stronger the leadership skills, the greater the potential for success of the project. This leadership, however, is not simply the utilization of power and authority: it also requires respect. A team may follow instructions based on fear. Project managers who earned respect have led the more successful projects with which we have been involved. As with any organization, the choice of leader is often more important than the individual skills the business may be able to muster.

> By Method and Discipline are to be understood the marshalling of the army in its proper subdivisions, the graduations of rank among the officers, the maintenance of roads by which supplies may reach the army, and the control of military expenditure.

Clearly, every organization needs rules and procedures. There also have to be appropriate levels of authority established. From our experience, however, and many of you may recognize this, these rules are often ignored on a daily basis. The exception is when there is perhaps a major bungle or an external audit.

The main reasons for failure are not that rules were not in place, but that the rules had been established without any recognition of the working reality. They were also frequently not supported by either the right level of resources or the tools to achieve the desired outcome. Therefore, when problems arose, they could be traced back to failures of the business processes rather than any intent to fail.

Developing the right methodology in the project environment is important. As we have already seen, in the global market the world changes and so do the requirements of the operation. A rigid discipline could result in its application being counter-productive.

This view of the business process has become more accepted in recent times as organizations recognize the need for control and flexibility. As such, it is important when creating a project team to understand what is needed and ensure that the processes and instructions are clear, to meet the needs of the organization as well as the project.

The adopting of business process as opposed to volumes of procedures makes it much easier to focus on what is necessary rather than on strict compliance. Identifying the variations which may be needed to meet customer needs or local conditions is crucial if the team is to understand how to proceed. The principles may be common but every project has its own peculiarities that must be satisfied.

These five heads should be familiar to every general: he who knows them will be victorious; he who knows them not will fail.

These issues are not new, and while they are addressed in many works on management and projects they often get overlooked. In the world of projects, having a clear strategy that addresses the key elements must be the cornerstone of any operational process.

Developing an initial strategic plan then redesigning it as more knowledge becomes available makes sense. Surprisingly, in many organizations this practice often falls very short of the mark. This is particularly relevant when looking at the front-end activity of marketing and sales of major projects. The sales operations often focus on opportunities and the salesman's role is to identify these. Practice has shown that applying this first level of filter to these opportunities will then result in high levels of rejection. This is not popular with the sales teams, but in our view is essential to ensure that resources are used wisely and risks are identified early.

One of the common statements in the initial stages of any development is that 'we don't have the answers', which is seen as a justification for not starting the analysis. In fact, most projects have inbuilt failures long before they reach a contract – usually because the research and risk mitigation did not become part of the capture process. The 'landmines' are thus planted in the contract and at some point they will explode.

The traditional concept many will recognize is the idea that any problems will be solved during execution. If we do not address these five key areas, as captured by Sun Tzu in Moral Law, Heaven, Earth, the Commander, and Method and Discipline, then the likelihood of project success is slim.

Therefore, in your deliberations, when seeking to determine the military conditions, let them be made the basis of a comparison, in this wise:

Which of the two sovereigns is imbued with the moral law?
Which of the two generals has most ability?
With whom lie the advantages derived from heaven and earth?
On which side is discipline most rigorously enforced?
Which army is stronger?
On which side are officers and men more highly trained?
In which army is there the greater constancy both in reward and punishment?

By means of these seven considerations I can forecast victory or defeat.

The more knowledge you can accumulate, the greater the chance of success. It is also true that the more you recognize what you *don't* know, the more likely you will be to try to close the gap. If you have no view of how to win, then you are almost certain to lose.

Projects are very complex operations, bringing together many often disparate parties, skills and resources. In the global market place they are influenced by many adverse factors. Winning a contract must be based on being able to execute it successfully. Trying to win without a game plan will result in chaos and failure.

These basic elements are the starting point; as we move forward the complexity will grow. It should be remembered that evolution created both the giraffe and the horse, so which approach you take must evaluate what makes sense in your circumstances.

It is also important to recognize that in the development stage of a project you may be facing not only the demands of the customer but also your competitors. Therefore the potential for failure is increased. To be successful you must know what is needed to satisfy and win the customers' backing, but also the strengths and weaknesses of those in competition with you. A winning strategy should bring together the right ingredients for the task at hand to meet your objectives and the challenges of the market.

> The general that hearkens to my counsel and acts upon it, will conquer: let such a one be retained in command! The general that hearkens not to my counsel nor acts upon it, will suffer defeat: let such a one be dismissed.

Having had experience of many organizations it is interesting to evaluate what they considered to be their advantages. Too often companies create an inflated view of their standing in the market. This self-assessment then promotes self-confidence, which in turn leaves opportunities for both customer and competition. False confidence is one of the major factors of failed projects.

Exploiting one's own strengths without understanding the external pressures and issues is almost certain to leave one exposed. First, one must assess the risks and objectives, then look to see what advantages one can capitalize upon. It is certain that your competitors will be doing a similar analysis, and your customer will also be developing expectations. To win, one must be confident of being equipped to succeed, but at the same time one needs to look for opportunities to exploit unusual approaches. If all the players are using the same rules, then competition becomes pure commoditization.

Success will on many occasions come from taking up an alternative strategy. It is relatively easy to follow conventional paths, but this is not likely to assure a winning combination. Many heralded generals have reached celebrity through unexpected actions; and many business ventures have enjoyed similar success.

The more an approach varies from accepted practice, the greater the need for a good strategy well understood by those who have to execute it. Having the best players does not necessarily make for the strongest team.

> While heeding the profit of my counsel, avail yourself also of any helpful circumstances over and beyond the ordinary rules. According as circumstances are favourable, one should modify one's plans

In the business world, it would perhaps be considered unethical to use deception. This statement should be qualified, however, because this must depend on one's opponent. It would probably not be a good marketing strategy to appear incompetent or ineffective to a prospective customer.

On the other hand, when considering your competition, perhaps the less of a threat they perceive you to be, the more likely they would be to be less conscientious about their own approach. As a customer one might find it helpful to appear disorganized, while retaining internally a very clear focus on strategy and objectives.

The main issue here is related more to how you want to be perceived and what advantage you may gain from such an approach. This again is dependent on the relationship that is envisaged going forward, since the more devious one is the more difficult it would be to build up a collaborative relationship in the future.

In any negotiation it is preferable not to disclose ones true aims or targets. This issue will be discussed again later. If, however, one is looking to build partnerships or alliances it is crucial to develop these from a position of openness. The principle behind any strategy must be to limit the exposure of one's plans while at the same time creating an environment that opens opportunities for you to exploit your strengths.

The objective throughout these original Sun Tzu writings is to focus on the development of a winning strategy and win before battle is joined. The less obvious your strengths at the outset, the more valuable they are as tools for success. On the other hand, when your strengths are what a potential customer is looking to evaluate, then any confusion is detrimental. That is why in this adaptation for the project world it is critical to understand the nature of the multidimensional opponents involved.

> All warfare is based on deception. Hence, when able to attack, we must seem unable; when using our forces, we must seem inactive; when we are near, we must make the enemy believe we are far away; when we are far away, we must make him believe we are near.

As we have already considered, the project world – as with many areas of business – can be very complex. Once a business strategy is in the public domain one is generally forced to take more of a reactive position. It is therefore essential that one maintains maximum confidentiality for as long as possible. In large global projects this is often difficult, as these projects span many operations around the world and often require external partners. The same can be said of many internal projects where the development may have an impact on sectors of the organization or a perhaps long-term external commercial edge.

It is common for the true nature of business ventures to be veiled by false messages or indicators. Customers have developed projects in the market while in fact planning some completely different scheme. For project sales people this becomes a major issue when trying to establish which projects to follow.

The procurement environment is often equally challenging in this respect, where selections may already have been made but the market is played either to confuse or to aid negotiations. It is a risky ploy, since once established as a methodology future support may be restricted or less valuable.

In general, the concept of keeping the opponent in an unprepared state is easy to convert to many differing applications in the winning and execution of projects.

> Hold out baits to entice the enemy. Feign disorder, and crush him.

It is not difficult to align one's thinking in the business world with the concept of gain. The whole principle of business is the creation of wealth or value for those who have a shareholding in the outcome. The difficulty in the project world is the need to maintain the focus on what services the customer needs. A customer will only buy what is considered to add value for them. Unfortunately, in the execution of projects it is often the goals and aspirations of individuals that are delivered.

The project team, as was said earlier, is in most cases a collaboration of specialist skills and resources. Many times the overall aims of the project strategy get lost in the specialized focus of individuals. If projects are to be successful, all participants have to be working to a common goal. In the past, the desire, for example, of a designer to deliver the best that can be achieved as opposed to what is needed has resulted in delays and cost over-runs. In reality, the participants should see the potential for gain, whether they are customers, partners, suppliers or the project team.

The second aspect of this message is less meaningful except once again in the arena of negotiations, perhaps, or the competition's perspective of your participation. Having established this, it is perhaps worth noting that in some projects benefit for all participants can be achieved by the creation of confusion among external parties, where the outcome is of less concern to their objectives, which are not aligned to the project. Certainly within both large corporations and political environments, confusion can be a very positive tool.

> If he is secure at all points, be prepared for him. If he is superior in strength, evade him.

Choosing ones opponent is a key factor in any development strategy. For example, the multinational customer who is established and well organized is unlikely to be flexible in his or her thinking. Clearly, those who are strong present a more difficult challenge in some respects than those who are more entrepreneurial in their business focus.

The major organization has many facets and functions within its infrastructure, and there will be both functional protectionism and status associated with any decision. These barriers can at times be in conflict with the major objectives of the overall organization. They are very real when it comes to major development projects.

The more established and successful the opponent, the harder it becomes to maintain focus on the aims of the project. It is also more difficult to introduce alternative thinking into the business process. Many times the obvious solution is ignored in favour of the one that fits the internal aims of a particular fraction.

The question of who is strongest is yet another area of potential conflict in establishing a viable strategy and successful outcome. If you can avoid those who are strong, you can influence the outcome more directly. Strength can be relative, however, in a business environment, where technology may have a greater influence than size and knowledge can be more crucial than market share. Experience has more value in a risk analysis than simple financial power. At the same time, abuse of a position has to be measured against the stature and nature of the opponent. Customers, for example, may be wrong but they do not like to hear that, so presenting a solution the right way could be more productive than relying on your perceived strength.

> If your opponent is of a choleric temper, seek to irritate him.

The development of business is based above all on the establishment of relationships. It is also generally true that most people in business try to develop relationships that work for them. The use of reverse emotion is a common strategy for negotiations. In a true relationship it is also valid to show your feelings.

When developing a project strategy the approach of creating anger in one's opponent can assist in generating an adverse or disorientating reaction. Anger is an unstable reaction and can cause confusion, during which an advantage can be exploited.

When one's opponents are over-confident and thus often unreasonable it can make a significant difference to your position if they are made angry or frustrated. It is at these times that their own strategy may be ignored in an effort to make their position stronger or to validate their position. Such carelessness can be turned to your advantage.

With the frustrations that can come from major global projects it is worth remembering the importance of maintaining your own position by not reacting to direct or indirect conflict. It should always be acknowledged that for any strategy you employ there will be a counter-strategy in place.

Perhaps one of the most significant frustrations, however, is likely to come not from a direct intent but more from cultural differences that may exist. The style of operations in other places in the world can be diametrically opposed to those of your organization. It is therefore important to understand the driver behind the positions and not to react to the outward display.

> Pretend to be weak, that he may grow arrogant.

The customer is always right. We all understand the principle but often forget the reality in practice. The customer may have many failings but at the end of the day he or she is the reason for any project. Whether this is an internal development or a market-led opportunity. The easy way to help a project fail is to take up a position that puts the customer in a weak, or perceived weak, role.

This is particularly relevant to the supply chain, where the experienced supplier tries to dominate the customer's thinking. In many cases there is a clear superiority of knowledge and experience but the moment this is displayed, the supplier creates his/her own disadvantage. It may also be true that while the supplier may consider his know-how to be greater, in fact the customer knows what he or she wants to do and has the ultimate responsibility for the operations.

It is also a common failing with internal projects that the evangelist is so convinced of his/her goals that the users are ignored. This behaviour will ultimately cause friction and result in project failure. A buy-in by the participants is crucial to success.

In the life of a project there will be many conflicts and differences of views, both with proposed internal solutions to problems as well as the propositions being placed before the customer. Winning an argument, whether technical or commercial, is of little value if customers feel they have lost. There will be other challenges where your position, is weaker and even though you are justified you may lose.

Even in negotiations when playing from a position of strength the real skill is to leave the other party with the feeling of superiority and that they have won. The common failing in many situations like this is to win the points but this often results in losing the battle.

> If he is taking his ease, give him no rest.

Those who have worked out in the East will be accustomed to the style of meeting and negotiations. Patience is an absolutely essential requirement. When time is not on your side you will become frustrated and perhaps elect to make decisions that are not to your advantage.

The issue of long-term projects will be reviewed in more depth, later but it has to be a factor in the development of any project strategy that you consider the implications of duration. Timing, energy and resources are a key facets of any project plan, and understanding how you intend to manage these issues is critical.

For the opponent who has no time restraints, the success of the project may not be driven by the same factors as the group trying to deliver the result. It may also be a consideration that fractions within the organization may have different drivers. Attrition is a significant tool in the business armoury. The more impatient you are, the more likely it is that you will concede to demands. Therefore, in establishing any project strategy it is important to understand the real pressures, both internally and externally.

It is therefore very important to have a clear perspective from your position and build the appropriate elements into your plans. On the other hand, where you have the choice, avoid making choices too early, thus limiting your opportunities. Being in control of the selection process and able to choose your timing might add significant value to your end game.

In any game, the more tired the opponent, the greater the opportunity there is for you to take advantage. The counter-position is also valid, therefore plan for the eventuality that delays may be part of an alternate scheme.

> If his forces are united, separate them.

In any business venture, alliances are a strong asset. This becomes even truer when one looks at the interrelated nature of global projects. Developing and executing projects on a global stage depends very much on maintaining the focus of the many parties involved. In fact, at any level of project activity success relies on the interaction of many disparate groups, both internal and external to the organization.

Often one's opponents also have the same pressures, whether they are customer or competition. Many times the internal conflicts between the commercial, technical and operations groups can be very strong. Within the project team these conflicts have to be controlled and managed. Failure to present a united front in line with a common strategy will result in delays and costs implications.

The tactic of division may work to your advantage, say within a customer or supplier organization, provided you understand the rules of engagement and the relative power structure. It is a key part of any strategy that you understand who the key players are and their value to you achieving your goals. On the other hand if conflicts are apparent these need to be recognized and often managed by you to bring about your desired result.

Like many tactics in business, division is one that needs careful management and defence when focused against you. One needs to be aware of the variable outcomes that may result. Division should only be employed if the result will enhance a strength that will provide an advantage. For example, a technical strength may be exploited by cultivating the technologists, but unless you can also find a commercial edge the effort may be in vain.

There may be an alternative and that is to find the collaborative route focused on joint objectives. In many ways, this has greater opportunity to be exploited but is much more difficult to orchestrate. It should be remembered that in battle there is one winner, whereas in business there can be multiple winners.

> Attack him where he is unprepared, appear where you are not expected.

Success in any venture often relies more on timing than any other factor, so surprise or innovation can be key competitive edges to be developed. Assessing when to move and when to divulge your hand is a major part of the business game. The project strategy, from concept through contract negotiation and execution, must validate the best possible use of knowledge and resources.

On the one hand, competitors should never be given enough time to mimic your ideas and approach. It would be equally important that they also have little time to divide the customer's focus. Strategy in this regard relies on timing and secrecy, whereas understanding the right time to present innovative concepts to the customer may be instrumental in closing out the competition.

The supplier market may require a completely different approach to obtain the best advantage and to maintain control of strategy timing. Too often the key route for information is not the customer or the competition, but what the supply chain is being asked to provide. This is particularly critical in the engineering world, where reverse engineering may be possible with very limited information. In these crucial cases it may be an option to build an alliance with a supplier.

Understanding and planning for key time-related issues must be part of any project strategy. Judging when and how to use that knowledge will be a major factor in achieving the success of the project. When implementing the unexpected one must, however, be careful not to create an impression of panic or disorganization. There is a balance that must be maintained to ensure you will meet the objective.

> These military devices, leading to victory, must not be divulged beforehand.

Projects are complex activities, and the development of an effective strategy is necessary to ensure a successful outcome. Wherever you may be in the capture or execution cycle, however, one's opponents will also be developing their own approach. The efforts to create a winning solution will be lost if your strategy falls into the hands of your opponents.

Maintaining control becomes more difficult the larger and more complex the project becomes. Large military operations are often divided into many parts in order to ensure that very few individuals can see the full picture. This approach has been used in big, risky business ventures, particularly in the case of hostile takeovers or the launch of new products.

In developing a strategy for the project, clearly the first objective is to have absolute clarity for the main players. If the project is to succeed there must be no gaps in the execution. Deciding what should and should not be in the public domain has to be evaluated on a case-by-case basis.

In the majority of organizations the business processes and functional approaches are disciplined reasonably well. As a result, because the 'how' is understood, the 'why', 'where' and 'who' may not be as critical at the capture stage. The strategy can therefore address the critical points within a closed network if secrecy is a key factor. When it comes to execution there has to be clarity of vision and objective to avoid confusion and failure.

> Now the general who wins a battle makes many calculations in his temple ere the battle is fought. The general who loses a battle makes but few calculations beforehand. Thus do many calculations lead to victory, and few calculations to defeat: how much more no calculation at all! It is by attention to this point that I can foresee who is likely to win or lose.

The maximization of opportunities or the failure of a project can in most cases be traced back to the lack of an adequate strategy, resulting in many participants not being able to understand their roles or the necessary interactions with the other players. In most cases success does not come from the effective execution but is anchored in the capture strategy leading up to project release or contract award.

A team game is never won simply by putting a group of top-class players on to the field; often those with less skill but better team interaction will triumph. This is the case also in the project world, where the team has to be focused on a common objective and work together. Developing a sound strategy that is understood by all the players and executed under clear direction will ensure that every opportunity is considered and exploited.

At the same time, a strategy is about the identification of risks and creating the appropriate measures to mitigate those risks. Project management is about leading a motivated team and managing risk. It is a complex world of issues, all of which need to be assessed and addressed. To attempt any project without a clear strategy is to invite failure. If the strategy is valid and flexible, communicated to those who need to know, then success, while never absolutely assured, is certainly more probable.

Given the complexity of the business environment, the importance of creating an effective strategy to meet the many challenges should not be underestimated. The battlefield is both volatile and varied, and those who aim to achieve success should be looking to base their activities on strategies that are comprehensive and at the same time dynamic.

Many times we have seen organizations expend considerable effort to build strategies that reflect their internal assessment of the world, and then lean lightly on these to focus the ongoing activity. A strategy has little value if it is only based on internal data and does not take into account the widest possible available information. It would be even more wasteful to expend effort to develop a strategy then fail to follow it through in the organization or project for which it was planned.

The effective use of strategic thinking should embrace every aspect of the business culture as an integrated part of the operation. Strategy that is created but not communicated is worthless and unlikely to meet its objectives if it is not cascaded down through the organization. Each functional group within the business must not only execute its activities within the overall strategy, but should also be using a strategic approach to match, if not all, of its activities.

At every level of an organization or project team the opportunity to exploit the strengths and weaknesses of one's opposition exists and should be pursued. Success seldom comes from power alone, and power if used without strategic thinking could be a liability, particularly for those who do not appreciate fully the landscape within which they are operating.

CHAPTER 3

Waging war

In the operations of war, where there are in the field a thousand swift chariots, as many heavy chariots, and a hundred thousand mail-clad soldiers, with provisions enough to carry them a thousand Li, the expenditure at home and at the front, including entertainment of guests, small items such as glue and paint, and sums spent on chariots and armour, will reach the total of a thousand ounces of silver per day. Such is the cost of raising an army of 100,000 men.

In the development of projects, time is always a major challenge, not only the time required to complete each project, but also the management of time and resources. The linear extension of time over the life of a project is perhaps the project's worst enemy. Every project when it is planned is generally based on an optimistic programme, which is often never achieved.

Structuring a project for the long haul is no easy task and is an area that too frequently gets ignored. Planning the way to execute a project effectively is only one aspect; establishing a controlled contract close-out is a crucial part of the activity. Many projects, while successful in their initial objectives, ultimately fail because insufficient strategic thinking has been given to the closure.

In general, the shorter a project, the more effective it will be. Thus with internal development projects it is often wiser to work with many smaller sequenced projects than with one 'big bang'. People get tired or burnt out and as a result, towards the end, a project may start to falter. For major development projects, the problem is magnified and the risks greatly increased.

Large engineering or construction projects may span many years. In fact, the gestation period often exceeds their execution time. This sets several significant challenges for the long-term management of these ventures. The greatest of these is how to keep a team motivated, whilst you close out the project effectively. This is particularly pertinent when dealing with, say, customers whose natural style is to base their approach on attrition. Burn-out can be a major concern.

> When you engage in actual fighting, if victory is long in coming, then men's weapons will grow dull and their ardour will be damped. If you lay siege to a town, you will exhaust your strength. Now, when your weapons are dulled, your ardour damped, your strength exhausted and your treasure spent, other chieftains will spring up to take advantage of your extremity. Then no man, however wise, will be able to avert the consequences that must ensue.

We all know that when we are tired we do not function at our best. Long-duration projects can have the effect of becoming less and less effective, and thus the final outcome will not be as successful. Planning for this is a difficult but necessary part of the project strategy. Since, clearly, the less effective you are, the greater the chance that your opponents will be more forceful or the current risks within the project will grow exponentially.

The dilemma is that, having built up an effective team with the right balance of skills, it is hard for any project manager to let them go. Better to have someone on the team in whom you have confidence, but this is less effective than bringing in someone new. The balance has to be planned into the programme of work.

In the same vein, time is also money and as a result, when projects drift their resource burn rate increases. One of the key factors in many less successful projects comes from the desire to keep a team in place for as long as possible. The net result is that planned costs and resources are not used effectively and ultimately grow.

It is therefore important during the development of a strategy that the focus is maintained not simply on the primary task but also on how to maintain efficiency during the execution and how to close out with greatest effect. The traditional 'S'-curve of a project always reflects an extended tail. Closing the gap on the last 5 per cent of activity is often the most costly.

> Thus, though we have heard of stupid haste in war, cleverness has never been seen associated with long delays. There is no instance of a country having benefited from prolonged warfare.

Therefore, in developing a strategic approach, one has to consider the advantages and disadvantages between time and execution. Many projects could be done better and in a more refined manner, but there is a price to be paid for perfection. This has to be balanced against the value of the outcome.

Death by analysis inflicts many organizations: a process where decisions are delayed by procrastination and the desire for a definitive result. The truth in most cases is that long before the finite outcome, the conclusion was already clear. Therefore further efforts expended could not be justified against the residue of improvement that could be achieved. This is an important aspect, particularly in engineering projects.

Engineers by nature and training seek perfection and will focus their efforts on reaching the best possible solution they can imagine, whereas in most cases the solution initially in place would be sufficient to satisfy the needs of the project. One of the big issues is when a project has been sold and it is then redesigned to make it more elegant but with no consideration of additional cost and time implications.

Short projects are more readily controlled and costs/resources more easily defined. It is a necessary discipline to understand that, in general terms, the shorter the time, the lower the cost. At the same time, if the project gets out of balance, reducing the time spend on one area or function may have a detrimental effect somewhere else in the programme. Understanding this can ensure that the correct strategy is put in place.

> It is only one who is thoroughly acquainted with the evils of war that can thoroughly understand the profitable way of carrying it on.

It is generally accepted that for every positive there is a negative, and it is no different in the world of projects. The aim of a project strategy, whether in the capture or execution phase, is to consider the impacts of each potential approach. There is no 'one size fits all' solution, and it is therefore important to understand the disadvantages of your plans as well as the potential advantages you may have considered exploiting.

One approach that has been used with some success is to utilize a separate project team to analyse and question the strategy that has been developed. We all suffer from a belief in our own ideas, and often filter out the potential negatives later if they don't fit our plan. This is particularly appropriate to the whole spectrum of risk analysis. For example, a salesman would not naturally give prominence to the downside of any market prospect, since his role is to obtain new business. On the other hand, the project execution team will often take a 'first pass' review and focus on the potential for failure, because that builds a safety net for their future activities.

The truth, as always, is somewhere in between, and developing a strategic view of the project should be based on achieving the right balance. There is always a risk in any business venture, and to avoid risk completely is virtually impossible. In fact, in an effort to exclude all risk one may actual create risks, such as loss of business.

Risk management is the backbone of project management, therefore understanding and addressing or mitigating risk is the principle challenge.

> The skilful soldier does not raise a second levy, neither are his supply wagons loaded more than twice.

This concept is very true for the project landscape and is often forgotten in the excitement of getting a new project off the blocks. This comes up particularly when looking at so-called 'fast track' projects – those that are targeted for completion within very tight time frames. The inclination is to throw resources at the project from day one and push forward any aspect that can be progressed.

The reality is that if a period of strategic review and planning is initiated, then the strategic plan will identify the true critical path. Failure to put effort into planning will ultimately result in repeating work and misuse of resources.

It is easy to adopt a philosophy of 'right first time' but in truth there will always be room for something to go wrong. This is certainly so when applying parallel engineering, where the normal sequential process is squeezed to improve overall timing. Customer changes and supplier information will seldom, if ever, be correct or available first time. The result will inevitably create overlaps and wasted effort.

To use resources in the most economic way and gain the best time advantage it is necessary to utilize the planning and strategic approach skilfully. There is much discussed in operational manuals about critical path analysis, but often this is ignored in the heat of the moment and the euphoria of initial project start-up. Effective use could avoid waste and delay, while enhancing the outcome of the project.

To many organizations resources are a valuable, and often scarce, commodity and they must be integrated into a value proposition in the most cost-effective way.

> Bring war materials with you from home, but forage on the enemy. Thus the army will have food enough for its needs.

Many times the debate has centred on where a project is to be based, and traditionalists will argue that everyone under the same roof is the only way forward. In reality, this is seldom practical, and certainly in the modern era of global communications, not necessary.

The concept of outsourcing is not new, nor in many industries is the idea of partnerships and alliances. These approaches are very pertinent in today's global market. Manufacturing operations have learnt their lessons and realized that to maintain a competitive edge they need to source globally. Building equipment as close as possible to the ultimate destination reduces logistics costs and can save time. In the project world this has to become a part of the strategy, in both the winning and execution of contracts.

This is also a major consideration when establishing a risk-management strategy, since moving outside one's comfort zone might have competitive benefits but unless the approach is managed well it could create significant risks to the execution of the project.

Local sourcing becomes a major factor with overseas projects, particularly those associated with government infrastructure developments. In many cases where international agencies are involved in the funding the need to help develop local skills and employment can be a controlling factor. Clearly, however, such changes require a solid understanding of what can be done, the skills that exist locally and any training supervision that may be required.

Therefore while the strategy may be sound, the evaluation of the risk implications must also be assessed as part of that strategy.

> Poverty of the State exchequer causes an army to be maintained by contributions from a distance. Contributing to maintain an army at a distance causes the people to be impoverished.

For most organizations, the procurement of materials and equipment, together with the logistics of delivering these to their ultimate destination, represent the major part of the cost base. Yet in many cases this aspect of the activity often receives a minimal amount of attention. The actual logistics operation may receive even less attention and in the long run cost the project dearly.

Major projects can be won or lost based on the organization's ability to exploit the supply chain. No matter how good procurement operations may be, these can be negated by a poor understanding of both the physical and documentary requirements for delivery. The safe and timely delivery of products should carry as much importance as any other aspect of the project. In fact, managed well these activities can add to the overall success of the project.

In project terms the efforts of the team and the investment of resources may put considerable strain on an organization, but this could be wasted if the whole picture is not considered. The further away the destination, the greater the risk and the more important is the development of a strategy to avoid failure.

A great effort may be undertaken to develop the best possible engineering solution, but if this is done without consideration of sourcing and supply it may all be in vain. The execution of a project and thus the strategy must be a holistic programme, integrated to optimize all aspects.

> On the other hand, the proximity of an army causes prices to go up; and high prices cause the people's substance to be drained away. When their substance is drained away, the peasantry will be afflicted by heavy exactions.

In basic economic terms everyone generally understands the principles of supply and demand. This affects all of us on a daily basis in some form or other. For the project, which is perhaps structured around a high external spend, understanding this is crucial. If it is not managed properly it may certainly exhaust contingency and profitability.

There are several prime areas for consideration in this respect, which must be included in the overall strategy. The first is procurement planning, to ensure that maximum advantage is developed from the supply market. This must be integrated with the project to consider every aspect from supply of information to enable scope development through to local supply and storage needs. Alongside the financial aspects of what to spend where, and when to maintain the project flow while improving profitability.

The closer the supplier is to your needs and the less time you have to make a choice then it is certain that the cost base will change. This is the first rule of marketing and sales. The supplier may influence your choice but at the same time limit your options. Therefore, if you want to control the process, the understanding of timing and interdependency is crucial.

If projects are driven by overseas local investment, then the options and control may be even further complicated, forcing you into a captive market. This is not new, but is often not part of project forward thinking and strategy. It should always be remembered that the sales strategy you want to employ could also be the strategy of your suppliers.

If suppliers or specific products are critical to your programme then bringing them close can be costly without pre-selection agreements or alliances.

> With this loss of substance and exhaustion of strength, the homes of the people will be stripped bare, and three-tenths of their income will be dissipated; while the government expenses for broken chariots, worn-out horses, breast-plates and helmets, bows and arrows, spears and shields, protective mantles, draught-oxen and heavy wagons, will amount to four-tenths of its total revenue.

The major challenge in any project is to forecast accurately what will be needed to execute the project and then to contain the costs and resources within the budget limits. The greatest of these issues is the external expenditure that goes to the supply chain. In a large engineering project this can easily reach 70 per cent of the contract cost, and therefore any negative movement will have a significant effect on final profitability.

While there may be a drive to conclude the project or meet its delivery milestones, this should not be done without constant reference to the overall projections of the completed venture. In the excitement of a project profitability may well be ignored but inevitably this will lead to reduced profit and thus be a drain on the organization.

The failure to plan resources may also create pressures within an organization. This will in turn limit a project's success when key skills are not available when they are required, or are taken away at a crucial time. Long-term projects are particularly vulnerable to this risk, and maintaining a programme often becomes a question of which project is allowed to falter.

The development of project close-out plans is as important as the need to start with the right emphasis. Developing critical path networks should provide the true route and resource exposure that can reach a satisfactory end within the restraints of the budget.

Projects have many differing objectives, but the main one is to deliver value to the organization: success in a customer's eyes may be viewed internally as a failure in terms of the organization's overall goals.

> Hence a wise general makes a point of foraging on the enemy. One cartload of the enemy's provisions is the equivalent to twenty of one's own, and likewise a single picul of his provender is equivalent to twenty from one's own store.

In considering the strategy for a project and preserving one's own position and profitability, the key external areas in both cases, must be the supply chain and the customer. Where it is practical, and acceptable, the greater the number of your activities that are shifted to become the responsibility of others, the better. This has the effect of reducing risk and cost, while at the same time reducing the drain on your own resources.

In many cases this can be done during the pre-contract stage, where it has the effect of reducing your overall cost base. In the post-contract stage it will have an immediate effect on bottom-line profitability. It should not, however, be done simply to shift the load, but rather in a constructive way where both parties can gain from the change.

Major disputes over responsibility within a project can be seen as creating significant risks to its overall success. Projects waver while these problems are being debated and resolved. There can often be a negotiated outcome involving a transfer of responsibility and some commercial adjustment. Very few large contracts are ever fully defined at the contract stage, but set key parameters and thus leave some aspects to be resolved during the execution phase.

The overall goal should be to aim for the most effective solution that aids the project's outcome. Since the eventual success of a project will at various stages be dependent on the parties involved, an equitable solution may ultimately be more beneficial than maintaining the starting position.

Often the parties in a contract find they have, for example, better bargaining power in a particular circumstance but choose to maintain a rigid viewpoint. In the longer term, a collaborative perspective could add more value to both sides.

> Now in order to kill the enemy, our men must be roused to anger; that there may be advantage from defeating the enemy, they must have their rewards.

Most long-term contracts have a number of stages when there is a power shift between the parties involved. In the case of procurement, the power generally sits with the purchaser until an order is placed. After this point, the success of the parties depends on the performance of the seller as much as the purchaser. In the majority of cases, the interests of both are only served by the overall success of the project.

In looking at many projects, the overall success has often been compromised by short-term actions that have sought to take early advantage of a situation. As the project progresses, a power shift occurs and past approaches are brought back into the equation.

It should always be part of the project strategy to consider the end game and not the individual battles that occur along the way. This does not mean that either side has constantly to take a soft position, but they should engender an approach that looks to overall gain. If one party or another takes an aggressive viewpoint and primes the opponent to react at the first opportunity, eventually both will fail and so will the project.

In a business environment the common interest is for maximum commercial gain and delivery to the shareholders of either the planned or improved objectives. If all parties receive their planned reward or better, then their focus will be maintained for overall success. If there is no recognition of their needs, the likelihood of success is low.

It is important that all players appreciate the drives of the others and concentrate on final success for all rather than short-term opportunism that might be structured more around personal goals than project success.

> Therefore in chariot fighting, when ten or more chariots have been taken, those should be rewarded who took the first.

It is always difficult to create the right incentives within projects and for the people within them. Customers and suppliers have an equal role in the outcome. In projects that are spread over several years, maintaining the impetus is hard. In general terms, most people and organizations respond better to reward and recognition than to threats.

Building the right ethos for a project may come from being generous towards early wins. Certainly, this approach often wins within organizations. The tendency, however, is to remain cautious to protect the long-term perspective, and this may in time have a counter-productive impact.

There has to be a balance and a confidence that all parties will maintain an open attitude. Clearly, in the early stages of a project when large capital expenditure is being processed there is the maximum opportunity for gain. The recognition of competitive advantage and innovation should be the focus. Whether driven by supplier or customer if improvements can be gained by sharing know-how then it makes sense to share the reward.

Within a project it is always a challenge to offer reward or acknowledgement at the individual level. Because of the nature of the project it is unlikely that any single individual could or will alone affect the outcome. The project management role is one of seeking the best possible result through the integration and ownership of the team. This challenge may be further complicated when considering alliances and partnerships.

True success will come from the whole team being rewarded or acknowledged for their joint contribution.

> Our own flags should be substituted for those of the enemy, and the chariots mingled and used in conjunction with ours. The captured soldiers should be kindly treated and kept.

On several occasions we have mentioned the development of alliances and partnerships. This approach can, and has been shown to, produce exceptional results in major development projects. As the complexity and variability of global projects increases, so does the need to configure project teams from many organizations. Unfortunately the traditional approach to customer and supplier relationships often undermines what could be a very successful teaming.

The nature of a business is to maximize its own advantage at the risk of reducing that of venture partners. As outlined earlier, in the life of a project the power shifts and as it does so the opportunity for harnessing joint skills and resources may diminish.

Many project have greatly improved their chances of sanction or the overall outcome by working together with traditional adversaries. Innovation and the sharing of skills, knowledge and resources can exploit opportunities that might be lost in traditional structures. Therefore building teams that can focus on the outcome rather than on individual success can provide longer-term benefits for all involved.

But even under a traditional arrangement there is room to consider and exploit an improved relationship. In the project world, the success of the project is the prime goal, and when diverse individuals are brought together from within an organization they focus on the objectives for the project. The same can, and should, be achieved for the customer or supplier associated with the project.

The end-game should be more important than the individual positioning or image of the parties. The most successful projects will be those driven by customers who encourage all the players actively to pursue ownership of the project goals.

This is called, using the conquered foe to augment one's own strength.

Competitors can be partners if the rewards and risks can be sold to them as being of greater advantage. This challenge is where most alliances fall down and ultimately cause the failure of projects. Customers who may be considered as opponents can also benefit from integrated projects.

Maintaining a closed mind to the possibilities of working in an alliance may in the longer term weaken your position. Strength is often very fickle in a changing market place, and thus to rely only on one's existing position may reduce opportunities in the future.

It has been written many times that one should keep one's friends close and one's enemies even closer. The truth is that, in this application, one is only reflecting a negative relationship. In the world of international business and corporate mergers one's enemy might be your colleague tomorrow. Even so, the integration of specialists can strengthen your own position and may also produce more profitable results.

Trying to define an opponent in the business world is often difficult and may create a single-minded approach that precludes alternative strategies. Success is generally a combination of your strengths and weaknesses matched against those of others. If by building alliances one can increase the chances of gaining a project or executing it more effectively, then such an approach should be developed.

The key to any successful venture is to focus the maximum resources available on the project's outcome. There should be no limitation to this concept except where in doing so the longer-term corporate aims may be diluted.

In war, then, let your great object be victory, not lengthy campaigns.

This is also true for the world of projects, since time and effort have no benefit if success is not the outcome. It is of no value achieving satisfaction in the method of executing a project if the result of the project is deemed to be a failure.

The common failure of projects is to fight the customer or the suppliers so much that in the end the project is unsuccessful. It is also of no value to win arguments and score on points if one fails to achieve the original goals that had been set.

There are very few occasions when a project is viewed as successful but does not reach the desired outcome. This may seem an unnecessary comment, but should be considered in terms of looking at many overly bureaucratic organizations. The restrictions put in place are often outdated and counter-productive. The actions of the project team are measured against compliance with procedures rather than the success of the result.

The business world is set to drive targets and goals, not methods, provided such methods are maintained within ethical boundaries. The objectives of a project should not be defined by artificial rules that promote a lack of ownership or initiative. There should be an ethos ensuring that the players look for effective options and develop their strategy accordingly.

The world of projects is very difficult and for many organizations historically is not an area of which they have a background. Where projects are a common way of working, maintaining a degree of flexibility of approach ensures that opportunities are not overlooked.

> Thus it may be known that the leader of armies is the arbiter of the people's fate, the man on whom it depends whether the nation shall be in peace or in peril.

For project management, there is no easy way; one is dealing with both people and organizations. Leadership and the development of effective and meaningful strategies are crucial if a project is to be successful. These strategies must be based on satisfying both the project and the corporate objectives.

In developing a winning proposition, the key elements of the strategy must be defined before the team launches into activity. Ensuring success means that these approaches are fully recognized at the start of the execution phase. Failing to identify what is necessary before starting the implementation phase will probably leave the prospect or project floundering after a short time. Alternative success will only be possible by devoting additional resources to meet objectives, which will certainly reduce the overall profitability.

Business operations and projects will probably draw on wide range of capabilities and resources, both internal and external, and programming these essential elements before launching a project is crucial. Once activities or a process are in motion there will be little opportunity to drag it back on track without some negative impact. It is clearly important to identify these resource requirements when developing cost profiles aimed at meeting the objectives.

The project team is dependent on having leadership focused on achieving clearly defined goals, and supporting the team in meeting these objectives. Developing integrated planning is a key factor in ensuring that the appropriate skills and resources are defined and scheduled to meet an optimized approach. These plans become the central point upon which every member of the venture should be able to focus his or her individual contribution.

The execution strategy must be focused on a wide range of issues and must address these to ensure that the maximum benefit is achieved. It should also be clear that many aspects of the project require both internal and external acceptance. The project manager must lead and drive the team, while managing complex relationships with customers, partners and suppliers. Each will have a potential impact on the final outcome, and thus understanding the interaction of these relationships within the overall strategy is the key to success.

The objective of a business venture is to be successful and not simply to have the most well-managed and visible operation. In our experience we have seen organizations that have very well established operating and reporting programmes. The danger in some cases is that compliance takes precedence over the needs and potential opportunities that may be presented. This is a very complex environment, which requires that the team is both properly trained and focused towards the end-game, while at the same time being ready to adapt to change and innovative in its solutions.

The strategic approach should provide for innovation both in developing alternative propositions for the customer but also to meet and adapt to the changing business environment within which these will be delivered. The paradox is that, the more innovative the approach the greater the need to consider the widest possible strategic perspective and ensure that all those involved have a clear picture of how to deliver any alternative that is outside traditional thinking.

CHAPTER 4

Attack by stratagem

In the practical art of war, the best thing of all is to take the enemy's country whole and intact; to shatter and destroy it is not good. So, too, it is better to recapture an army entire than to destroy it, to capture a regiment, a detachment or a company entire than to destroy them.

Strength is relative and it is better to develop allies than enemies, whether they are customers, suppliers or even occasionally competitors. This is also true in the project world, and the traditional concept of battling every party will eventually result in a project being less successful or missing opportunities that could be exploited.

Many major contracts have faltered because of a desire to be seen as dominant. In the final analysis, the problems that are encountered often stem from a lack of understanding and co-operation. This should not mean that either party has to be weak or always opt for concessions, but exploring the benefits of a collaborative approach can produce more valuable results.

As has been outlined before, the power in any contracting environment has a habit of fluctuating between the parties at various stages in the venture. Therefore in any buyer/purchaser relationship, the focus on the end result is often more important than any individual peak or trough in the relationship.

This type of approach is not, however, an easy road to follow or master and requires a clear vision and strategy among the participants. What may initially be considered strong opponents may weaken themselves by trying to maintain the high ground.

The supplier relationship is of particular importance in this regard, where too rigid a focus – for example, on the cost – may ultimately result in higher costs overall. Continual pressure to reduce prices may hide the true value, which is in the reduction of costs. Understanding the strengths and value of the players is crucial in developing an effective strategy for any project. A supplier that is forced to the wall may provide a limited contribution overall. In the longer term, what each learns can be turned to greater joint advantage.

> Hence to fight and conquer in all your battles is not supreme excellence; supreme excellence consists in breaking the enemy's resistance without fighting.

In most cases there is never a single point for negotiations. In fact, for long-term projects there will be a series of clarifications and a shifting of goals. It is therefore unlikely that a sustained attack can deliver the end results that are needed. Success comes from good negotiations where everyone feels they have won, or contributed to the outcome.

The skill of the negotiator is to achieve the desired result, not to win on points. The art in any project is to focus on the end-game and avoid conflict with the parties involved. This again does not mean that either side has to adopt a soft approach, but every venture will ultimately be a series of compromises and joint actions. The final success of the project will provide, or *should* provide, benefits for all.

Clearly there will always be those occasions where the mutuality of the objective has to be ignored because of some contractual impasse, but these situations are rare. Most business activities rely on a foundation of relationships, and to maintain these parameters in a productive way requires skilful dialogue not confrontation.

Many times the optimum outcome is clouded by a desire to establish superiority. The desire to win a battle then becomes more important than the eventual result. Strangely, this situation happens more often within organizations than it does between different organizations. Since in the latter case there is often more focus on the long-term outcome as opposed to internally, where positioning and internal politics is focused more individually.

In the project world, the number of parties involved can be extensive and the opportunity for conflict greater. The gratification of achieving a satisfactory result is, however, perhaps the most important driver. The challenge then is to maintain position and deliver the best return, and in this the project environment offers daily opportunities for the really skilful negotiator.

Thus the highest form of generalship is to balk the enemy's plans.

The early bird catches the worm, or so it is said, and in the world of projects this is surely true. The earlier the involvement, the greater the opportunity to formulate an understanding of the requirements and customer needs in order to respond effectively.

Building a sound knowledge of market trends and customer investment strategy is crucial, and critical to understanding one's own strategy and developing an approach that will be successful. The essence of any business venture is to create propositions that offer something new and will add value for the customer or supplier. Customers often ignore the supplier investment strategy in their own plans but as these can be essential ingredients in the final outcome, so perhaps ignoring them could be counter-productive.

When faced with competition there is a similar need to address the market before the approach has time to be copied. Taking the advantage in any business project has to be balanced against being able to deliver what is promised. Many business ventures start with a sound idea but fail to recognize the infrastructure required to close the trading loop.

In the negotiation environment the element of surprise is a key to controlling the outcome. The more time provided for consolidation, the greater the opportunity for positions to become crystallized, which in turn will make discussions more complex.

Superiority has to be considered a transient feature: when buying, the less time provided to the opposition the better, but when selling the reverse is probably more advantageous. Therefore in any strategy one should consider relative strengths and position oneself accordingly.

Most important, whatever role or position one is in, the key factor is to understand the implications and benefits of moving quickly and being confident of the outcome.

The next best is to prevent the junction of the enemy's forces.

If the opponent is strong it is better to undermine his or her confidence and alliances, but never by devaluing your competition. One poor strategy used in the selling process is to promote the failings of others rather than elevate the advantages of your own approach.

But many customers will encourage this situation, mainly as a ploy to apply leverage to existing partners. This approach can be exploited by a newcomer but often results in significant investment and few successes.

Where a customer has preferences in approach these can often limit where a newcomer can intervene. It is also common that, in large infrastructure projects, level-two players may already hold positions of strength with the end customer. This can either be local political influence or operational comfort. To dislodge these incumbents can be counter-productive, since ultimately you may find them preselected for your final solution by the customer.

Attacking an alliance may be a costly and negative approach, but attacking the close relationship and shifting the alliance to your proposition can be a closing factor in securing the project, building a solution that ultimately brings the customer preference into your approach and presents a more acceptable package. It should always be remembered, though, that if successful one may be forced to work with a party you had previously been attacking and as such the relationship may be difficult.

> The next in order is to attack the enemy's army in the field.

In a sales context there is always a problem in identifying the power bases within one's opposition. In customer organizations, particularly multinationals, there are often many fractions. Thus one can be considered favourably in some areas and viewed very aggressively in others. It may not be the overall organization that one has to challenge, but only one part of it.

In many cases this may be the power of the purchasing department versus the technical group or operators. Before one attacks it is crucial to understand where the real power is, and if the battle is worth winning. Similarly, within supplier organizations the stresses that exist internally may be pulling against your objective. In many politically driven countries, for example, there may be differing objectives and responsibilities.

In such cases while the overall goal may be to satisfy the customer, the obstacles within functional groups or political rules may be acting against you. Each of these bodies could be considered as separate armies, and each requires a different strategy to ensure a successful outcome.

As in any conflict, one must first understand the relative strengths and positions, and if possible seek a strategy that avoids conflict. Often it is better to isolate an issue than to charge forward. This can also be seen with internal projects that cut across various functional strategies within organizations.

What makes the project world so interesting is that during the life of a project there is never only a single opponent, and as things progress the target may change. This we have referred to previously and should always be a consideration. Once one decides to attack there is often a course of events set in motion that cannot be reversed, therefore any action and strategy must look beyond the immediate challenge.

> And the worst policy of all is to besiege walled cities.

Few business ventures can operate with a siege mentality, though over the years major organizations have embarked on strategies of attempting to control the market. In many internal development projects and mergers the siege mentality can easily be identified as disparate groups or functions trying to secure their position.

It may be considered that long-term projects could be related to the siege concept. These cases, particularly infrastructure and aerospace projects, may take many years to complete. As a result, the relative positions of the parties involved are locked into a programme that contains resources and drains them simultaneously.

This concern in the project world often leads to a strategy of preservation of resources for the long haul. As a result, the early direction of key activities is deferred or delayed having an impact of defeating the true objective. In most projects their success is governed by the first quartile of activity and it is during this period that success is gained. Even worse is the philosophy of not spending until there is a contract, and then finding that key issues have been overlooked. This will often happen when capture and execution groups are segregated.

The other factor that seldom gets the attention it should is that long-duration projects will also drain the energy of those trying to execute them. Time is a costly commodity, and the desire to reduce costs will often override adequate resourcing, with the effect of burning out the key players.

If a project is long-term it should be viewed as many shorter stages or individual battles rather than one long challenge. The programme and resources should be assigned appropriately to ensure a consistent and functional approach from start to finish. Failure to see the long road has caused many projects to flounder.

The rule is, not to besiege walled cities if it can possibly be avoided. The preparation of mantlets, movable shelters, and various implements of war, will take up three whole months, and piling up of mounds over against the walls will take three months more.

Viewing the project as a complete entity will lead to a lack of focus further along the trail. Assuming a quick win will in most cases create a strain that will result in failure, whether this is in terms of profitability or resources. There has to be adequate time spent on planning once a strategy has been developed.

Many projects teams leap into action on day one and find some three months later that the route and resources they selected were inappropriate. Often even the strategy is ignored in favour of seeing rapid progress. The end result will be rework and waste.

Every project, once initiated, should go through a validation process to ensure that there is a full understanding of the aims and a valid strategy. Then the planning process and team building needs to start, ensuring that the appropriate skills, tools and people will be made available.

In the project world there is no substitute for proper planning, and the longer the projected duration of the project the more important this aspect becomes. Even short-duration projects should not be allowed to rush off spending resources without appropriate consideration of what has been targeted and who is going to do the work.

Where necessary, even training may have to be considered in the early days. Many times projects fail because in the initial enthusiasm the goal was to get bodies involved without first considering the skills and capabilities that existed. As a result, in the latter stages when costs are escalating and progress is slowing one finds that the early gains have been eroded. Adequate preparation and planning is the cornerstone of all successful projects.

The general, unable to control his irritation, will launch his men to the assault like swarming ants, with the result that one-third of his men are slain, while the town still remains untaken. Such are the disastrous effects of a siege.

It is easy to see where a good general and good project manager have (or should have) similar attributes. The essence of project management is leadership and effective use of resources. There are many organizations that ignore this principle and look only for a project manager who portrays the most aggressive approach.

Once again, the good project, and thus also the good project manager, is the one that uses resources well and considers the long-term outcome. Maintaining pressure yet at the same time ensuring that effort is both recognized and rewarded, while always being productive. If the project team gets exhausted in the first months, then the project will ultimately suffer. The majority of people want to be useful and constructive, but if they see their efforts being wasted they reduce their input.

At the same time, it is also important that when there is a need to turn up the heat, the team recognizes this and follows. Projects tend to be cyclic in their needs and thus while it is important to conserve resources and effort it is also important to use them when necessary.

In a fast track engineering project, which may require a degree of parallel engineering, this balance becomes difficult to maintain. In these cases it is important to focus on critical path analysis and ensure that any overlap is minimized. Whatever may be needed, it is crucial to maintain communication with those involved and ensure that they understand the drivers and risks.

People are a key resource for any project, and must be used to best effect. The perception of progress may be a factor in many projects, particularly where the customer may be looking to support external funding, but even in these cases there has to be constructive expenditure. This is the challenge the project manager has to meet while ensuring that the true effort and resources are utilized appropriately.

> Therefore the skilful leader subdues the enemy's troops without any fighting; he captures their cities without laying siege to them; he overthrows their kingdom without lengthy operations in the field.

The challenge in any business venture is to follow the principle of martial arts. Turning the strength of the opponent to your advantage should be an underlying aim, and in the project world it should be a goal.

Very often the first view of any business challenge is to consider how strong one's opponent may be. The next step should be to look at where this strength can be redirected, and to focus on the potential that this new channel could develop. In many cases, for example, the use of a contract and legal measures can be quite daunting, but when analysed against each party's real needs the threat can be turned to advantage.

Strength is relative and should not always be assumed to be on the side of those who threaten its use. In many cases, suppliers have special skills, and while they may be considered as being at the mercy of a major customer, they may be crucial to that customer's success.

To complete a project to meet the aspirations of both parties and within the restraints of cost and resources is a major challenge, and to master the difficulties of local cultural and political pressures takes the execution to another level. The concept of winning without a fight is not one that many understand or deploy; assuming that the strong will prevail but, as many have seen, it is the clever that usually triumph.

Working to attain collaboration and developing a win–win approach takes considerable effort, but may more often than not provide more meaningful results.

All these issues are addressed throughout these writings, but the clear message to any project team is to value time and resources: since once they are expended they are lost, so they should be utilized with care.

> With his forces intact he will dispute the mastery of the Empire, and thus, without losing a man, his triumph will be complete. This is the method of attacking by stratagem.

As a project team must be viewed in a holistic context to ensure that every aspect of the project is supported, so the success of the project must also be viewed holistically. While the principle aim of any project must be to add value to the organization, whether by internal development or commercial business, it should always aim at meeting the multiple objectives of the customer.

A project that delivers within the agreed budget or contract price may be viewed as a success by the CFO (Chief Financial Officer), however, failure to meet the other parameters may be counter-productive in the longer term. Similarly, a project that meets delivery targets and costs but fails to meet performance objectives may be deemed a failure.

Profit may be the key driver for any business, but sometimes the marketing impact of a single focus can limit future opportunities. It may also be that for marketing reasons a refined technical solution may provide a market edge, and the cost implications maybe outweighed by the benefits of market position.

The clear definition of project goals is crucial, and the focus on meeting these parameters must not be diluted. This is particularly true in terms of a project with an extended time-scale. As the costs grow and the margin becomes depleted the overall objectives get lost in a targeting of cost implications.

The truly successful project is the one that meets all its intended goals, and in particular leave the customer satisfied with the outcome. In many cases, failure to meet time and cost restraints can be discounted by a customer who finds a more effective solution than originally intended. In others, the position can be reversed, a situation that often arises in highly technical projects where the interaction of engineering drives a project beyond the practical needs of the customer.

> It is the rule in war, if our forces are ten to the enemy's one, to surround him; if five to one, to attack him; if twice as numerous, to divide our army into two.

The key to any project, and thus the need to create an effective strategy is to ensure that the resources and approach deployed provide measured response. This requires the careful analysis of the opponent and a controlled application of the appropriate team.

Each of the three options suggested assumes that there is a single opponent but, as we have discussed, there maybe multiple elements that must be addressed and satisfied. Therefore the obvious and direct approach may not be the most successful.

It is also, as outlined earlier, that even within the opposing organization there may be differing camps with alternative objectives. Understanding the relative strength and impact that these fractions may have is a crucial part of developing the right strategy.

This comes to the fore when developing a negotiation approach, where wielding the big stick may in the long run be detrimental to the desired outcome. When it comes to negotiations, the stronger side often starts from a position of strength but ultimately finds itself losing the overall objective or creating an environment that in the longer term can deflect from the prime goal.

What is certain is that there is no 'one size fits all' solution, and the role of the players is to understand the full implications and objectives. Maintaining this total perspective is often a hard task in many organizations, particularly where the project concept is not in the normal business mode.

Within a project, the need for a team approach is most important if the overall project aims are not to be hijacked by certain players having their own viewpoints. This again often comes to the fore in the debate between, say, engineering and procurement, where the responsibilities are clearly defined but the best outcome can only be developed jointly.

> If equally matched, we can offer battle; if slightly inferior in numbers, we can avoid the enemy; if quite unequal in every way, we can flee from him.

The true skill in any business environment is to chose your targets carefully and then focus where you see the best opportunity for success. In the project world this has to start in having a good and meaningful evaluation of the market opportunities. The costs of developing and supporting a major project can be very significant, and to chase a prospect that is not a real opportunity is a waste.

When the real prospect has been identified, one needs to evaluate the relative strengths and weaknesses that may govern success. This means looking at all aspects and implications, and in the global market these are more complex than simply price and delivery. There should also be a good understanding of what drives the customer, and where one may be able to add or leverage advantage.

The development of a project execution strategy should start at this stage in order to establish and validate one's capability of turning the prospect into a winning proposition. If one ignores the downstream needs and impacts while preparing a contract for a customer, one will inevitably create a potential failure.

Deciding which approach has the best chance of success has to take into account the strength not only of the customer but also the position of the competition. If you consider you are strong without really measuring your position, you may create an approach that is in fact weak. In a case where all parties may be equal, this will drive you towards creating an approach that is perhaps more collaborative.

It is hard for organizations to accept that they may be weak or at a disadvantage in any given market. To ignore the facts will certainly drive one down a route that is likely to fail. In such cases, the best strategy might be to create alliances or bring in partners that can complement one's own strengths and develop a unified proposition. It is also true that, when considering the competition, one tends to think others are generally more skilled or influential. In most cases this is fear, not fact.

Hence, though an obstinate fight may be made by a small force, in the end it must be captured by the larger force.

Flexibility should be the watchword for all project-type business operations, and it is vital in the global context. Being able to respond to customers' needs in a constructive way often means suppressing a natural urge to consider one's own organization superior.

Many organizations with long histories of technical competence and experience are driven to present propositions that fail to recognize the customer's own background. In such cases, despite the fact that there might be a good reason for such an approach, a customer will incline towards those who respond to his/her perceptions and experience.

On the other hand, those who take a totally complicit viewpoint run the risk of being sucked into approaches that ultimately will result in failure. Often the salesman will support this compliance approach to keep the customer satisfied, a contract will result, and when the salesman has responsibility for the execution it then becomes an operations problem.

The most successful salesman is one who never agrees with the customer, but also never disagrees either, manoeuvring discussions to a point of compromise or agreement. It must always be the end-game for the customer to consider that they have achieved the best possible outcome.

In the project execution phase, the hard-and-fast approach, standing intransigent against all requests, is also flawed, since at some point there will be a need for some form of concession, which will ultimately be refused.

In the case of many government contracts, particularly those with foreign governments, the attitude of always being right can be detrimental to meeting the end-game. Therefore, sometimes it may be more beneficial to concede even when right is on one's side. Being stubborn in any situation will ultimately lead to loss of advantage at some stage of the relationship.

Now the general is the bulwark of the State; if the bulwark is complete at all points, the State will be strong; if the bulwark is defective, the State will be weak.

Project managers are the front line of the company and may be seen to act in a similar way to generals. Certainly, there are many commonalities in the two roles. The effective management of projects will therefore strengthen the organization in many ways. The role, however, must always be driven by the business objectives of the organization and not the aspirations of the individual.

This element of project management is often ignored as the project sets out to establish and achieve its goals, which sometimes inadvertently conflict with the organizations business strategy. It is crucial that any execution strategy that is developed is linked clearly to the goals of the business. Many projects that have been deemed failures could have been successes but for conflict within the organization.

When organizations are driven by their project group they must invest in that resource and ensure that its project management teams are properly focused on the objectives. On the other hand, an organization may be strong in every functional aspect, whether technical or commercial, but if it does not have sound project management that can integrate and direct these skills it will fail.

In the global market, where few organizations can support all activities, or where there is a need to build temporary organizations, the role of the project team and its leaders becomes a fundamental element of the whole business.

Effective and strong leadership, together with the knowledge and skills to meet the challenges of the market, can make all the difference between successful organizations and those that must fail at some point.

There are three ways in which a ruler can bring misfortune upon his army:

By commanding the army to advance or to retreat, being ignorant of the fact that it cannot obey. This is called hobbling the army.

By attempting to govern an army in the same way as he administers a kingdom, being ignorant of the conditions which obtain an army. This causes restlessness in the soldiers' minds.

By employing the officers of his army without discrimination, through ignorance of the military principle of adaptation to circumstances. This shakes the confidence of the soldiers.

But when the army is restless and distrustful, trouble is sure to come from the other feudal princes. This is simply bringing anarchy into the army, and flinging victory away.

The success of a project must also depend on the effective support of the management towards the project manager and the project team. Clearly, leadership only comes from an organization being prepared to delegate authority and responsibility, ensuring that once the game is in play the channels of command are not compromised.

This may seem somewhat simplistic, but in cases where projects have been deemed failures it is often because of the conflicting instructions that may be issued from outside the project team. As was highlighted earlier, projects by their very nature are holistic groups incorporating many functions, where the individual drivers of the customer being interpreted and focused into a composite solution. When external instructions are forced into this platform for specific functions or internal pressure groups, then the overall strategy becomes vulnerable.

The challenge for the project manager is to hold an agreed line and execute it within the confines of an agreed strategy. If there are multiple influences, then the command and control function collapses and the project is destined to fail. This lack of joined-up thinking is quite often a factor in the failure of projects. In such cases either the information used in the decision-making process or the methods of execution conflict with the overall strategy.

Projects need clear rules and uncompromising attention to the authority and responsibility of the project manager.

> Thus we may know that there are five essentials for victory: He will win who knows when to fight and when not fight. He will win who knows how to handle both superior and inferior forces. He will win whose army is animated by the same spirit throughout all its ranks. He will win who, prepared himself, waits to take the enemy unprepared. He will win who has military capacity and is not interfered with by the sovereign.

In summary, the success of a project can be captured in these five basic elements of a structured strategy. If this framework is supported by an organization, then the chances of meeting the objectives are greatly improved. Building these into the strategic thinking of the organization is the key to developing an approach that can generate a significant differential between one's company and the opposition.

Understanding when it makes sense to pursue a prospect is the hardest of challenges, particularly in a tough market place, but chasing lost causes will eventually drain the capacity to tackle real opportunities. Ensuring that one has a solid basis for execution and a good understanding of the relative strengths and weaknesses in order to win is equally important, and this will form the background for an effective strategy to maximize the eventual outcome.

The development of an approach that assesses the most effective use of resources and focuses on the cost–benefit analysis linked to the critical path of the project will maintain momentum throughout the life of the project. Ensuring that each member of the team is able to contribute to their fullest extent by understanding where they fit in and what the impact of factions will be.

The underlying need for any project is to maintain a sound strategy, and a clear command and communications chain will keep the multiple project players locked into the project plan. In an environment operating in a global context and built around a virtual organization, which is not limited by geography or location, the need for integrated management and communications is crucial.

The earlier one takes action and less ready the opposition, the more opportunity there will be for success. Those who wait to respond to the market will generally be disadvantaged by the competition. Developing a business strategy that looks beyond current thinking can provide a competitive edge, which may only exist for a limited period before the unusual becomes the norm and one has to move on.

While business strategy and project strategy should always be linked and be the focus for the project manager, there must always be a clear authority and responsibility assigned to the project team. These factors will ensure that the project team has a true focus on its objectives and the customer drivers. What ever the strategic programme consistency in the management structure is important to ensure that the team has unimpaired direction and support towards success.

Hence the saying: If you know the enemy and know yourself, you need not fear the result of a hundred battles. If you know yourself but not the enemy, for every victory gained you will also suffer a defeat. If you know neither the enemy nor yourself, you will succumb in every battle.

The basic need to develop and execute a project is to have a sound understanding of the market place, competition, customers and oneself. And the latter has to be considered a key feature to ensure that projects are planned realistically and executed successfully.

The more one knows and understands the drivers and pressures, the more opportunity there is to find innovative solutions and advances to customers that will attract them. Realistic perspectives of one's own capabilities and those of the opposition must drive such skill and knowledge assessments.

Success will not come only from firm and established procedures, but also from the ability of skilful professionals to work within consistent frameworks that allow for adaptability and change. At the same time, the more knowledge one has of the opposition, the greater the prospect of adopting approaches they are unable to challenge.

Projects are complex arrangements involving many players, and to achieve success one has to minimize the number of variables that may arise. At the same time no project is likely to be risk-free, and the project team must maintain an effective strategy of risk management. The mapping of business processes allows organizations to fully understand their activities at every level and to refine their approach to optimize focus. In a project environment that may involve several organizations, these process evaluations can be even more crucial if the integrated approach is to meet its objectives and capitalize on its combined skills and resources.

Failure to understand these critical points and to build a structure that supports the deployment of resources and to control them is fundamental to their ability to be successful. Through the individual success of the team members and task groups will come the overall success of the main venture. By constraining the ability of individuals to feel successful and be recognized for that success one limits the probability of overall success.

CHAPTER 5

Tactical disposition

The good fighters of old first put themselves beyond the possibility of defeat, and then waited for an opportunity of defeating the enemy.

All business bears some degree of risk and in general terms, the greater the risk, the higher the return. The management of these risks is what sets good companies apart from bad ones. Global projects are a particularly dangerous arena, where risk management is the main underlying responsibility.

The more risk one can take on and manage well, the greater the differential one has with the competition and the more opportunity to be the customer's choice. The customer also has risk to manage and the more they can transfer to their suppliers, the less vulnerable their development becomes.

Risk identification, and more importantly mitigation, is one of the cornerstones of project management; the greater the skill in this regard, the better chance of a successful project. The management of risk starts with the first identification of a project prospect and continues through out the life of that project. At every stage, the evaluation and implementation of counter-strategies has to be the role of the whole project team.

Perhaps the greatest opportunities also come from identifying where others have missed vulnerabilities through poor risk management, and this can be turned to one's advantage. Next to costs risks and responsibilities are the key features of contracting in the project the world. Most negotiations will centre on the passing of risk between the parties.

The biggest risk for most business ventures, however, is to adopt a risk-averse culture, which will stifle valuable opportunities and create a major risk of rigidity. Even worse, this approach will stop innovation and the lateral thinking attitude that is necessary to build or try alternative ideas. Risk management skill is the difference between success and failure for most projects. Risk-free projects are the ones anyone can do.

> To secure ourselves against defeat lies in our own hands, but the opportunity of defeating the enemy is provided by the enemy himself.

The more secure you are in your risk management strategy and capability, the more vulnerability there is created for your opponent. Most projects are complex configurations of skills and resources, whether one's own or those of partners, and as such are very susceptible to the creation of risk. In a global market, political and cultural issues can increase these risks exponentially. The better one understands these risks, the more opportunity there is to establish opportunities from them.

If your risk management approach is sound you will proceed with greater confidence. The reverse is also true: if you are unsure of your position and thus build high contingencies, it is likely that you will lose out to those who have a broader understanding.

The essence of project management is to create a risk-aware culture that focuses not on the strengths but on the vulnerabilities you can identify. Then ensure that the team and all actions are centred on implementing appropriate responses.

Therefore, the more confident you are, the more risk you will be prepared to undertake and thus the stronger your marketing and execution position. Many organizations fail to recognize this and as a result suffer a weakened position in any business venture.

The stronger the risk management culture the more robust will be the platform on which business, and in particular projects, are undertaken. The more integrated the appreciation of risk in whatever form, the more likely the project team will be to push the envelope in terms of exploiting opportunity.

Risk-averse organizations tend to engender a blame culture, which in turn will undermine the confidence of the team and dilute effort and flair. Competitiveness is relative, thus the stronger you are, the weaker the competition

> Thus the good fighter is able to secure himself against defeat, but cannot make certain of defeating the enemy

Over-confidence, however, can also be dangerous. If a person believes they are beyond the impact of risk, they will certainly fail to recognize those risks that exist. At the same time you cannot and should not underestimate your opponent's ability to assume risk.

In any business situation, the rules that you play by and the knowledge you have may also be available to your opponent. Many times, traditional assessments of opponents have been based on historical performance, and many times this has been proved wrong. As outlined earlier, the market changes and the pressures of that market can induce a new approach from others. Therefore, just when you think they will accept greater risk, or not, they change position and your strength is defused.

Therefore, understanding the business landscape and the risks it has within it is as important in developing your strategy as it is in understanding the strategy of others. In many games the winning team often plays poorly but wins because of the failure of the opposition. It is also a common problem for this to be taken as a success when in fact it is a failure, apart from the record books.

It may in some cases be that your confidence will force the other side to take on more risk than they had previously considered. Exploiting this tactic can at times be beneficial, but it is clearly a risk in itself. It should not be assumed that your confidence would always be viewed favourably, since in some situations it may create a negative impression and thus be counterproductive.

Therefore, the assessment of risk and the position taken may be geared towards success but it is not likely to be a consistent tool with which to unseat one's opponent. Understanding it and developing one's confidence will certainly improve the strategic position taken.

Hence the saying: One may *know* how to conquer without being able to *do* it.

The more risk taken, the greater the probability of success, provided it is known how to manage that risk. The chances of success may be improved but the final outcome can never be guaranteed. You may be able to predict the result with a greater degree of confidence, but one cannot ensure that prediction is correct.

Some risk can be calculated, and in most case business judgement is used to understand the implications. In many cases the risks can be covered by insurance, as is often the case by governments to cover political risk when supporting local industry. Some risk may be so great or improbable that one may decide to take a positive position in any event. Alternatively, the failure to take the risk may be more risky than the proposition.

This last case is one that should always be watched for in others. For example, in the project one may look to pass as much risk to the supplier as possible. The supplier, being desperate for orders, is prepared to assume unrealistic levels of responsibility, with the result that they become more vulnerable and may fail. The effort to shed risk has in that case created a new risk for the project. Once again, the understanding of the risk profile and a realistic assessment of it should be part of the risk management culture.

In some cases, lack of experience on the part of the buyer may push them to try and force a supplier to take on liabilities that are out of proportion to the return they can expect. The strength of the buyer then forces the supplier to withdraw. The aim may have been correct but the result is that a good supplier has been lost and this has perhaps brought new risks with untried suppliers.

There are many counter-balances in the deployment of risk-management strategies, and therefore certainty of success can never be absolutely assured. The project team must understand and focus on maximum sustainable benefit.

> Security against defeat implies defensive tactics; ability to defeat the enemy means taking the offensive.

The stronger one's position, the more likely it is that opponents will take risks, and the more risks they take the greater their chance of failure. Alternatively, if their risk-management approach and mitigation strategies are better than yours, then ultimately they may be more successful. This is the paradox of the business world.

In general terms, the more robust is your standing in the market, and the more established your capability, the greater the opportunity to wait and let the opponent come to you. In any situation throughout the project if you do not have to concede to risk then don't, so long as you really understand the implications of standing firm. As we have already highlighted, the objective is to win the war, not the battle. Therefore a defensive position may be only a short-term solution and sometimes counter to the long-term aims.

In similar vein the organization that takes a defensive position on risk may well find itself losing out to a more risk-aware opponent. There is a delicate balance to be maintained and it is the management of this that is likely to define the result. Since it is never possible to eliminate risk entirely, a purely defensive position is probably unworkable.

On the other hand, when you face a situation that against all reasonable benchmarks not likely to be successful then taking an offensive position may be more practical. This is a key tactic in negotiations, for while the attention goes on the issue that you must lose, other issues become obscured.

The pros and cons of when to run and when to fight are related more to tactics but these can only be properly assessed and developed if one has a sound understanding of the risk profile. As any project progresses, the positions alter and thus a risk-management programme must remain dynamic at all times.

> Standing on the defensive indicates insufficient strength; attacking, a super-abundance of strength

All business strategies must be established against the background of both the organization and the marketplace. When one has a full order book and a healthy marketplace, there is less of an appetite for risk. When the marketplace is hungry, the reverse is generally the case. Unfortunately, when organizations are feeling comfortable they seldom expend resources on developing capabilities to handle the hard times, and when those hard times arrive, they are unprepared.

Clearly, when an organization is not confident of its risk-management capability, it becomes defensive. This in turn leads to a weakness of position in the marketplace with the result that, often by a negative culture, it produces risks. When organizations are strong in risk management they are able to exploit their position in any market.

When considering a strategy, whether with a customer or a supplier, the reverse position is of greater interest: understanding where others see their risks and being able to address these provides a platform for exploiting their needs.

Taking a proactive approach to sharing risk with a view to benefiting both parties can often exploit negative risk. What makes you strong may make your opponents weak; therefore, by combining capabilities it may be possible to create even greater added value for the other party, which in turn will add value to your own position. This can be a major factor when considering complex projects, involving contributions from a number of parties.

In the project world the opposition may be a combination of factors beyond all the primary players. In such cases, the combined effort of managing risk and sharing responsibility may be more appropriate than individual stances or strategies.

> The general who is skilled in defence hides in the most secret recesses of the earth; he who is skilled in attack flashes forth from the topmost heights of heaven. Thus on the one hand we have the ability to protect ourselves; on the other, a victory that is complete.

The biggest risk within a project is in not addressing risk. The balance must be maintained between the optimist and the pessimist. Each takes a view of the world, but from diametrically opposite positions. The optimist will ignore risk on the basis that if one moves fast enough one will overcome opposition by speed. The pessimist takes the view that if nothing is done, the risk will disappear. Both are clearly wrong, but since projects tend to bring together a variety of people there surely will be some of each type included.

The role of project management is to take a holistic view of the project and assess risk from every direction, then develop a strategy that takes into account the most effective route to minimize or mitigate the risk, but maintain the project's probability of success.

Project success must be a common goal, and the approaches and practices must be driven by this common aim. While individual skills and attitudes may evoke particular interest, it is the team that will ultimately win through. The collective responsibility towards risk management is crucial if the objectives are to be realized.

The strategy for managing risk has to be one that combines the skills of all and ensures that no actions are taken that are driven solely by individual concerns or aspirations. The interdependence of projects makes them interesting environments within which to work, and it is the recognition of this within the team that will ensure an effective risk profile.

> To see victory only when it is within the ken of the common herd is not the acme of excellence. Neither is it the acme of excellence if you fight and conquer and the whole empire says 'Well done!'

The lower the risk, the greater the challenge from competition since if there is no risk then there can be no mastery of it. If one has a level and risk-free playing field it will probably be only strength and endurance that prevails. Therefore skill and differentiation will have little impact on the potential for success.

The mastery of the project environment provides a platform for approaching opportunities with high risk and one would therefore anticipate higher returns. The development of any project must be structured around the proper assessment of the vulnerabilities of the task, together with a sound strategy to manage the risks involved.

The essence of any strategy is to place the organization in a position of strength and confidence such that it can undertake challenges that others may avoid. The balancing of risk and return can be significantly improved if the project has a valid and robust risk mitigation strategy.

Many times, what is seen as a successful project and used as a benchmark for the future has in fact derived its success from an inflated comfort zone. This can often be seen in cases where, for example, the baseline cost estimate of the project was heavily padded. Thus, when the project proceeds, a favourable outcome is certain. This is not true success, and will create future risks from over-confidence, of both the organization and individuals involved.

Projects are complex and challenging environments, which can create great satisfaction from a good result. Understanding the risk profile and meeting those challenges engenders true satisfaction and demonstrates real skill.

> To lift an autumn hair is no sign of great strength; to see the sun and moon is no sign of sharp sight; to hear the noise of thunder is no sign of a quick ear.

Risk management is not simply about mastering obvious challenges. It is about understanding those issues, that are not obvious, or may be hidden or result from upstream issues within one's strategy. The concept of 'if it's easy anyone can do it' should be the underlying mantra for any project team.

There are many forms of risk within the project landscape, ranging from the impact of error through to those that perhaps only the psychics among us could see and avoid. The risk envelope must be viewed not only from the simplistic perspective of relating current or historical practice to challenge but also from the unpredictable nature of the business environment.

It is relatively easy to define a risk where one may be looking to extend the performance of known technology. This can be measured and evaluated.

A degree of comfort may be attained through the duplication of critical functions, greater testing, or extra caution, say, in manufacture, or additional spares. The same risk, however, may be amplified beyond acceptable limits depending on the end location. If a product fails in a hostile environment the impacts in time and cost if the required skills or parts are not readily available can lead to a more risk-averse approach being needed.

Therefore, the perspective of risk, however small, may be a factor of resources and environment rather than complexity. The risk scenario may be further multiplied by political and cultural pressures, which may have a dramatic influence on recovery plans.

What is also clear is that what may be a risk in one location may be insignificant in another and vice versa. A sound risk profile must therefore look not just at what is known, which is manageable, but also, and perhaps more importantly, at what is *not* known and therefore unmanageable.

> What the ancients called a clever fighter is one who not only wins, but excels in winning with ease.

The impact of globalization has been to stretch the knowledge and experience of many organizations. As traditional markets contracted and future projects were only available in the wider world, so there was a natural movement towards them. Conceptually, those that had been successful at home in traditional markets assumed that this business model could be transported.

There is certainly no substitute for experience. Too often, however, that experience is focused in a few key individuals or gained in other environments. In the same way, established methodologies may provide a sound basis for developing an approach, but they might not have the degree of flexibility to address new markets.

One of the exciting features of working in a major development project world is that no two projects are ever identical. Therefore, while the framework may be the same, the risks and opportunities can and will vary to a greater or lesser degree. This may even apply when considering identical projects in the same location, since variables among people and politics alone can completely change the risk profile.

Perception and untested assumptions are the two major factors in failed projects, and when developing a risk strategy these issues must be investigated fully, for what succeeded in the past may be a significant risk the next time around. In the case of both organizations and individuals, their past record of success is only an indicator of their capability, and if that capability was gained in a less complex market place it is no guarantee that those skills will prevail in the current venture.

As the business landscape changes, so the approaches must also change; and to ignore a future based on a successful past record may invoke greater risk. The real skill is to be able to manage risk through adaptability.

> Hence his victories bring him neither reputation for wisdom nor credit for courage. He wins his battles by making no mistakes. Making no mistakes is what establishes the certainty of victory, for it means conquering an enemy that is already defeated.

Therefore, if a project is to be successful it must establish a valid programme first to identify the range of risks inherent in the venture. This must be followed by an effective strategy to manage the elements of risk that fall outside normal business practice.

The process of risk management must be an integral part of the project culture and the business processes that are employed during its execution. Success will not simply be a result of effort and past experience but of a focused approach to dealing with those elements of the operation that can, individually or cumulatively, impede progress and the eventual outcome.

As has been suggested, the validation of an organization's or an individual's skills cannot be measured simply against past success if that result was within an environment that did not reflect a similar risk profile. The practices that have been developed in the past should, however, provide a sound structure to identify and manage these unstable influences on the project's operation.

As the marketplace and challenges increase, so must the risk elements of the project, and those focused on establishing a solid strategy and recognition of risk will place themselves in a winning position. Failure to approach risk in a proactive and disciplined manner must eventually disadvantage an organization and move the advantage further towards their opponents.

Risk is integral part of the business world, and it is only the degree of risk and how it is managed that influences the winners and losers. Risk can be exploited and the suggestion that the brave will inherit the earth is not intended to reflect a careless approach. Projects and those involved, whether in internal developments or business ventures, must be made risk-aware and adaptable.

> Hence the skilful fighter puts himself into a position which makes defeat impossible, and does not miss the moment for defeating the enemy.

Since, therefore, risk is an inevitable part of the project environment, it must follow that risk mitigation must be an integral part of the project operation. As we have defined it, risk may come in many guises, some direct and others more random or the result of earlier choices made by the project team.

The development of a risk register provides an ongoing record of what has already been established and what proposed strategy would be employed to counter the threat. A common failing is that during the pre-contract phase of a project up to negotiation and contract, many issues will be identified and incorporated. These may include key elements of a winning proposition based on an assessment of acceptable risk. If there is no record of these and negotiations have not eliminated them, then the risk carries forward into execution almost like a time bomb waiting to explode.

What cannot be seen or is not known cannot be dealt with or managed. A key feature of the project process must be the continued maintenance and monitoring of existing and newly established risks. This must be fully detailed and available to all the project team, since in many cases the strategy that has been evolved may be the responsibility of others to execute.

Mitigation may come in many forms, requiring action, preventive action or insurance in some context. In other cases it may simply be the need to acknowledge their existence. This latter type often falls within the scope of contingency or reserves being established for an eventual claim solution.

What is certain is that in very few cases does real risk go away of its own accord. Therefore understanding the conditions within which the risk can be handled will greatly increase the chances of success.

> †
> Thus it is that in war the victorious strategist only seeks battle after the victory has been won, whereas he who is destined to defeat first fights and afterwards looks for victory.

It can therefore be assumed that adequate monitoring and action in respect of risk can greatly enhance the chances of implementing a successful operation. It is likely that a sound risk-management strategy and programme will underpin the business objectives and assure the achievement of the project goals.

There are many who are very effective at finding solutions when something goes wrong or some new factor is introduced into the arena, but the real skill is to avoid potential problems by taking a proactive approach. Meeting the challenge when there is time to adjust rather than when there is a failure will have a major impact.

If one waits until there is no choice of action, then the likelihood is that the only solution available is not the most cost-effective or efficient one. This can result in higher costs, delays, and even perhaps a less effective technical approach. If it involves a customer it may generate at the least a lack of confidence and at the worst, possible claims. In the case of a supplier one may have to give away previously hard-won commercial advantages.

Understanding and managing risk also provides a solid basis for taking on even greater challenges and being successful. Risk should not be viewed simply in a negative way, since effective risk management can open the door to new opportunities. Since all projects generally involve some degree of risk to reserve finance, the more confident one is of the identified risks, the more flexibility is created.

Risk provision in many cases will also place a cap on the level of exposure the project can endure, so mitigating or controlling some of the risk can release resources and funds for other opportunities. The right mitigation strategy means a greater chance of success.

> The consummate leader cultivates the Moral Law, and strictly adheres to method and discipline; thus it is in his power to control success.

Risk management is the responsibility of the whole project team and must be focused on the aims and objectives of both the customer and the project. The project manager must be responsible for ensuring that the overall output and approach to the project remains within the objectives of the business organization. This structure ensures that in Sun Tzu's terms, 'the Moral Law' is maintained and the rules kept.

Those within the project that abdicate responsibility for managing risk or ignore the strategy in favour of localized initiatives will not only place the project at risk but may also endanger the overall organization. As risk is a multifaceted beast, so the management of it must be a collective approach and responsibility.

If project teams are well practised and disciplined in the risk management process the success of most projects can be assured. The teams will identify and implement mitigating solutions at the most effective point.

While all involved must take a proactive role in the risk process, there has to be a single point of responsibility and it falls to the project manager to monitor and direct, ensuring that the structure and form of all action reflects the holistic needs of the organization and customer.

Risk management must be viewed positively and approached with the best knowledge, skills and experience that are available. In this way the project can be executed effectively and driven to even greater success. A stable process will also help to ensure that when there are unexpected changes the team can react with a unified approach and be adaptable.

There can be only one direction for the project and the risk process within it; any deviation is likely to create even more risk and expose it to a greater possibility of failure.

> In respect of military method, we have, firstly, MEASUREMENT; secondly, ESTIMATION of quantity; thirdly, CALCULATION; fourthly, BALANCING of chances; fifthly, VICTORY.
>
> MEASUREMENT owes its existence to EARTH; ESTIMATION of quantity to MEASUREMENT; CALCULATION to ESTIMATION of quantity; BALANCING of chances to CALCULATION; and VICTORY to the BALANCING of chances.

These five rules can easily be applied to the risk-management process and management. There are many risk analysis programmes, which range from the very simple to highly complex, and each will satisfy different applications. They all, however, rely on the basic steps to evaluate and condition.

As has been outlined so far, the key first stage is to understand the business environment and the objectives and requirements of the project. This we have defined as *the earth*, and in a global context this can be extremely complex and far-reaching since it has to take into account economic and political variations within a global matrix of cultures and customs.

The next stage is to identify the many risks that may be anticipated and collect these together under a comprehensive process such as the implementation of a risk register. It should then be possible to *measure* the extent of risk, which is likely in each case. In a business context, virtually every risk can be converted into a commercial impact, basing the cost penalty or risk on the perceived extent of liability. Certainly there will be some risk that should not be measured in commercial terms, such as loss of life or the impact of long-term pollution. In more recent times, the growth in concern for corporate social responsibility and the wider context of sustainability have added a new dimension to the whole arena of risk profiling.

Clearly, not every risk will reach its full cost impact. In very complex contracting contracts there is generally an accumulation of liability that will set a maximum overall risk. Therefore, some individual risks may be considered on a cumulative basis. An *assessment* of risk probability can then be derived that considers the likelihood of the event and magnitude of the individual and cumulative liability or impact. Again, these liabilities may be more indirect, such the reflections of market acceptability between returns to the shareholders and the perception of customers and consumers.

From this overall assessment one can proceed to *calculate* the level of impact on a scale from high to low. This leads to the creation of solutions or responses to these situations and establishes the cost of any mitigation strategy. A *comparison* of the mitigation cost versus impact will define an acceptable degree of risk, which, if managed correctly, will lead to success.

A victorious army opposed to a routed one, is as a pound's weight placed in the scales against a single grain.

The onrush of a conquering force is like the bursting of pent-up waters into a chasm a thousand fathoms deep.

Creating a sound risk-management strategy and implementing a robust programme to manage the issues through the daily pressures of the project will establish a background that will allow the team players to work proactively. It is essential also to establish a good level of communication so that everyone understands the roles they are required to perform. This will generate confidence and commitment from the management, and in turn will cascade to the team, creating a proactive approach and platform that will underpin success.

When the team understands what has to be achieved and each has a clear view of his or her part in the implementation of a mitigation strategy, the project can then proceed at a fast pace. The full weight of the team and its supporting organizations can be focused on results. If the process is not well defined and structured, progress will be slow, as each stage has to be assessed and cross checked more carefully, with the result that such an approach will produce a project where individuals are risk-averse and it is unlikely to meet its objectives or be successful.

Risk management is not only the challenge of project teams; it is a fundamental element of success. Those who feel confident of the path they take will proceed with haste and seize opportunities. This does not mean that one should be looking for a risk-free operation, which is highly unlikely in any event. The key to success is in creating a culture that recognizes that risk is a fact of life but identifies these risks and designing a programme that allows them to be addressed effectively. The failure to adopt an effective approach engenders a team where those who are nervous and unsure will be hesitant, which in turn is likely to generate even greater stress and uncertainty, with the probably of creating an even more risky environment.

Therefore, the production of an effective risk-management strategy should be addressed early in the development of any project, and supported throughout the execution and completion cycle. It is a major challenge for business management but can be the defining factor for success.

Energy

The control of a large force is the same principle as the control of a few men: it is merely a question of dividing up their numbers.

Fighting with a large army under your command is nowise different from fighting with a small one: it is merely a question of instituting signs and signals.

To ensure that your whole host may withstand the brunt of the enemy's attack and remain unshaken, this is effected by manoeuvres direct and indirect.

There is a clear need within the project team for a structured framework, discipline and an understanding of the objectives and goals. There is also a need to exploit the skills and flair of the individual team members within their range of experience. The key to effective project management is to balance the level of command and control with empowerment to ensure that the maximum advantage is realized from innovation and creativeness.

Project operations that ignore individual contributions and ideas will generally be less successful, since many opportunities will be missed against a background of rigidity. Personal satisfaction and drive are key components of any organization and should be encouraged within acceptable guidelines. There is also a serious risk if individuals are prevented from challenging the status quo, so that ownership becomes devalued. Creating an environment that supports lateral thinking requires careful management and trust.

When dealing outside the project team in the marketplace, predictability is one of the biggest risks. If one's opponent can predict one's approach or reaction to any given event, they are in total control of your destiny.

The novel approach or implementation of lateral thinking can make the difference between success and failure. A frame of mind and project culture that accepts this concept will also allow the team to absorb more readily external influences and change, thus driving a dynamic view that can adapt to most situations.

The challenge, then, for any project manager is both to promote new ideas and to maintain an overall disciplined structure.

> That the impact of your army may be like a grindstone dashed against an egg, this is effected by the science of weak points and strong.

The implementation of effective tactics is crucial to the overall success of any business venture and we shall explore this more fully later. The essence of any strategy must be to create the optimized approach to the task at hand and to apply the most innovative solution to the challenge.

The traditional or heavyweight approach may be effective in meeting the initial goal but will it in strategic terms provide the long-term desired result? For many organizations, it is often very difficult to stray from tried and tested routines. The project team, however, can create much of their approach based on the necessary reaction to specific conditions and pressures.

Focusing the strategy and tactics within a project must be a combination of tested norms and rules, an understanding of customer needs and preferences, and be balanced against current market pressures.

For example, if a customer is focused on low cost and the competition has a low cost approach, then the presentation of a high-cost/high-tech solution will be unlikely to succeed. This clash often occurs within traditional organizations as their comfort zone is based on historically proven products. For the project team, the challenge is therefore not the customer but rather internal prejudice.

Many times within an engineering environment or project this conflict of technical opinion can drag the project down. It creates a significant imbalance when tendering for projects, and cost and time pressure when it arises during the execution period.

Innovation must be part of the culture if project teams are to meet the challenges of the global marketplace and be successful.

> In all fighting, the direct method may be used for joining battle, but indirect methods will be needed in order to secure victory.

Surprise and innovation are key tools within the business world, and many cases can be cited where a successful organization has moved quickly and with flair to wrong-foot their competitors. The project world can adopt similar alternative concepts to win contracts and improve position during the execution phase. Clearly, promoting this approach has to be done within a context of skilful teams, effective risk management and a culture of open-mindedness.

In relationships with customers and suppliers, battles should be avoided. Surprise and lateral thinking are likely to have far greater success. Confrontation generally burns energy and resources, and will tend to force positions to become entrenched much earlier in the debate. The whole point of developing a sound strategy is to conserve resources and maximize opportunity.

Innovative approaches have to be constructed and developed properly. They also rely in most organizations on establishing a buy-in from the less adventurous. It should also be recognized that management generally does not like surprises, even pleasant ones if the result has not been predicted. Therefore, internally, the project team has to prepare its ground carefully and take into account fully the counter-positions that will be raised.

Surprise from the customer perspective is also a key issue and must be tempered with consideration as to how it will be received. Many parts of the world have very rigid structures, both within operations and in the political and cultural environment that surrounds them.

Therefore, in any strategy, the project manager must consider both the positive and negative implications of any actions contemplated, but this should not stop the team from considering options.

> Indirect tactics, efficiently applied, are inexhaustible as Heaven and Earth, unending as the flow of rivers and streams; like the sun and moon, they end but to begin anew; like the four seasons, they pass away to return once more.

Those organizations that are rigid and firmly structured are inevitably constrained by their approach. It must follow therefore that those who are not constrained can develop far greater flexibility of thinking and action, thus being better-positioned to create opportunities rather than simply reacting to those that arise.

In the world of global projects, the computations of influences and pressures are limitless, and so is the need to be able to assess multiple options in response. When one looks, as an example, at just the political landscape in many parts of the world, there is very little stability. This can generate both long- and short-term issues for the project team. Leadership changes can force operator organizations to regroup overnight. Agreements that have been ratified previously become void, leaving issues exposed.

This instability is often used very effectively as a negotiation ploy to interject an alternative approach and counter earlier trends. It should follow, therefore, that the project must structure its strategy in this event to ensure that risks are minimized. Interestingly, what one culture would consider unorthodox behaviour another would consider a normal approach.

The perception, then, of what is unorthodox can be the result of the experience baseline that is used. This arises when one crosses industrial sectors within the business world and can even happen within sectors that have grown up in different climates. Custom and practice can be very localized, and can often be a focus for innovative thinking.

Therefore, the wider the range of vision the project team has, the greater its capability to consider a much greater scope of options. Maintaining a dynamic approach throughout the programme is critical if opportunities are not to be lost through static thinking that avoids the option of challenging the corporate standard practice.

> There are not more than five musical notes, yet the combinations of these give rise to more melodies than can ever be heard.
>
> There are not more than five primary colours (blue, yellow, red, white and black), yet in combination they provide more hues than can ever be seen.
>
> There are not more than five cardinal tastes (sour, acid, salt, sweet, bitter), yet combinations of them yield more flavours than can ever be tasted.
>
> In battle, there are not more than two methods of attack, the direct and the indirect, yet these two in combination give rise to an endless series of manoeuvres.
>
> The direct and the indirect lead on to each other in turn. It is like moving in a circle, you never come to an end. Who can exhaust the possibilities of their combination?

Within the project environment, one of the most interesting and most crucial, activities, is the development and use of critical path analysis. First, since it is necessary in order to optimize resources and time, one must ensure that the focus of effort is effective. The second, and more complex, use of this tool is in its ability to be used to challenge traditional thinking.

Most planning activity is done with a methodical and logical approach. Each activity will be timed, sequenced and resourced to meet a specific target. In the normal progress of the project, events will inevitably arise which delay part of the process and this often results in an extension of the completion date. The common solution then is to look at the balance of the activities and either compress them or flood them with additional resources. This approach is intended to ensure that the completion date will be maintained, but a side-effect is generally additional cost.

The second approach is to step back and consider the unthinkable. By stepping outside the normal logic can one create a completely new logic, identical parts and resources being configured in multiple combinations to try to discover new options without increasing risk? From experience, the more novel approaches did not arise out of traditional brainstorming sessions but came from circumstances where the traditional planning structure and some immovable event caused those involved to adopt a more eccentric approach. The challenge comes from the recognition that if you cannot win by using the existing rules then you must change the rules.

It may also be a vehicle for developing alternative commercial approaches. Our commercial thinking is also governed by trading logic. Reverse critical analysis can provide a focus for concessions that in the longer term could be more profitable. These often emerge from considering the 'if only or wouldn't it be good if' particularly when trying to assess where the key edge could be developed for a customer problem.

> The onset of troops is like the rush of a torrent which will even roll stones along in its course.
>
> The quality of decisions is like the well-timed swoop of a falcon which enables it to strike and destroy its victim.
>
> Therefore the good fighter will be terrible in his onset, and prompt in his decision.
>
> Energy may be likened to the bending of a crossbow; decision, to releasing of a trigger.

There is no doubt that speed and focus can move projects forward and generally improve on the initial objectives. The role of the project manager is to build an environment and culture within the team that promotes commitment, team spirit, open minds and the utilization of individual skills.

Every project, to be successful, must be supported by a cohesive team. Since by its very nature of being a virtual organization its strength is in creating a concerted unique approach. The stronger the single focus, the greater chance it has to meet its objectives. The momentum that can be achieved by keeping all the players together will force the pace.

Time is the killer in all projects: the more time is spent, the greater the cost. At the same time, if adequate time is not allowed, then individual initiative will come into play and the unity of approach can easily fail. The longer one allows things to take, however, the lower the efficiency and in the end the project will fail in one or more of its main objectives. This is particularly true when projects are nearing completion and teams are held together to provide comfort and availability, but at the same time they often show a sharp drop in productivity.

The targeting of activities and clear direction enable the team to concentrate on the key issues. Management of definable tasks is a crucial part of the project management role and most people respond best to having a clear task to complete and the challenge of a finite time-span and fixed budget. They also become most creative when asked to meet a challenge and being given the responsibility to do so.

Therefore, focus, speed and purpose provide the ingredients for success. Utilizing innovative approaches can enhance these facets to stretch the envelope of objectives. They must, however, be managed to avoid the negative impact of being allowed to operate in chaos, or becoming the primary objective and overlooking the core aims. Innovation is a crucial part of building sustainable development, since traditional approaches will eventually offer no opportunity for differentiation.

However, the more eccentric the idea, the greater the need to ensure the development is undertaken within the constraints of tried and tested business cultures. The dot.com boom showed, for example, that many innovative approaches were unsustainable because they ignored the basics of business delivery rules and customer satisfaction. Every new idea has to be challenged, and when accepted, integrated into a robust programme.

> Amid the turmoil and tumult of battle, there may be seeming disorder and yet no real disorder at all; amid confusion and chaos, your array may be without head or tail, yet it will be proof against defeat.
>
> Simulated disorder postulates perfect discipline; simulated fear postulates courage; simulated weakness postulates strength.

It should always be recognized that every positive has a negative, and that negatives in others can create significant advantages for oneself. This principle was the mantra of the martial arts development in that to recognize one's own weakness and the strength of others creates a greater opportunity and strength in oneself.

This concept can be applied throughout the project world. At the same time it must also be accepted that careful attention to the counter-position is crucial. Too much unnecessary discipline creates apathy and a tendency towards ignoring the rules, which may be impractical. Fear of rejection suppresses new thinking. Management by edict weakens the capability of the innovative team player. Each has to be balanced in the team and exploited in the outside world.

Over-confidence is always a risk in organizations that have a very successful track record, and this can be an influence on the project team. The same can be seen in one's opponents, and this should be a target for developing a project strategy. The project team, in most business ventures as in life, is generally only judged on its most recent performance. Exploiting the over-confidence of others can certainly add spice to a venture.

The challenge of the business and project environment can through experience create an atmosphere of complacency, which will ultimately make the team less effective and more vulnerable to the changing face of the market. The model that worked previously may face critical flaws in a new context ,and thus the concept of revalidation and periodic testing must become an integral part of the culture. While much of any venture may be common to others, there will always be a vital element that is peculiar to that particular venture.

The role of the project manager and leaders within the team is to ensure that while the approach is grounded in custom and practice, it does not become stale. This is a particular risk in very extended projects, where for example, the pace of the customer may be slow and the tendency is to respond by slowing down one's own activities. The impact of this is very often reflected in poor efficiency and inability to pick up speed when necessary.

There has to be a balance in terms of work that might be affected by the delays of others, and that which can be completed and stockpiled effectively. The control of resources and outputs or deliverables is always a constant challenge for the management of any business venture.

Hiding beneath the cloak of disorder is simply a question of subdivision; concealing courage under a show of timidity presupposes a fund of latent energy; masking strength with weakness is to be effected by tactical dispositions.

The balance between discipline and a cultural framework that promotes creative thinking is a difficult one. There is a school of thought which suggests that chaos can engender progress. It also, however, has the inherent risk of building a structure of anarchy. Any project organization must have clear guidelines within which to operate. This organizational issue is a difficult one, because not only must it allow free thinking, it must also allow for the capabilities of the individual team members.

The strength of a good project team is in its ability to function not as a collection of specialists but as a unified group with a common aim. The skill and talent required to create this team culture is not one that is found in every manager. Therefore, in the selection and training of project managers, organizations need to look for more than technical competence. It is also important to ensure that, in nominating individuals for the role, they are considered against the parameters of the specific project. For example, the approach of one customer may be totally different from that of another, and as such the methodology employed to be successful will also be different.

Team-building has become standard terminology in the business world, and to some extent overworked as a concept. It is, however, most important in the project world to ensure that the common focus and interdependency is developed and exploited. The drive towards success and the shape of the organization have a major impact both on each other and on the eventual outcome of the project.

Therefore, to exploit the skills in the market, the project team must be both organized and liberated within a structure that can respond to the needs of the individual project. This is a paradox that many in management fail to recognize, and as a result they often do not enjoy the fullest commitment from their teams while thinking that they have built up a robust process. The most skilled and independent thinkers will always be at the top of any manager's list, but limiting their participation through being over-cautious or putting in place command and control structures that do not allow for any degree of self-motivation will eventually devalue their efforts.

Thus one who is skilful at keeping the enemy on the move maintains deceitful appearances, according to which the enemy will act. He sacrifices something, that the enemy may snatch at it.

By holding out baits, he keeps him on the march; then with a body of picked men he lies in wait for him.

In a volatile and variable global market, the route to success will be greatly enhanced by presenting a face that is obvious and traditional, while in the background the project team have to exploit the unexpected. A sound balance must be developed between tried and tested approaches and the innovation necessary to combat the changes in the political, economic and cultural traits of global markets.

In any venture the game can be won by appearing to be taking a well-worn path while being ready to introduce novel approaches that can offer an attractive alternative. By adopting a traditional approach the opponent would contest any situation from a similar standpoint and thus provide the lateral thinker with an advantage.

Innovation focused on an extended perspective of market drivers and customer needs will create a business environment that allows the forward-thinker to prosper. Provided that, at all times, any new approach or concept will be tempered by the right level of risk management. In this context, the opponent will always be ready to take the benefits that are offered and often not appreciate the longer strategy that lay behind it.

Any new idea will be resisted by a traditional market and must therefore be evaluated and developed properly. The more traditional the market, the harder it will be to create acceptance for innovation. The project world, by the nature of its flexibility and variability, is ideal for testing novel ideas. These must, however, be based on a concept of a value added proposition that can enhance the position of the other party. This may be in cost development terms or completion times, and therefore time to market. If these parameters are fully developed and exploited then the winning solution will have greater chance of acceptance.

> The clever combatant looks to the effect of combined energy, and does not require too much from individuals. Hence his ability to pick out the right men and utilize combined energy.

The onus therefore for the project team and in particular the project management is to build appropriate teams. These groupings must be able to function utilizing the best individual skills but more importantly maintain a common focus on the objectives.

Project managers must select team players and drive them towards a unified goal, encouraging innovation within a structured framework that seeks to ensure focus without rigid discipline. By promoting greater flexibility the team will challenge to traditional concepts and evaluate the less tried routes against a background of risk awareness.

The power of the team should not be under estimated, as the common focus will generate a will to succeed that is generally way beyond that of the individual. The confidence that comes from group responsibility and interdependence will ensure that even stretched goals can and will be met.

The collective commitment will encourage individuals to seek alternatives rather than rely on traditional paths. The result being that new challenges can be met with greater commitment and the biggest obstacles can be overcome.

In a traditional market when the rules have been well defined over time and the playing field has been levelled to the point of commonality then only the innovative solution will provide an advantage. Innovation can expose new and greater opportunities both for the immediate task and for the future.

The real challenge for the project manager is to build the confidence in the team through ownership not control, since the latter will only engender conservatism.

> When he utilizes combined energy, his fighting men become as it were like unto rolling logs or stones. For it is the nature of a log or stone to remain motionless on level ground, and to move when on a slope; if four-cornered, to come to a standstill, but if round-shaped, to go rolling down.
>
> Thus the energy developed by good fighting men is as the momentum of a round stone rolled down a mountain thousands of feet in height. So much on the subject of energy.

In any business venture, the future rests not in what has been done in the past but in what might be done in the future. Maintaining a methodology that is backward-looking will seldom enhance the performance of a project. If there is no impetus to change, then there will be no acceptance of change and little chance of innovation being exploited either as a team or by an individual.

In a changing market, the variables will be many and the pressure to retreat into the comfort zone will be great. If the leadership is not able to promote new thinking then the team will not be prone to consider risky options or opportunities. If one does not evaluate the less obvious route, then the result will be predictable and the chances of success reduced. The more predictable one's approach, the easier it will be for those in opposition to pre-empt one's approaches and thus create their own alternative solution and give themselves a competitive edge.

If one recognizes that change is part of the business environment, then an appetite for change must be a pre-requisite for coping with that challenge and developing approaches providing a profile that others either cannot understand or emulate. If people are not challenged they seldom maintain the status quo, in fact even in standing still they invariably fall backwards, the end result being failure rather than stability.

The project manager of any venture must consider these implications when building a team, and the organizations behind them must also recognize and support the selection based on the degree of variability that exists. These must be consistent with the challenges to be addressed.

The challenge within many organizations is that innovation is often promoted and encouraged, but not supported in real terms. The larger the organization, the greater the prospect of self-interest and conservatism overriding innovative approaches in favour of low-risk strategies. Similarly, many initiatives have been given a high profile as a means of exploiting innovative thinking across the organization but investment is not made available to test new ideas.

The project environment is one where, because of its specific and often isolated nature, innovation can be exploited or tested without encroaching into the wider organization. The extended enterprise, which is built up through the incorporation of alliances within the project, provides even more opportunity to develop new ideas through blending alternative thinking across organizational boundaries.

The key responsibility of any leader is to encourage those they lead to take ownership of the challenge and work towards creative solutions. The more innovative the approach adopted, the greater the chance of being ahead of the competition, and thus eventually being successful.

CHAPTER 7

Weak points and strong

> Whoever is first in the field and awaits the coming of the enemy, will be fresh for the fight; whoever is second in the field and has to hasten to battle will arrive exhausted.

The development of a sound strategy is merely academic if not translated into the appropriate implemention tactics. It is accepted that tactics must follow a strategy, but at the same time the strategy must be established to enable the tactics to be deployed. It is therefore crucial that, in the creation and finalization of the strategy approach, due consideration is given to the question 'How?'. Strategies not linked to practical implementation have little chance of success.

The business marketplace is a tough battleground, and as in any conflict the first competitor to decide the terrain often has the advantage. This is particularly important when moving into the global arena, where historical business relationships are less well established. When operating in your own comfort zone, being reactive is perhaps less of a disadvantage, but in the wider context only the proactive will create new beachheads.

In long-term projects it is essential that one's preparations are made early and one's approach is well grounded, to maintain a constant proactive approach. The programme will change many times as a project progresses and those who are settled in their position and ready to adapt are more likely to succeed.

Major development projects seldom mature overnight; they generally take many years to evolve through a complex gestation period. Building the right strategy and maintaining it over the longer term is a significant challenge. As projects do crystallize, refinement of the strategy must also come, and alongside this must be a balance of the tactics and approach that has been developed. Too often, the strategy becomes disconnected from the practical assumptions that have been made.

Strategy and tactics are interconnected and must always remain in sync during both the development of a project and its implementation.

> Therefore the clever combatant imposes his will on the enemy, but does not allow the enemy's will to be imposed on him.

The essence of any business venture, as with any military conflict, is to ensure that the opposition has established their game plan before you, by action or inaction, declare your strategy. The tactics that are deployed often enable the opposition to interpret your strategy, so it is important always to ensure that the approach you take does not disclose your solution until it is beyond being challenged.

The best approach to any situation that is less than clear or straight-forward, is to make a disjointed series of requests for information. The traditional market approach of issuing specific requirements in the form of tenders is often then supplemented by specific questions in which the real objective may be discerned.

When establishing negotiation strategies it is often the style to call the supplier to your arena, to both limit their preparation time and constrict their decision-making time. We shall look at this area more closely later, but what you see is an attempt to bring the debate on to your territory rather than meeting the opposition in their comfort zone, where they may be more relaxed and ready to trade.

When there is a dispute during the execution of a project it is common practice to leave the difficult issues to resolve themselves. For example, when claims are in the air no one wants to make the first move for fear of damaging their position. Risk analysis of claims may well show that over time the strongest position can be diminished. This is certainly the situation, when late supplier shipments delay overall completion. Thus it is to the suppliers' advantage to delay, and force a debate only when it improves their position.

The true skill in the project management field is to evaluate when to play and when to hold a position. If the longer-term result is likely to be detrimental, then pull the opposition into the debate earlier.

> By holding out advantages to him, he can cause the enemy to approach of his own accord; or, by inflicting damage, he can make it impossible for the enemy to draw near.

All business is, or should be, focused on gain or profit, which can be either in immediate cash terms or market share that can build a long term after sales maintenance and spares operation. Therefore, in all cases the focus is gain, but the reverse can also be true, in that the greater the opportunity for gain, the higher the chance of risk and potential failure. It is this that often stymies true innovation, which in turn may ultimately be to the disadvantage of those who may themselves gain from innovative approaches, particularly if they adopt a style that inherently forces risk towards the other party.

The real advantage, and therefore potential for gain, is the development and presentation of propositions that will ultimately provide a greater benefit for the customer. This can also be turned around when dealing with suppliers who, if encouraged to be more proactive, may secure a longer-term relationship and sustainable profit streams. What is likely to deter them will be a failure to recognize their commitment after the initial benefits have been realized.

It must always be recognized that in a traditional market there will be a natural reluctance to consider new styles of relationship or business model. While new methods may in time be beneficial, they do come with a greater share of risk. Therefore, when presenting innovative solutions, it is important to ensure that the benefits offered and the risks involved are properly balanced.

Risk and reward contracts have shown that in the right circumstances and with appropriate development, they can provide valuable benefits to all parties. These must, however, be developed in a structure of confidence between the parties. As the global complexity of projects increases, these arrangements are likely to increase, and project management must understand the implications when considering such approaches.

> If the enemy is taking his ease, he can harass him; if well supplied with food, he can starve him out; if quietly encamped, he can force him to move.

Tactics are the ways in which the true skills of any individual, team or organization exploits their capability. It is the deployment of strategy and approaches that focus on the weaknesses or strengths of an opponent and turn them to one's advantage.

It is clearly an advantage to focus on the more vulnerable points of the other side, but at the same time, if one recognizes opponents' strong points, then one's tactics and strategy can be adjusted to avoid potential areas of conflict, or to turn those strengths to one's own advantage. It should always be remembered that similar analysis could also be conducted by opponents regarding your own position.

The relative positions of competition in the market can be seen as one example where their strength can be used against them. A close relationship in a particular market will often be viewed as an impenetrable stumbling block. Yet the reverse may be true, in that a customer might initially look to validate his or her chosen supplier, but given an attractive counter-proposal might view the competition as being more interesting to them.

We have mentioned before the traditional stance that shows an organization to have a valid track record. However, the confidence this creates also has the negative side, in that being comfortable does not necessarily promote innovation. Similarly, when organizations are short of work they may take on propositions involving high risk in order to fill production gaps. This position can be exploited but must also be carefully watched since desperation may force them to cut corners and the long-term outcome may result in failure for both supplier and customer.

There are many situations where this approach can be developed and used to one's advantage, but as always, risk and reward need to be viewed simultaneously.

> Appear at points which the enemy must hasten to defend; march swiftly to places where you are not expected.
>
> An army may march great distances without distress, if it marches through country where the enemy is not.

The outward perspective of your organization and its strategy are key features of taking best advantage of the marketplace. When the competition does not see you as a threat they are likely to take less care in meeting your approaches. If you have no past experience in an area it will be assumed that you are not a serious contender. It may also be assumed that, because you do not have appropriate local resources, your proposition is inherently flawed.

This is a very comfortable position to be in, since it provides an opportunity to develop a strategy that is not obvious and therefore may not be matched directly. This issue is one that often arises in the global market, where it is seldom practical to be all things to all people. Many times when, for example, Western companies tender for business in the Far East they will be deemed to be 'no threat'. This perception must be considered a strategic advantage, but must also be developed with appropriate tactics both to shield the intent and ensure that, if successful, the work can be executed.

The cornerstone of such a strategy has to be the building of strategic alliances with local resources that can provide a novel addition to one's own skills. There can be no substitute for local knowledge, and the deployment of a partnering approach may provide the unexpected edge for victory. Clearly, such a ploy must be developed with care, to ensure both the correct selection of partners and the confidentiality of the strategy.

The latter part of this strategy is hard to maintain in a business environment where most, if not all, information can be gained at a price. It is often, therefore, a strategy to deploy subterfuge, developing parallel strategies and ensuring that it is a misleading tactic that is made public.

The art of employing sound tactics is that they are not seen until it is too late for the other side to counter.

> You can be sure of succeeding in your attacks if you only attack places which are undefended. You can ensure the safety of your defence if you only hold positions that cannot be attacked.

The art of all relationships is to ensure that you are able to deliver what you say, and stand by whatever position you declare. Most strategies do not fail in their creation but in the failure of the organization to follow through in the market. This occurs very often in large global organizations where there are many interested parties involved, and frequently in the world of global projects.

In today's market, many of the global players operate from multiple centres and these often have specific technical responsibility, leaving local relationships to geographically placed operations. Therefore, when the demands of a region conflict with the global programme, there is a tendency to break ranks and follow local drivers, with the net result that the strategic advantage is lost in the application of local tactics. For real success, the strategic viewpoint and tactics must be consistent.

It is also true that, when a position is established, all those involved should support it. Many times the conflict that is exploited by customers stems not from their own skills but rather from the inconsistent application of an organization's strategy where local or functional tactics vary from what is accepted as the norm.

A common example may be seen in the role of sales and execution, where the short-term objectives of the salesperson is not aligned to the aims and strategy of those who must execute the project. Whereas one's opponent may take the advantage it is likely to be one's own organization that misses the opportunity.

In similar vein, one must be ready when taking a strong position to follow through. Empty threats will eventually undermine the perspective of the market.

> Hence that general is skilful in attack whose opponent does not know what to defend; and he is skilful in defence whose opponent does not know what to attack.

In any relationship, and in particular those in the business arena, the selection of teams and specific players is important to ensure success. In general terms, the greater the number of lawyers that go into a room, the less probability there will be of an outcome. So in the case of disputes and claims, the lawyer makes the best defence, whereas in commercial discussions it is the lateral thinker who finds the workable solution. In a technical debate, the engineer must take the front line. In each case, however, all must be aware of the full picture.

In setting one's strategy and implementation tactics it is important to understand the nature and style of the opponent. For example, in those parts of the world where trading is a way of life, the tendency will generally be towards commercial players, since it is likely that every encounter will be one of negotiation. There is a danger of this approach in some of the countries where local government and regulations may overturn commercial agreements. This is often a ploy.

In the industrialized world the primary exchanges will be technical preference and debate. Thus it will be the specialists who lead the charge in any exchange. Often this leads to conflict when two opposing technologists disagree. It is also more likely in these environments that there will be greater dependence on contractual relationships. Which brings out the lawyers and accountants.

In general, lawyers in fact commit very few contracts, and most disputes are solved before they get to court. Therefore the strength of a legal position, or contractual rights, is often a basis for conceding a challenge. If the true impacts of dispute is evaluated, it may often be seen that strength rests with the side that has most at risk. Thus the solution may be less difficult to predict.

> O divine art of subtlety and secrecy! Through you we learn to be invisible, through you inaudible; and hence we can hold the enemy's fate in our hands.

In all aspects of business, the advantage rests with the side that is less easy to predict, since this prevents the opponent from being able to set out a winning counter-strategy. Therefore, in all case of creating business relationships it must be a key to success that one's strategy remains confidential. In most cases, the less is said the more is learnt. In the project world this is always true since in most cases a project will involve many different organizations, often with a group internally as well as external partners and suppliers.

Developing a major project will require the interaction of many different parties and maintaining confidentiality becomes a challenge. Creating misdirection can help, but the duration involved in developing major project ventures often makes it virtually impossible to contain all information and debate.

The reverse is also true that if one can establish which way the competition is likely to proceed, it is possible to adapt your approach to counter their advantages. It should always be remembered that what works for one side also works for the other. Strategy should not be developed within a single perspective, which is often the case.

In any form of negotiation, the game is often won not by the strongest player but by the side with the least visibility. Similarly, technical solutions, which can provide significant commercial advantage, must be deployed only when there is no chance of counter proposals. Recognizing that in a global business context the advantage of any technical approach has in reality a limited life span before the competition adopts or surpasses the innovation.

It is often the case that, when suppliers target a company, they avoid dealing with the commercial front of the organization but focus on those who may be able to disclose through technical discussions, even inadvertently, a clue towards the proposed approach. Many times, conferences and industry associations provide an arena where discussions may be held out of context but provide valuable indications of directions and developments.

In all cases, strategy must be developed to maintain the surprise factor and take advantage of the market.

> You may advance and be absolutely irresistible, if you make for the enemy's weak points; you may retire and be safe from pursuit if your movements are more rapid than those of the enemy.

The effective execution of a project rests in the ability of the team to maximize its capability and be flexible enough to take advantage of situations as they become apparent. Once an opening has been established it is important to ensure that time is not wasted in capitalizing on the opportunity.

The challenge for many organizations is to create a project environment that is not constrained solely by procedures. Few projects run to time, or will at least certainly encounter variations caused by the many external influences that may arise. Clear focus on the end-game and a constant review of progress will enable the team to adapt their tactics to meet variations on the surface.

If the team is convinced that its approach is correct, it should not falter in moving forward. It is often the conservatism and bureaucracy of organizations that prevents them from taking full advantage of any given situation. It may also be true that in many cases the chosen route meets with a solid defence or obstacle.

A structured withdrawal from a position is always difficult, particularly when the team has made a major push for acceptance. In these cases it is wise to ensure that, for every proposition pursued a defensive position is also established.

In all business relationships, confidence is a major factor and thus when presenting a position one must show commitment. The tactics of pushing forward must always be supported by a position that allows you to pull back when appropriate. This is certainly one of the major skills of negotiators, who must never be seen to retreat.

Customers and major organizations are often slow vehicles to get started and even slower to stop. Managing the situation to maximum advantage is a challenge.

> If we wish to fight, the enemy can be forced to an engagement even though he be sheltered behind a high rampart and a deep ditch. All we need to do is attack some other place that he will be obliged to relieve.

The challenge for any organization is to drive into a captive market where one's competition has established a strong foothold. When obvious moves are made into that market you can be sure that every effort will be made to keep you out. In these markets one needs to be subtle and develop strategy carefully, ensuring that you do not show your position too early.

When meeting a particular issue it is important to understand the importance to the other side. In many cases, disputes arise over technical issues for no reason other than that it is the particular favourite topic of the other side's specialist. In major project developments this becomes very clear when the operators come into conflict with their own development teams. The project players can find themselves being drawn into disputes that in fact are the customer's internal debates.

It should always be part of tactics when addressing an issue to try to detect the strength of feeling and power. Intelligence is a key facet of any business venture plus the development of approaches that will enable the stronger players to succeed with your support.

Highly specialized suppliers often fall into the trap of supporting a position based on their greater knowledge. This superior knowledge may be real but can often be counter-productive when dealing with, say, a customer's engineer who has a very strong opinion. Often the game is lost by not understanding where the power lies.

Alternatively, significant advantage can be gained by developing a neutral approach, but at the same time prompting the need for resolution. The key outcome rests more often than not on which decision will be made in the shortest time, and this is where the project team should focus.

> If we do not wish to fight, we can prevent the enemy from engaging us even though the lines of our encampment be merely traced out on the ground. All we need do is to throw something odd and unaccountable in his way.

Choosing which disagreements to meet head-on and which to deflect is the skill of the project team, whether with a customer or a supplier. Occasionally this can even be related to an internal issue, which in turn may affect the project.

In a sales context, for example, the best salesman never says no. They may offer multiple alternatives or even dance around the subject for hours, but if they say no, then ground is lost. Conflict seldom brings any great benefits but much time can be wasted in defending a position or trying to recover a relationship.

When considering the competition it is always best to have them believe one is taking a specific route or development. The further this is from the actual proposed approach the better, provided it is logical, since any unreasonable approach will be seen simple as a guise and ignored.

In a global market it is often difficult to decide when to battle and when to retrench. It may be that in many cases one has no choice but to defend one's position. Clearly, whenever possible you should only enter a fight that you are prepared for and can win.

While it may not always be possible to defer the meeting of a challenge, it is often possible, using skills in relationship management, to turn conflict into collaboration. The only conflicts that should be addressed head-on are those where all other avenues have been evaluated and discounted.

If an alternative conflict that brings about collaboration can be created, all parties can benefit from joint success and improved relationships. This is often the case when working with major projects and the customer's team. Their needs and objectives can be subject to internal conflict, and helping them helps your organization.

> By discovering the enemy's dispositions and remaining invisible ourselves, we can keep our forces concentrated, while the enemy's must be divided.

Structuring an approach to get the opposition to come to you should enable you to define their approach, while maintaining the confidentiality of your own ideas. In this way it is ensured that you maintain the advantage. In all cases, the greater the view one has of the market and the competition, the less knowledge they have of one's ideas, and the greater one's opportunity for success.

The main difficulty with this concept is, of course, that one's opponents will also be trying to establish a similar strategy and employ similar tactics. Again, the methods for determining the opposition's strategy may, and often must, be by analysing the indirect rather than direct information.

For example, to judge whether the competition plans to create local alliances one needs to understand first what options are available. In most industries there are few local companies with an appropriate background. When approaching these organizations, one may find they already have exclusive positions in place.

By analysing a customer profile you may establish that historically there are connections between certain supply sources and your competitors. It may even be that specialists used by the customer have their own alliances in the market place.

Tactics will be defined more often by what one does not know than what one does. Every exchange must incorporate the undercurrent issues that need to be defined or explored.

If you are to be successful it is important to be ahead of the game and understand where others may place their strength. From this a proposition can be detailed that will differentiate you from the rest. In the project world, if rules are rigidly defined then the outcome is reduced to commodity pricing rather than the exploitation of skills.

> We can form a single united body, while the enemy must split up into fractions. Hence there will be a whole pitted against separate parts of a whole, which means that we shall be many to the enemy's few.

Once the strategy and tactics of your opponent have been determined you then have the possibility to focus only on a winning solution. The more widespread the possibilities, the greater the area of focus and thus the less focused your resources. It is the skill in setting the strategy and deploying resources that enables smaller, specialized organizations to challenge and succeed against much larger competition.

It is often assumed that large organizations have the greater skill base and knowledge, and are more able to undertake the management of risk. In fact, this may be less true than most people would expect, since in many cases these larger organizations find it hard to be innovative and flexible. Therefore, success may be dictated by the application of tactics using a much reduced resource base.

The alternative can be to create the right combination of alliance partners who can jointly establish a proposition making them the equal of much larger groups. The added advantage of such a tactic would be to confuse the competition into a level of comfort based on their assessment of the scale of organization you may need. In today's global marketplace and under the investment pressure that faces many large organizations, the clustering of smaller but specialized and complementary operations provides a flexible business model that works well within the project concept.

The tactic of building specific relationships to address a current objectives means that these can be adapted to suit any geographical or cultural barriers. This approach is in direct opposition to the larger conglomerate that needs to optimize its internal resources and cost base before considering the focused needs of the challenge.

The key issue is to define which are the main avenues to be developed and which will ultimately be the deciding factors. In most projects, and particularly those on the global stage, the drivers may be extremely varied. By focusing on the prime issues and exploiting them you may be able to concentrate your efforts.

In the engineering project world it often breaks down into commercial, technical, operations, local politics and environmental impacts. If you try to satisfy all you will certainly fail, and if you concentrate on the wrong factors you are also likely to fail. Therefore, the outcome of any project is more likely to be decided based on exploitation of focus than by weight of numbers.

> And if we are able thus to attack an inferior force with a superior one, our opponents will be in dire straits.

The greatest risk in any major project, and in particular those open to the global market, is the effective support of the supplier base. In most cases the external supply involved in most major projects will represent between 60 per cent and 90 per cent of the costs. Failure to have the correct strategy in place and to manage this portion of the project will certainly have an impact on the chances of success.

The strategies for handling this major activity can be many, and the tactics to minimize the potential risk represent even more opportunities. It is normal in most traditional organizations to look upon the supply chain as a necessary evil, assuming that the only mechanism would be to squeeze every supplier to the bone in order to reduce costs. Certainly this can be successful in the short term, but on highly technical integrated projects the reverse can easily happen. The crippled supplier who is an integrated part of your solution may fail and bring the whole project into risk.

Alternatively there is the possibility of building a network of key suppliers even at the pre-contract stage. These specialists may then provide many additional opportunities and benefits that can be optimized to improve your position. Not least of these would be security and speed of technical data, along with established costs and known risk profiles. The addition of a network of allies in some parts of the world can also improve the influence that can be applied locally. There may be opportunities for sharing risk, and improving financial management, through an integrated view.

The focus for a networked supplier base is then on the outcome of the project and resources are freed to focus on the more difficult challenges. Tactics must be developed to ensure that the right balance is maintained, but certainly there will be opportunities to be exploited in both traditional and the collaborative approach.

> The spot where we intend to fight must not be made known; for then the enemy will have to prepare against a possible attack at several different points; and his forces being thus distributed in many directions, the numbers we shall have to face at any given point will be proportionately few.

Once again, it is crucially important to maintain a secure strategy and effective disposition of tactics to ensure that no predetermined approach can be detected. To spend resources and effort to develop an approach and then to publicize that approach to the market will certainly waste resources. At worst, those who realize from where your thrust is coming may determine the outcome.

The more potential options your opponents have to consider, the greater their risk of diluting their efforts and missing your winning strategy. It is also important that they do not understand from your actions what is important to you, since this will also be high on their agenda in order to be successful.

It may also be useful to look at the development of project tasks and evolve tactics that focus on manageable elements. The larger the challenge, the greater the pressure to try and solve all issues at the same time. The net result of this approach will be to reduce the focus and probably miss the one key issue that predetermines failure.

Taking any project, the true number of 'show stoppers' is often very small, since in general most things in a relatively organized operation *will* happen. Not necessarily exactly as planned, but generally within acceptable limits. It will be the small item that is missed or fails that will cause the greatest impact.

In all project matters, the best approach is to divide and evaluate at the lowest possible level then focus maximum attention and resources on the key issues that will ultimately determine success.

> For should the enemy strengthen his van, he will weaken his rear; should he strengthen his rear; he will weaken his van; should he strengthen his left, he will weaken his right; should he strengthen his right, he will weaken his left. If he sends reinforcements everywhere, he will everywhere be weak.

In developing a project and setting the right tactics for the individuals and the team overall, it is crucial to have a holistic view of all the requirements. Many organizations are defined by function and created with the best available specialists. Yet the project by its very nature is a virtual entity, built of multiple skills and resources. In many cases the overall project brings together multiple layers of suppliers, and success does not depend on any single unit.

Decisions within a project must be governed by the appropriate analysis of all factors, which are then focused on the drivers and objectives. Each element may have many interactive impacts and unless they are all considered the outcome will be based more on luck than on skill.

The project management role must be to ensure that whatever tactics are put in place are based on a sound strategy and the team operates as a unified group, always considering those on either side or further downstream. For large projects reaching from design to implementation, this is crucial.

When a project takes into account all needs and objectives, the only surprises will be those that could really not be anticipated. Unfortunately, this is seldom the case, and most failures result from individuals or elements of the organization not considering a rounded view of the project.

The development of a risk-management strategy and the effective implementation of tactics in the market can easily be wasted if the overall focus of the project team is not prepared in all directions to meet the challenges of the objectives and the volatility of the global market. There can few that do not appreciate the need for a consistent approach that supports every aspect of the strategy and implements tactics in specialized areas that underpin the overall aims.

Unfortunately, experience has shown that in many cases this recognition falters when challenged by internal agendas and priorities that do not see the project as the prime responsibility. This conflict is one that executive management needs to address and to allow the project a degree of autonomy.

> Numerical weakness comes from having to prepare against possible attacks; numerical strength, from compelling our adversary to make these preparations against us.

The global engineering project is a risky beast and those who do not recognize the risk or who choose to minimize it will certainly fail, together with those who choose to take no risk at all since they will probably not stay in the market. The whole essence of project management is about risk management and mitigation.

Risk is only dangerous if it is ignored. The majority of business risks can be evaluated and suitable tactics employed to rationalize and protect against possible impacts. Success in the market will be gained by those who chose to understand the risks involved and have developed the skills to manage those risks in an appropriate manner.

Thus, in developing successful projects and in their execution, an integrated approach to deploying effective risk management tactics is paramount. These may be during the pre-contract stage, or during the actual implementation of the project. The more risk you are prepared to manage, the greater the pressure you apply to the competition and the more possibility you have of influencing the customer.

The mitigation of risk has already been outlined and can occur in many ways. The more defensive you are, however, the greater the pressure you place on yourself. Thus being confident in the way the project teams operate and their ability to identify and play the risk game, the greater the chance you have to win.

The whole business world revolves around tactics, and success is often measured in relation to the failure of others. Therefore, if one wishes to hold the higher ground one also has to be prepared to develop more effective strategies and implement them with tactics that create greater pressure on opponents.

> Knowing the place and the time of the coming battle, we may concentrate from the greatest distances in order to fight.
>
> But if neither time nor place be known, then the left wing will be impotent to succour the right, the right equally impotent to succour the left, the van unable to relieve the rear, or the rear to support the van. How much more so if the furthest portions of the army are anything under a hundred Li apart, and even the nearest are separated by several Li!

The critical nature of developing a sound strategy is to understand where and when to go into battle. The tactics of the conflict can vary, and depend on many different factors. What is for certain is that if one fails to comprehend the tactics of the opposition, then one will probably fail, but if with that understanding there will be success even in regions that are new to one's experience. By establishing alliances networks can be built up that can be more effective and flexible than those of opponents.

The reverse is also true, and in the complex world of global projects it is certain that if the strategic analysis route is not followed and one simply launches into ventures, these will fail. This can be assessed even for those business ventures closer to home in that failure to study the terrain and the opposition will eventually come to grief.

The implementation of project strategies and plans is an essential part of the project manager's role. When all the project team has a clear view of what is required and an integrated perspective of the project, they will not only be able to meet their individual goals but ensure also that they support the objectives of others.

The ability to predict the outcome of any project has many variables, and in the complex and volatile global environment these increase exponentially. It is therefore often surprising that organizations move forward without effective strategies that recognize the particular environment that is being faced.

> Though according to my estimate the soldiers of Yueh exceed our own in number, that shall advantage them nothing in the matter of victory.

Therefore, to assess a project it is not simply about the strength of one's organization and resources creating success. The outcome may be more dependent upon what strategy is employed and reflective of the approach taken in evaluating the risks and challenges set by your competitors.

The larger, more established organization being faced could be made vulnerable if a correct strategy is pursued, and converted into meaningful tactics by the project team. Success is then not simply a case of the weight of numbers, but more to do with innovation and capability.

Many significant engineering projects have failed because, for example, a small, specialist supplier was not managed effectively. Often the downfall has come from a failure to understand the logistics support required, or even what documentation is necessary. Experience can always succeed over power. This is the mantra of the martial arts specialist.

Strategy and tactics provide an equalizing effect, so that smaller, more flexible organizations are able to win in the face of large conglomerates. The multinational customer may find its power drained by its own infrastructure and decision processes, and government organizations can be crippled by the rules that cover their activities.

The flexibility of networked alliances can provide a global capability that brings to bear as much, if not more, skill than can established major corporations. This is certainly being seen in the potential of the Internet to link and integrate clusters of specialists and is certainly a business model for the future, where the experience of working in cross boundary alliances will provide an alternative approach to the monolithic company.

Success may be a factor of power, but it does not automatically mean failure for the flexible team. Power often creates a rigidity that more adept organizations can outstrip by speed, flexibility and agility.

> I say then that victory can be achieved.

The challenge for all project-focused organizations is to ensure success, but in a complex world this is largely a question of how the game is played. In very few markets can the success of a venture be assumed, but it can certainly be assisted by an effective application of strategy and applicable tactics. Naturally, this depends very much on the capability of the team and knowledge of the many influencing factors.

One interesting facet of projects is that seldom, if ever, are found exactly the same conditions. Therefore any assumption carries a wide range of risks, many of which cannot fully be predicted. It is also certain that a fixed traditional approach will only work in part, and the need for adaptability is crucial once the game is in play.

The correct assessment of the opposition's power and its challenges will provide a project execution plan that has taken into account most of the definable conditions. These are not simply restricted to technical and practical tasks, but also to those that might arise as the project progresses. There can be no ultimate guarantee of success, but the element of risk can be reduced by effective evaluation of potential risks.

The greater the disparity in size between opponents, the more innovative the approach needs to be. Identification of the weaknesses on both sides will provide the baseline for the development of a strategy and a blueprint for the appropriate tactics to be taken forward.

Strategy, planning and tactics are the cornerstones of successful project management. These will enable the correct identification of the required resources, skills and alliance partners. The chances of success will be improved, but the unpredictable will still happen and a watchful eye would anticipate these and modify the local approach within the overall framework.

> Though the enemy be stronger in numbers, we may prevent him from fighting. Scheme so as to discover his plans and the likelihood of their success.

In many aspects of project development and execution, challenge and conflict can be avoided based on perception rather than fact. This is the backbone of negotiations in that, if neither side knows all the answers, then the outcome depends on the skill of either to present their case more effectively.

Those less experienced will often seek to take up every challenge without evaluating the need to contest, or the value in winning. Certainly, where relationships have to survive lengthy contracts there is often a case for reviewing whether losing in the short term may be more profitable over the longer term.

It is also an assumption that the opponent may on the surface hold the stronger position and therefore a contest is avoided. The converse may also be true, in that when opponents feel they are strong they will not understand why one should press forward with a losing proposition. In moving forward, an impression of confidence is created that may on occasion undermine the other's confidence.

Customers always assume they have the upper hand but in most cases the potential for loss is greater for them than for the supplier they are squeezing. The supplier may also believe that they have a unique position of strength, but will falter if challenged.

In most cases of disputes during the life of a project, the best approach is to resolve them quickly, since the longer they prevail the more intransigent each side may become. In the event of a major dispute, a protracted approach is often more effective as such approaches tend to become bound-up in contractual debate and analysis. Occasionally, the cost of winning may in the end be more detrimental than to accept the position and proceed.

In all cases, the tactics deployed have to be assessed against the knowledge either party has, and the impact on the overall objectives. They must also be validated against the plan and resources, and deviations considered in a measured way to ensure that short-term success is not building in greater challenges for a later period.

> Rouse him, and learn the principle of his activity and inactivity. Force him to reveal himself, so as to find out his vulnerable spots.

Therefore, any action, whether planned or reactive, must always be evaluated to understand the impacts of the potential outcome. In business life we tend to do this based on personal experience and within our sphere of responsibility. In the integrated project world we need to incorporate inputs from others.

The route or solution elected to be used must not only follow the overall objectives of the project plan but must also take into account the potential plans of others. When the opponents' plans are understood it is often possible to seek an agreement that benefits both parties and follows a middle way. Project planners need to be able to assess not only the impact on their own organization but also on customers and suppliers.

When preivous risks and problems are appreciated, the current problem can be positioned in the right perspective. Very often the approach taken comes not from specific demands or needs, but rather is based upon historical knowledge of previous encounters. These may, in fact, have no relevance to the immediate issue, but simply colour the way it is viewed.

In studying the past performance of one's counterparts, it is possible to assess what is likely to drive them in the direction in which one needs them to go. This, for example, often arises in the selection of suppliers, since those that perform best are often the more expensive. The evaluation of which to choose then falls to the key drivers and the overall impact on the project. The safeguards chosen to build into a contract may be driven directly by the past interactions.

Effective tactics must have their foundation, then, in exploiting both the knowledge and experience of past behaviour, accepting that in general terms the traits of individuals or organizations seldom change dramatically.

> Carefully compare the opposing army with your own, so that you may know where strength is superabundant and where it is deficient.

The tactic for all encounters should be to create a position that draws out the opposition's approach without revealing one's own. If this were always the case, the likelihood of failure would be very remote. In reality, of course, this is never going to be the case on every occasion. Thus the challenge for the project manager is to define those activities and issues that are most critical to success and focus on those.

The process of getting others to divulge their plans and objectives is not an easy one. This requires considerable focus on the part of the team to watch all activities and share the interpretation of events. Certainly, on many occasions it will be the indirect actions that in fact show the real intent.

In dealing with suppliers, for example, their approach to defining when and how they intend to meet your objectives will lay down a platform of pinch points. When they fail to meet their own targets it is easy to take a stronger position and push for corrective action. In many organizations, the approach is often to dictate approaches instead of objectives and requirements. Thus, when the practical application fails to deliver, then the supplier will maintain that your input was the cause.

With customers, on the other hand, they will define their needs and objectives and allow you to provide a solution. As matters progress, the skilled project manager will identify his/her own pinch points and alert the customer to the impact of their action or inactivity. It is therefore crucial not only to follow your own progress but also to monitor that of others.

By anticipating the impact of action or inaction it is possible to predict the impact. Thus one can either take preventive action or present a defensive position that may force a change in direction or action.

> In making tactical dispositions, the highest pitch you can attain is to conceal them; conceal your dispositions, and you will be safe from the prying of the subtlest spies, from the machinations of the wisest brains.

There can be several applications in this regard, the first being that, in developing project concepts and solutions the advantage in the market will go to those able to fulfil a requirement. A more effective marketing approach is to analyse where a customer has a weakness or can benefit from a specific solution that fills an identified need.

In more normal relationships the project team must evaluate the skills and capabilities of their counterparts at all levels, together with an analysis or identification of special drivers. Developing the skills to handle any organization should incorporate a degree of power-mapping. This platform of relationship profiles will help one to understand ongoing actions and to predict actions and reactions.

Fulfilling the needs of a customer should be the mantra of the project team, but this must be done within the confines of what has been contracted. Where effective power structures and drivers have been identified it often becomes a process of realizing the aspirations of individuals rather than those of the organization. When considering tactical options the assessment should be made on the benefit of not fighting or supporting a particular position.

Where there may be a conflict of interpretation in, say, technical matters, these are often not based on contracts but on personal positions. Very often major disputes can arise within a project based simply on two opposing individuals' personal preferences. This is a key area for project managers to be aware of, since such a dispute, while having no contractual basis, can inflict serious delays on the project. In many cases there may have to be an acceptance that 'the customer is always right' even when, perhaps, the customer is, in fact, wrong.

Testing the ground and establishing both positive and negative routes enables the project team to move quickly through key issues and maintain progress, thus ensuring that the customer's perspective is seen as the prime focus. While this perhaps offers a less satisfactory overall solution, it is more effective in terms of maintaining progress.

> How victory may be produced for them out of the enemy's own tactics, that is what the multitude cannot comprehend.

The project environment is the classic formless or virtual organization being created and structured to meet an individual proposition. This approach is becoming more common since the introduction of the Internet, and is being greatly enhanced as the concept of alliances is being adopted.

The principal benefit is that, since most organizations cannot focus in every part of the world, and they must adapt to the conditions of the market and the requirements of any given project. This may be addressed by the creation of integrated organizations that are complex but which can be configured to meet the specifics of a development. The project model provides the framework for these multi-organizational structures and the concept is gaining greater acceptance.

To those competing for business in the global projects world, this flexible approach is both cost-effective and versatile. It is also very difficult for competitors to fully understand the configuration they may be up against. At the same time, the adapted cluster can carry forward elements from earlier programmes while incorporating essential specific local ingredients.

Developing these integrated groupings of alliance partners is a major challenge for project teams and requires a sound understanding of the difficult and complex management of relationships that is necessary. The major successes have initially come from customer-driven projects, and these have shown significant benefits even in conventional industrial markets. The wider application is, however, growing in the marketplace and the extended enterprise is becoming a strategic platform.

Clearly, whether forming a new integrated team with external partners or creating multi-company groupings the key to success will be found in establishing appropriate interfaces. The objective should always be to retain the detail of that approach in confidence and away from the market for as long as possible.

The challenge for the pre-contract team will be to convince conventional customers that these groupings of non-aligned organizations can work effectively together. There will clearly be those who see these configurations as being unstable. However, provided the security can be put in place, they can often offer a more proactive solution, particularly since each independent player is not in conflict with the others and will see overall success as being beneficial to all. This configuration approach is in contrast to the situation that is often less obvious within the divisional or functional boundaries of a single organization.

> All men can see the tactics whereby I conquer, but what none can see is the strategy out of which victory is evolved.

The driver for all projects is to find a solution that others cannot provide or even appreciate. The development of the right relationships in the market and working within these to create innovative approaches is crucial to success. Novel concepts and ideas should be kept away from the market until they are too late to be mimicked: at which point one needs to be thinking another two steps ahead.

Marketing is more than having the right product at the right time; it is about attracting the market towards a product or concept. The more flexible the organization, the more practical it is to take a look outside the box. Success is then driven not by reaction but by innovation.

The aim of the project team must be focused on considering how to out-manoeuvre the opposition from whichever direction it comes. Often such opposition may come from within, and thus conservatism becomes the challenge rather than the market place.

The application of tactical considerations in the development of strategy is critical, since most strategy fails because of impracticality and lack of suitable resources and skills. If the market is not to see where you are coming from, the structure and approach must be both varied and inspired.

Success, if it comes without design, is a fluke, and the more complex the market the greater the degree of luck is needed to win through. The alternative is to focus approaches from an alternative position and create novel propositions.

By following unconventional routes, tempered with traditional skills in recognizing and managing risk, the project team can present options and alternatives that others have not considered. Success is then a question of creating the future, and not trying to predict it.

> Do not repeat the tactics which have gained you one victory, but let your methods be regulated by the infinite variety of circumstances.

The more predictable your stance, the greater the risk that others will develop counter-approaches that anticipate your reactions. The opposite must also be true, that the more you are able to predict what others will do, the high your own chances of success. Therefore, in developing any strategy one must consider both ends of the spectrum and focus on the routes that are more unpredictable.

In long-term projects it is also likely that due to time and circumstances, where you start will seldom be where you finish. Few projects ever manage to maintain all their original plans and strategies. The true test of any project manager is to maintain or improve his position within an ever-changing world.

The global market can move in diametrically opposing routes overnight. The pace of change is unprecedented and communication capability as never before. An organization that is not able to respond will surely fail, and with the pressures that exist this can happen faster than ever previously experienced.

Put simply, the nature of global politics and economics can introduce overnight changes that will throw most projects into disarray. The management of large projects in this environment must be able to respond, and quickly. By understanding what the impact is of any given change, and by being flexible enough to meld the team into a new direction enable the project to remain focused.

Those who manage by rules will quickly lose control when the unusual occurs. Projects must be a smart combination of discipline and innovation, together with a clear ability to recognize change and move with the current of the time.

> Military tactics are like unto water; for water in its natural course runs away from high places and hastens downwards. So in war, the way is to avoid what is strong and to strike at what is weak.
> Water shapes its course according to the ground over which it flows; the soldier works out his victory in relation to the foe whom he is facing.

Therefore the project organization and approach provides the ideal plat-form for the application of alternatives and adaptations. Production-based organizations struggle to establish global structures, which are by nature prone to be rigid, with distribution constraints. They are hindered by long-term investment, training and employment issues. The mobility of produc-tion capability often constricts those who have the foresight to log short term economic or political changes.

Projects, on the other hand, can often be developed as one-off entities, which can adapt to both market and global changes. The establishment of project team need not be location-focused but can integrate resources from across the globe, selecting an appropriate configuration to meet the current challenge, and mobile enough at times to ride significant local or global influences.

The flexible approach can allow the project team to blend with the cultural, economic and political restraints of the market. It has no fixed format other than the establishment of best practice, which ensures an appropriate level of discipline while retaining multiple options.

By studying the market and the competition, successful organizations can develop the flexibility to reflect a position that exploits the limitations of others. Thus it will inevitably be the actions of the opposition that dictate the outcome of any venture as one exploits their approach and conceals one's own.

> Therefore, just as water retains no constant shape, so in warfare there are no constant conditions. He who can modify his tactics in relation to his opponent and there by succeed in winning, may be called a heaven-born captain.
>
> The five elements (water, fire, wood, metal, earth) are not always equally predominant; the four seasons make way for each other in turn. There are short days and long; the moon has its periods of waning and waxing.

The skill of the project manager and of his/her team is in developing the right tactics to support the strategy that has been established, together with being able to adapt to the market and the occasion with varied and innova-tive approaches. So, as the business landscape changes, so must the tactics of the team or organization.

There must always be an underlying discipline enabling the team to recognize when changes occur or may arise in future. The most challeng-ing aspect of leadership is to balance the need for order while the encourage-ment of an ethos of creativeness or even radical thinking. This combination is hard to control but rewarding when successful.

The most successful projects that have been seen often started from a point of saying 'why not?' The market will often be unable to identify the shape that is being created until it is to late to take an opposing position.

The need to foster the pioneer spirit within any organization is crucial to success, and within global projects it must be considered essential. Those who have worked on ground-breaking projects, either technical or innovative in other respects, will know the energy that can be created. Tactics, which may never have been tried, become commonplace and the team thrives on the challenge.

Strategy without action is as worthless as action without strategy, as each aspect fails to deliver. The combination of the right strategy and effective implementation can provide outcomes that exceed the expectations and efforts of individual components.

The effective linking of sound strategy and innovative tactics requires a special style and critical focus on the leadership. It is essential that managers of projects are selected very carefully, and then provided by clear support from the executive.

CHAPTER 8

Manoeuvring

In war the general receives his commands from the sovereign.

Having collected an army and concentrated his forces, he must blend and harmonize the different elements thereof before pitching his camp.

Whatever structure is considered appropriate, the outcome of any venture in the project world will be dependent on the style and capability of the leadership more than any other issue. The management of an organization may set the objectives, but it will be the project management that takes this forward through strategy and implementation. The main challenge for any leader is to convert vision into reality.

Management must provide clear direction and objectives, along with empowering the project manager with the authority and resources to meet the aims and commitments. Many times, problems within projects are generated not from the market but from internal multi-level influences being forced into the project agenda. The global project environment and the very nature of project teams being created for specific needs means conflicts of direction.

Since projects tend to bring together many separate functions, and often external organizations, the demands from outside the team can be numerous. Failure to recognize these potential conflicts and assign responsibility will lead ultimately to confusion.

The project management of complex major ventures is a tough challenge. The skill is not simply in understanding the task, but in creating a unified approach merging the right resources and capabilities.

The project manager's role is to bring these many elements together and ensure that they remain focused on the job at hand. The task requires more management skill than most business activities, since the team generally has little time to blend and must be effective and productive right from the start.

The challenge of leadership is to inspire and direct their team in all respects, providing support and mentoring in addition to the traditional command and control role, particularly when operating within a virtual organization where the traditional social interaction of co-location is replaced by distance and often linked only by communications technology.

The more global organizations become, the harder it is to build the normal interfaces of social teaming. Even more complex is the ability to exert influence and leadership when operating at a physical distance. The project environment has been addressing the challenges where non-aligned organizations work in collaborative alliances.

After that, comes tactical manoeuvring, than which there is nothing more difficult. The difficulty of tactical manoeuvring consists in turning the devious into the direct, and misfortune to gain.

For projects that span long periods the difficulty is always to maintain enthusiasm and commitment among the team. Few, if any, project managers are able to undertake every task themselves, though some will try. In the end, the success of a project depends on the contribution of the team, and maximizing this contribution is a key function of the project manager.

Careful consideration must be given to the pressures of long exposure to a given task. Projects frequently reach plateaux resulting from burn-out. Skilled personnel, like any machine, need time for maintenance, and the demands of challenging projects can easily drain even the most hardened. Task management therefore is not simply a question of good planning to reach the project's goals but should also recognize the impact on the team.

Focused tasks with short-term targets will enable all the players to see some immediate return for their efforts. This in turn, will it is hoped, give them the chance to recharge their batteries. Rotating the tasks of key individuals is another possibility, though often this becomes difficult when customer confidence in an individual gets in the way. It is important, however, for individuals to be able to focus on a series of stages rather than one long haul.

The game plan of the project manager must also to be creative in looking at problems as challenges, and keep the team focused on solutions. All projects will inevitably encounter problems, and in many of a more complex nature may take years to resolve. These are likely to drain even the most enthusiastic of team players.

The skilful manager will look to turn problems into challenges, and adapt them to the team's advantage. Thus they will create new drive at every level of the team. The innovative approach and open-minded perspective will aid this challenge. This often requires a change in culture that looks not to assign blame for problems but to stimulate wide-angle thinking which can exploit the problem.

The reality of a complex business operation is that, however experienced and skilled the players, there will always be situations that catch the team unawares. The traditional command structure relies on maintaining authority through power and assigning responsibility.

This is part of the military culture that often fails to map across into the commercial world because in the army the structure is very rigid and must remain so to ensure a unified approach on the battlefield. In a commercial environment, clearly the majority of players are there by choice and deliver the best results when operating in a semi-free power profile.

> Thus, to take a long and circuitous route, after enticing the enemy out of the way, and though starting after him, to contrive to reach the goal before him, shows knowledge of the artifice of deviation.

The difficulty with any strategy is to make the going hard for the competition and as easy as possible for one's own team. The benefit of building a wider project group including external partners is that the majority of one's own skill is invested in managing others. As the pressure is maintained, the internal load becomes less. In this way your team will remain ahead of the game.

The supplier market will generally invest considerable effort in order to secure business. Often this can be a pre-emptive activity, which reduces the load on the project team. It must be recognized that this approach only works if the reward is there and achieved. For critical components or equipment, the development of alliances will provide extended resources at little or no cost. The benefit will only be realized, however, if duplication of effort is avoided, and this requires an alternative methodology to the traditional approach.

Therefore, the project team must focus more on planning and managing activities than on trying to accomplish everything. This is always hard in an engineering environment, since by its nature the tendency is to want to get into the detail. In the main context, most equipment is better understood and exploited by those who build it. The drive should be towards performance requirements. In this way the project role is to link 'black boxes' and ensure integration rather than define every element specifically.

The task for the leadership is not simply that the project manager is to maximize the benefits of this approach and keep the project on track. Turning designers into process managers requires special attention to the monitoring of effort and a degree of discipline within the team. If managed well, the net result is a greater focus on completion and less emphasis on output. Thus the team is always closer to the end-game than is the competition.

> Manoeuvring with an army is advantageous; with an undisciplined multitude, most dangerous.

There is no doubt that the complex world of global projects is a tough environment in which to work. Those who take on mangement roles know that, and expect that the rewards will reflect the return on investment. Whether at the corporate level or down through the project team, project managers must recognize not only the commercial returns but also the humanistic needs of the team. The first concern for any leader should be the well-being of his or her staff. They are the project manager's key resource and their performance will largely dictate the success or failure of the project.

The interesting dilemma for any leadership is that organizations respond to risk and reward, whereas people generally respond better to satisfaction and recognition. Therefore, within a project the role of project manager has to deal with these two ends of the spectrum. At the organization level, when dealing with customers or suppliers the same principles will apply and the more experienced practitioner will recognize and exploit both.

In selecting and managing a supplier, it must be remembered that the key ingredient is people, and that these external resources have the same drivers as your own. If anyone ever calculated the number of people outside their own organization that could influence the outcome of their project, the number would be staggering. The management of these relationships to the benefit of the project is crucial.

At the team level, it is important that everyone's contribution is recognized, and that effort is rewarded. If people gain satisfaction from what they do, they will exert greater effort, which in turn will build towards a successful result. The most effective leader is the one who takes credit from the performance of his team, compared to the one that takes credit for the team.

If you set a fully equipped army in march in order to snatch an advantage, the chances are that you will be too late. On the other hand, to detach a flying column for the purpose involves the sacrifice of its baggage and stores.

Thus, if you order your men to roll up their buff-coats, and make forced marches without halting day or night, covering double the usual distance at a stretch, doing a hundred Li in order to wrest an advantage, the leaders of all your three divisions will fall into the hands of the enemy.

Resource management is a critical part of the project manager role, and building an appropriate profile for the task at hand will significantly improve the probability of success. For most projects, the key time for action is in the early stages, when most of the key decision and actions are needed to set the pattern for what follows through the life of the venture.

Too often the tendency is to focus on profit maximization in the early phases of the project. Thus resources are constrained and the required skills limited. In the majority of cases, the cost and impact of this approach will be felt throughout the project and almost certainly dilute the chances of success. The converse can be equally damaging in that resources are thrown at a project, particularly one on a tight schedule. The result is that much of the work is developed in parallel and will need to be reworked, or resources are wasted to the detriment of long-term need.

Even for so-called fast-track projects the first step should always be to take time out to ensure that the objectives and strategy are in place and properly understood. Without this initial review and the establishment of a project execution plan, the likelihood is that both effort and resources will be consumed without gain. It is also a key failing of project managers that they, for the sake of comfort, hold on to key personnel long after they have completed the majority of their work, for fear of not having them immediately available. A balanced and considered resource plan is essential to success.

The stronger men will be in front, the jaded ones will fall behind, and on this plan only one-tenth of your army will reach its destination.

If you march fifty Li in order to outmanoeuvre the enemy, you will lose the leader of your first division, and only half your force will reach the goal. If you march thirty Li with the same object, two-thirds of your army will arrive.

We may take it then that an army without its baggage-train is lost; without provisions it is lost without bases of supply it is lost

The key ingredients of a project plan are task, time, cost and location. Each of these has a significant effect on the profile of a project team, but together they can create a complex and difficult challenge. They need to be matched against skills, resources and business processes and, more than anything else, supported by effective communications.

Certainly the more remote the development, the greater the pressure on all involved, since the further the operation from the home base, the more significant the impact of even minor problems. What may be solved in minutes locally may take weeks to overcome in some distant location. This applies not only to tasks related to the project, but also to those who are sent to undertake the work.

The project management approach must recognize not only the magnitude of the task but also the methodology of executing it. In today's world, communications capability is often overestimated, with common use of phone and Internet access. The position changes when the telephone lines are cut for long periods. This is when local leadership becomes particularly important, and the full understanding of the strategy and plans, as local action is still needed to fit the bigger picture.

While it may be true that people are driven by recognition and satisfaction, if their employer cannot feed or pay them, the emphasis will quickly change. If people do not have the correct tools they will be distracted from the task. When many distant groups are engaged, the need for consistent methodology is crucial.

The project manager must consider all these aspects and ensure that the leadership provided is both driving towards the established goals and supporting those to whom the tasks have been given. Recognizing the roles of master and servant is a complex aspect of effective leadership.

> We cannot enter into alliances until we are acquainted with the designs of our neighbours.

The key to any strategy is to understand the game that is being played by others, whether customer or competition. Without this knowledge, one cannot employ good leadership and guidance. The role of management is to interpret the trends and data and formulate effective strategies.

The development of alliances can be a primary factor in establishing a sound project approach. These can be utilized at many levels, and the challenge for the project manager is to evaluate where alliances will aid the project and with whom they should be made. It may prove to be a significant task in itself just to blend the variety of internal opinions that will be needed to support the proposed approach.

The failure of many alliances is often not from primary failings on the part of either partner, but rather because of the internal negativity that the alliances attracts. Therefore creating alliances must first involve leading the organization towards an acceptable arrangement.

The conflict will come from many directions. First, the traditionalist who will not accept that any break from the old ways has any value; second, from those who see the development of a partnership as a threat to their own role or position; and thirdly, from those who have an alternative preference for a partner.

To proceed without internal support will place the project at risk and is likely to negate any planned benefits. The leadership requires an identification of needs and the potential opposition's focus. Then one has to establish realistic benefits and measurements that can be validated.

Collaborative alliances can add great value but they are not easy routes to follow, and without understanding the drivers of others will be destined to fail. Since each partner has his or her own internal targets and objectives, these have to be integrated to some extent within the overall objectives of the project. The leadership therefore has to recognize these pressures when assigning roles, responsibilities and rewards within the project. The major challenge for any alliance is to maintain a common focus on the joint objectives and this becomes very complex when there are conflicts and failures.

It is easy to be a good leader when all is going well, but the mark of a great leader is being someone who holds the team together and focused when the chips are down and things are not proceeding to plan.

> We are not fit to lead an army on the march unless we are familiar with the face of the country, its mountains and forests, its pitfalls and precipices, its marshes and swamps.
>
> We shall be unable to turn natural advantage to account unless we make use of local guides.

The most important factor in successful leadership is that those who follow have confidence in the chosen route, and belief in their leaders. Therefore leaders must be able to show that they have greater knowledge and awareness of the challenges ahead. They must also be able to recognize and have faith in their followers.

A confident leader will always draw out the best in his/her team and project managers who can command respect will build on success. To be assured of taking the right route the leader must understand the terrain better than those who follow. Where it is deemed necessary to take a more obscure path, then the leaders must be able to define the anticipated advantage that will be gained.

In a team that is both experienced and innovative there are not likely to be many who will follow without question. If people are to give of their best, they need to take ownership of their tasks, and not simply to follow orders. When the strategy proposed is not clear, or perhaps appears to be wrong, they will challenge and then they need to be convinced. There will always be occasions when either time or confidentiality prevents open discussion, and this is where the past record will prevail.

When breaking new ground there needs to be recognition of the value that can come from local experience. Too often the over-confident fail to appreciate the intricate nature of local culture and regulations. This results in directives that become impossible to meet, and the standing of the leadership is reduced.

The project manager must use all available information to form strategies and where possible communicate all available information to the team. There are clearly those situations where only limited information can be conveyed, but if there is a practice of being open, then the majority will appreciate circumstances where 'need to know' has to prevail.

> In war, practice dissimulation, and you will succeed.
> Whether to concentrate or divide your troops, must be decided by circumstance.

A project will generally owe much of its success to the development and deployment of well-founded strategies. These will be created to exploit the weakness in others and to draw the competition into making the wrong assumptions. These strategies must be communicated to those who need to know, and certainly kept away from those who are the focus of the tactics.

Success will also be driven by the wide acknowledgement of effort and reward of those within the team, while every interface outside the team must be attracted by their individual potential to gain from the project, either by profit in the case of suppliers or value-added benefits for the customer.

The effective management of resources focused on the real issues and trained to the critical path will underpin the chances of a successful outcome. The excessive use of resources and continuous pressure will deplete energy levels and eventually be counter-productive.

Task management at every level within the team will maintain the focus on what is necessary. This must be extended to those external elements that are supporting the project, whether alliances or straightforward suppliers. They too must be encouraged to concentrate on the end-game to ensure success.

The establishment of clear responsibilities and lines of communication will enable the team to restructure its approach to meet changes in the market, without which success would be less assured. The opportunity to regroup may initially be considered a problem for some parts of the operation that are focused on early completion, but they must be made to appreciate the wider picture

These are the principle challenges for the leadership through the project manager: to maintain the balance across the venture, and to optimize the use of resources within the effective limits of the changes being faced.

> Let your rapidity be that of the wind, your compactness that of the forest.
> In raiding and plundering be like fire, in immovability like a mountain.

Leadership by itself will never be successful: it is the team that generates the effort, ideas and enthusiasm that drives a project forward. The project manager must create both the environment and the ethos that keeps the team focused on the overall objectives.

The team must be able to respond quickly and efficiently to the challenges and problems that will arise. They must have a holistic view of their actions and be ready to support not just their own tasks but also those of the other members, ensuring that all actions are clearly targeted towards the implementation of the project plan and the strategy that has been deployed.

When appropriate, they must take a slower pace and maintain the consistent approach that is required to succeed. When a strategy has been developed and agreed, it will surely fail if those charged with its execution take independent action, even if this is for for positive reasons.

The team must constantly be motivated towards the end-game, and the role of the project manager in recognizing when the pressure is too great it is essential. Public acknowledgement of special effort in any area will help to maintain commitment to the project.

Most important of all is the need to ensure that the team, whether internal or external partners, is concentrated properly on the single goal of joint success. This concentration will create a momentum that will be hard to resist, and which will tend to look at problems and challenges in a more rounded manner.

When the project manager has built a team, supported it properly and encouraged it effectively, it will deliver. The more effective the team, the greater the challenges its members will be prepared to undertake.

> Let your plans be dark and impenetrable as night, and when you move, fall like a thunderbolt.

To maintain discipline and focus while encouraging innovation and commitment is a skill that many project managers need to develop. Taking advantage of the marketplace and meeting the volatility it can produce is where strategic skills can be fully recognized. Creating a team that can respond quickly and effectively to these opportunities comes mostly from experience.

The approach to the outside world must appear grey and disorganized such that no one can predict where or how one will meet the challenge of the day. The harder it is to predict what one may do, the greater the opportunity to exploit the situation to the best advantage of the project. The commitment of the team and the recognition that its success is founded on its capability to enact the improbable and succeed must be underpinned by the awareness that when others understand one's particular approach it will probably fail.

Many times, an organization's approach can be seen long before any action is taken. This arises not from the intentional passing of information, but more often from private disquiet among the team that becomes public.

Project managers must also be decisive, since the biggest drain on resources and energy will come not from external pressures but from loss of pace internally. To maintain momentum within the team, decisions should be made quickly even if their implementation may be delayed. In this way, issues do not reverberate around, which simply wastes effort. If no immediate action is needed plans can be changed with good reason, but death by analysis will certainly tax the team and dilute their focus.

> When you plunder a countryside, let the spoil be divided amongst your men; when you capture new territory, cut it up into allotments for the benefit of the soldiery.

To both control and motivate a project team, the team members must see a clear picture of their roles and the tasks that are required to fulfil them. Each task within a project needs time and resources and will therefore have an impact on the schedule and costs. For major projects, this can be a significant trial for the project manager. If one waits until the end to establish the level of progress, the project will certainly be a failure. The effort involved in creating a monitoring programme can be great and thus often ignored in favour of rushing into action.

Designing work breakdown structures with assigned tasks provides a platform to maintain a proper view of a project's progress, as well as establishing individual or group benchmarks. Against these the team can easily see what they have achieved at any stage and will be able to take credit for meeting the plan within budget.

For the project manager, the strategy of the project can be measured and where necessary adapted to reflect the impact of changes. Focus can be maintained on budgets and forecasts against individual elements of the project. The tasks can be subdivided to whatever practical level makes sense, though it has been known for these to become so detailed that more effort goes towards mapping progress rather than on moving forward.

With this tool in place, the project manager has the ability to reflect on performance and give recognition at key intervals, thus the measurement of progress becomes a fillip to the team, not a bludgeon. It is then easy to ensure that the team is focused to meet the real needs rather than simply meeting individual objectives which may be of marginal immediate impact.

> Ponder and deliberate before you make a move.
>
> He will conquer who has learnt the artifice of deviation. Such is the art of manoeuvring.

Leadership strategy will drive the project team and define the probability of success. If it is built on good experience and reliable knowledge of the market and the competition, and recognizes the challenges ahead, it will form the basis upon which the team can proceed with confidence. The effort required may be large, but the rewards will be significant. It is not possible to make any journey without first defining where you are starting from, and then how you intend to reach your target.

Strategy must then be converted into realistic planning and this is often where many project managers flounder; not because they don't understand the tasks, but in their enthusiasm to be successful they set challenges that are not achievable. The result is that those who have to follow them perceive failure before starting and as a result do not exert their full effort. The impact of this needs no explanation.

Tasks and objectives must be within the grasp of those that have to meet them. They must be clear and measurable, so that even at the lowest level of the team it is possible for members to understand their own progress and contribution. Resources must be assigned consistent with the tasks to be met, and again one often sees this being ignored in favour of short-term savings opportunities.

If a project has been properly estimated and the finally agreed costs are realistic then if significant savings are subsequently made the project generally was in fact potentially at risk through an inflated price. Even more likely is that it will ultimately exceed its budget. Project managers may create a stretch or challenge for the team but this must be recognized as such.

If there is a sound basis for the strategy and valid measurement of progress then the end-game is clear before the race even begins. The chances of success are then greatly enhanced.

> On the field of battle, the spoken word does not carry far enough; hence the institution of gongs and drums. Nor can ordinary objects be seen clearly enough; hence the institution of banner and flags.
>
> Gongs and drums, banners and flags, are means whereby the ears and eyes of the host may be focused on one particular point.
>
> The host thus forming a single united body, it is impossible either for brave to advance alone, or for the cowardly to retreat alone. This is the art of handling large masses of men.

We have already touched many times on the issue of communication, and good leaders must place this requirement at the top of their list of concerns. One assumes that a visionary leader with wide experience has the ability to communicate, but the reality is that many are very poor in this regard. This becomes critical when dealing with project teams, which are by nature virtual organizations often spanning the globe, involving many cultural boundaries and even language barriers.

Projects, to be run effectively, must be integrated, which means that every contributor must know what actions they must take, and when. Questions must be answered with speed to ensure that circumstances do not overtake events. All communications must clearly define responsibility for actions or responses.

The explosion in communications technology has provided today instant access around the world in seconds. A single message can reach almost immeasurable numbers with ease and yet the impact in many business environments has been to impair the quality of communication.

The email has reduced the dependence on verbal exchanges and at the same time has opened channels that create confusion, indecision and lack of ownership. As the tool that should move the virtual organization to another level of capability has in cases had the reverse effect. Project managers must counter this by establishing an ethos of real communication.

> In night-fighting, then, make much use of signal-fires and drums, and in fighting by day, of flags and banners, as a means of influencing the ears and eyes of your army.

Effective communication will ensure that the project stays on track, and this means the appropriate use of all media. The human interface is still the one of choice despite advances in technology: people feel more comfortable and respond better when face-to-face. It is difficult to form relationships via electronic means. Even the video conferencing capability is measurably more successful once the parties involved have met each other.

Meeting the demands of modern technology while exploiting the basic instincts of people must be recognized by every leader, and in the project world it is crucial. Meetings may often be seen as expensive, but they enable the team players to make real connections with their counterparts.

The project must establish clear communication along with an adequate monitoring and recording capability. Over the life of a project a large volume of correspondence will be created. When projects are executed over a long period many of the original team may have moved on and their knowledge travels with them if records are not maintained in an orderly fashion.

The world may have become smaller in some respects with advances in technology, but limitless capability can also be the downfall of a project. When everybody is considered responsible, the reality is likely that no single person has a clean line of responsibility and problems remain in limbo.

Project managers must set the scene to ensure this does not apply. They must be communicative, and demand and reinforce this requirement across the whole team, irrespective of locations. The worst situation for any venture is that inactivity results from individuals assuming that a problem belongs to someone else.

This situation can be seen clearly in what we call the 'chain-email', where addressees grow exponentially but with no clear responsibility being maintained. The network of inputs grows to the point where nobody has a clear picture of the issue or the way forward. In the context of a global project or operation, this situation will be an early sign that the structure is unstable and needs attention.

> A whole army may be robbed of its spirit; a commander-in-chief may be robbed of his presence of mind.

The art of leadership is to create the right environment for one's organization to be successful, and to promote a position in the marketplace that ensures that the opposition is threatened by your organization's performance. These two key objectives are inextricably linked since unless one's team is successful, it will not perform to its limits, and if it is not performing better than others it will not be successful.

Nothing is a greater spur towards success than success itself. Teams that are successful will stretch themselves to even greater heights. Customers prefer to deal with organizations that have a solid track record as this gives them confidence. Competition is wary of challenging successful organizations and will back off or take on exceptional risk to try to dislodge them.

Therefore, the more successful one's organization, the more likely it will be able to proceed with less opposition, which in turn will push it towards greater success.

For the project manager, this challenge should be constantly in focus, and every effort must be made to ensure that the team enjoys its achievements. Recognition of effort and the success of the team will breed increased energy. Suppliers, strangely, also prefer to support organizations that are successful, even when part of that success may be a result of hard trading with them. This is a strong factor when establishing estimates, as in general terms preferred customers get preferential support.

Customers, once they select a supplier, look for two key factors by which they will judge success. First, that the supplier delivers what has been agreed with the minimum of effort on their part; and second, that they deal effectively with problems as they occur. Sound leadership must drive this message throughout their teams. In this way, opponents will always be at a disadvantage.

Now a soldier's spirit is keenest in the morning; by noonday it has begun to flag; and in the evening, his mind is bent only on returning to camp.

A clever general, therefore, avoids an army when its spirit is keen, but attacks it when it is sluggish and inclined to return. This is the art of studying moods.

There is a time to fight and time to hold back. Understanding the optimum point of contact is the role of leadership. To challenge when you are weak will place you at a disadvantage. To push forward and expend effort when there is no real advantage will simply waste resources. When your opposition is strong and energized is the time to seek alternative strategies.

Historically, projects have a tendency to be cyclic, to start with gusto, become drained over time and then gather momentum during the final phase when spurred by the prospect of completion. This is probably true in most areas of business, but in the project world, as opposed to a production environment, it is more crucial to understand the pace that is needed at the right time.

Long-duration projects suffer badly when the team has passed through the initial enthusiasm and is locked into the long haul. This is the phase when the project manager has to be most on his/her guard, since not only will productivity drop but focus also. In the first phase, problems and risks may be created because of over-enthusiasm and a desire to rush forward, and during the middle stage risk comes from over-extending resources and lack of attention.

The responsible leader will measure the performance of his team and balance pressure to even out the flow, injecting some variety into the work pattern and demands. The difficult balance is that, while discipline must be maintained to meet targets, the management style must also take into consideration where the pressure points may build if ignored.

Disciplined and calm, to await the appearance of disorder and hubbub amongst the enemy: this is the art of retaining self-possession.

An effective leader will recognize the 'temperature' of his team and adjust it to manage for optimum output. Leadership is a capability that is hard to define, and different challenges may require different styles of leadership, or even different leaders. It is seldom either practical or desirable in major projects to consider changes of leadership, since knowledge and continuity are important factors. Therefore, project managers must have the skill to adapt their approach to the circumstances of the day.

In selecting project managers, their particular style must be evaluated against the parameters of the task. It is not simply a question of technical knowledge and experience; it also requires an appreciation of the nature of the team and project's demands. For short-term, fast-track projects there is little time for mentoring or people management. Tasks must be clearly defined and executed, and disputes require quick and effective judgement.

In the case of protracted projects, demand is likely to require the same focus on the task management but more emphasis on human resource management aspects. In these cases, the project manager will be a key figure in the creation of human development and support. For while some task functioning can be programmed, many of the team will be in harness for extended periods. It is often a failing in project-based organizations that they commit people and then forget their obligations to develop their skills.

The role of managing a diverse project team and maintain a concentrated focus is challenging. Effective leadership must recognize and support its key asset: the team.

> To be near the goal while the enemy is still far from it, to wait at ease while the enemy is toiling and struggling, to be well-fed while the enemy is famished: this is the art of husbanding one's strength.

The mark of a good leader is that he or she will always look to place the team in the most advantageous position and implement tactics that should ensure success. In this way the leader will be able to draw far more from their teams than by simply pushing them forward constantly.

The art of project management is to take these principles and convert them into meaningful plans for the execution of the project. The project team must see that their individual and collective efforts are being used effectively. This will engender greater confidence and promote commitment to the overall objectives.

The target must always be to focus on what is important, and will improve the chances of success demonstrably. If this is clear to all involved, then the project will generally run smoothly. It is also crucial that the management and the project manager recognize that feeding corporate exercises outside the project that have no direct impact will also dilute focus and reduce commitment. This is seen quite often in cases of financial reporting.

The project manager must also ensure that his/her team is well-equipped, well-trained and appropriately experienced. This will ensure that team members keep their attention on the real issues. Thus when effort is called for to meet a particular challenge, the team can move with speed towards a resolution.

Exploiting the strength of the project team and supporting their efforts will place a focus on problems, challenges and the competition. If the team is not ready and those challenging recognize its weaknesses, the advantage will be lost. Mastering this element of project management will differentiate good from weak project managers.

> To refrain from intercepting an enemy whose banners are in perfect order, to refrain from attacking an army drawn up in calm and confident array: this is the art of studying circumstances.

Project managers must consider the benefits and risks in every planned step. Recognizing the strength of opposition or challenge and creating innovative solutions is the essence of the role. Managers' skill in undertaking the challenge will be seen and acknowledged by the team as sound leadership. When effort and resources are seen as being spent on issues or challenges that are felt to be losing tactics, their abilities as leaders will be questioned.

The team must always view its position as both valuable and considered; if not pressure will ebb and progress will falter. When a team gets burned out, the probability of success will decline. Clearly, there will always be occasions when an apparently illogical decision may be necessary, and it is at these times that the credibility of the leadership will be tested. If the rationale is explained, however, it will generally be accepted.

The ability of the project manager to display tactical leadership skills is critical to being able to carry the team forward and keep it focused on the project's objectives. Those who push teams towards well-defended and insurmountable objectives will lose credibility, and eventually control.

Selective tasking and resource allocation will enable a project manager to share the pressure and maintain focus. This is particularly important when there is a need to adapt to changing conditions, or to take advantage of observed changes in direction or tactics by others.

Leadership is not simply about driving forward; it must also encompass the ability to reflect the twists and turns that arise during a project's execution.

> It is a military axiom not to advance uphill against the enemy, nor to oppose him when he comes downhill

The project team must always be directed towards the optimum approach and deflected from making challenges that are unlikely to be successful. This attitude has to be developed by the leadership, in looking for alternatives rather than by blind obedience to a rigid plan. When faced with a conflict that would be hard, if not impossible, to win, the aim should be to find an alternative way.

In developing projects in the global marketplace there must be a realistic perspective on the probability of winning. This is often the dilemma between sales and execution. Sales people will see every opportunity as a potential success, whereas those faced with delivering the project may find the prospect improbable. The life of a project does not start from a contract but builds slowly from concept through to selection, and the failure of most projects can be traced back to over-optimistic assumptions made right at the start.

Leadership must be able to see the full picture, and be strong enough to be able to walk away if necessary. This is hard when the market is down, since every opportunity may be seen as filling a gap in the business profile. The reality is that projects you will not win or those with little chance of success should be abandoned early to avoid wasting effort or adopting risk.

In the same way as one should not put the project at risk, one should also consider the results of pressing suppliers too far. Those that are struggling in a tough market may take on more risk than they can handle. This might present an attractive proposition in the short term, but it must be understood that, if they fail, it will certainly damage one's own prospects.

The strong leader will assess these dilemmas and will often need to be brave in order to avoid the potential risks that may arise. Too often, the financial pressures within organizations focus on the immediate returns from aggressive negotiations and pricing; but this may lead later to more costly implications.

Do not pursue an enemy who simulates flight;
do not attack soldiers whose temper is keen.
Do not swallow bait offered by the enemy.
Do not interfere with an army that is returning home.
When you surround an army, leave an outlet free.
Do not press a desperate foe too hard.

Leadership has to be focused on creating an environment that promotes and supports the development of initiative and innovation. Clearly, this is the ethos that is needed by complex projects in the global market to drive forward and capture opportunities.

There is a risk in taking such a stance, and that is where one can find enthusiasm and drive being pushed beyond what is in the best interests of the project. As the professionals within the team will have their own views and points of focus, there is often a tendency to overstretch for the sake of professional pride. This happens in all areas and functions, and must be monitored and directed.

Technical specialists will frequently want to show their personal capabilities, and will debate and challenge long after the debate has been won. The impact of this may frequently create a backlash, either immediately or at some time in the future. The desire to score points is often the cause of conflicts beyond the position where it is adding value.

On the commercial front, the less experienced procurement person will want to dominate a supplier that has already met the demands of the organization. The selection and negotiation of a supply contract should be targeted at acceptable market levels. When pressure is applied to go beyond what is reasonable, the impact can be the loss of an opportunity if the supplier walks away – or worse, that at some point in the future the tables will be turned.

When one has achieved one's aims and understood the market, it is time to stand one's ground. The desire for personal achievement, or plain ego, which pushes beyond the edge can create a risks that a good leader must manage and direct.

Such is the art of warfare.

Successful projects, like any other ventures, depend on the capability and skill of the leadership. This is not the project manager alone, but must flow down through the task teams and to all interrelated locations.

Without sound leadership, a complex team will fail to maintain its direction or pace. Opportunities may be exploited and personal challenges met, but these must always be within the confines of the overall strategy. It is effective leadership that can maintain the right balance, allowing personal initiatives while retaining primary goals and targets.

Leadership is not just a case of setting rules and maintaining discipline; it must look at what is needed to inspire and drive the project teams to meet well-established objectives. It must also provide an environment where the team is integrated to ensure maximization of opportunity without increasing the existing risks.

Project managers need to ensure that their teams have the skills to meet the demands of the projects, and are tasked to ensure the optimization of the capability. The project team is what will make the project manager successful and the project meet its goals. These assets must be managed not simply by rote, but by example.

To get the best from people and alliance partners one must ensure that their efforts and contributions are both acknowledged and rewarded. Thus leadership must look beyond management and create an ethos that makes the team want to follow where the project needs to go.

There should be greater emphasis placed on the training and selection of project managers that can lead with experience and appreciation of the tasks to be achieved. All too often the roles of managers are created by default, time or seniority without recognizing the practical and different needs of leadership focused on the challenge at hand.

CHAPTER 9

Variations in tactics

In war, the general receives his commands from the sovereign, collects his army and concentrates his forces.

When in difficult country, do not encamp. In country where high roads intersect, join hands with your allies. Do not linger in dangerously isolated positions. In hemmed-in situations, you must resort to stratagem. In a desperate position, you must fight.

There is an inevitability in virtually every project that there will be changes, so when the project strategy is created one can know for certain that it will need to be adapted. Those who have worked in this project environment will understand full well the impact that change can have. The project may set up correctly and planned to perfection against a strategy that has taken into account all aspects of the tasks, objectives and market place, then orders to change are made, and every careful tactic has to be adjusted.

Change is generally considered in negative terms, therefore most projects prepare for its control. In fact, many adaptations can be reflective of opportunities to be exploited. The real focus should be on change management. This may seem trite, but most people view control as a policing function and when an opportunity arises the potential for benefit has ignored.

Many times the change is at the direction of a customer, but equally it can come from internal errors, design improvements, the impacts of market variations or to accommodate some commercial variation. Whatever the cause, the impact of change can have dramatic effects on the outcome of the project. Each variation will certainly generate a ripple effect and must be evaluated fully against the project's objectives and strategy.

Too often changes are viewed at a local level and accepted as part of the natural chain of development. It is only further down the line that the real impact becomes apparent, and generally when it is too late to reverse the approach. What may be considered unimportant in one part of the integrated project can mushroom tenfold in importance in another phase.

> There are roads which must not be followed, armies which must be not attacked, towns which must be besieged, positions which must not be contested, commands of the sovereign which must not be obeyed.

Every project team must remain acutely aware of the impact of change, and the project manager must ensure that the process of evaluation is firmly in place. Change can surface from many different areas, and if not recognized and assessed will ultimately have an impact somewhere during the execution phase.

This process of managing change starts right at the outset of a project, even before contracts have been put in place. This is often the most difficult time to monitor and direct, since, to conclude an arrangement when the heat is on, means that many issues are interlinked, and often the impact of a simple variation to the original concept and strategy can have a significant effect.

When change is identified there has to be a holistic view of the implications. These may not only effect internal operations but may also have to be considered in the wider context of project objectives. These variations must also be evaluated against customer impacts, because what may be seen as a change by one party, may be considered a normal development by the other.

It may also be possible that while a change may be outside any original agreement, the impact of challenging its validity may be greater than acceptance. It may therefore be more effective to trade than to fight.

The historical practices for many organizations with regard to change were to tender low and then adopt an aggressive policy towards every possible extra. Again, strategy must be balanced with relationships in both the short and the longer term.

Change can cripple a project, but if managed well it can greatly enhance the venture's outcome and success. The implications of change should be evaluated from both positive and negative perspectives.

> The general who thoroughly understands the advantages that accompany variation of tactics knows how to handle his troops.
> The general who does not understand these, may be well acquainted with the configuration of the country, yet he will not be able to turn his knowledge to practical account.

> So, the student of war who is unversed in the art of war of varying his plans, even though he be acquainted with the five advantages, will fail to make the best use of his men.

The project manager must maintain control of change and be able to recognize the advantages and disadvantages associated with any deviation to the strategy and plan. Since there will always be some variation, there must also be an attitude that ensures these variations are exploited and do not become obstacles in reaching a successful conclusion to the project.

Some change may not be material in terms of the final project completion, but may generate an impact on the way the project is executed. For example, government regulations may come into effect, or economic upheaval may force changes in the procurement strategy. The risk of changes in currency rates may be small, but extended over a project deferment could be significant.

Therefore, the project manager must be aware and ensure that his or her team maintains a close monitoring of the peripheral issues that can have an impact on the final project results.

It may even be that simple changes in personnel could by the nature of specific relationships cause immeasurable impacts. Very often the successful completion of a project may take much of its momentum from the individuals involved. In some parts of the world, both official and unofficial relationships are crucial. When any part of the chain is broken or changed there should be a review of the potential impact.

Project managers have to be tuned in to the possibility of change and be able to implement adaptations to their strategies and plans. If not, it may be that the changes that will occur will ultimately dictate the programme for the project.

> Hence in the wise leader's plans, considerations of advantage and of disadvantage will be blended together.
>
> If our expectation of advantage be tempered in this way, we may succeed in accomplishing the essential part of our schemes.
>
> If, on the other hand, in the midst of difficulties we are always ready to seize an advantage, we may extricate ourselves from misfortune.

Change in whatever form will create new dynamics for the project, and for the project team. Therefore these have to be treated with respect and assessed to the same degree that the original project was assessed. Strategic planning may provide some latitude in terms of cost, resources and time, but once these have been consumed the backwash will certainly impinge on the objects and aims.

Every aspect of the project must be considered and worked through. Too often, a change will be reviewed at a functional or local level and deemed acceptable, or not, without validating the impact on others. The positive and negative results of a change must be considered, and where necessary contingency plans established to counter any negative results.

In engineering projects, change is a way of life, since no contract is ever able to define a complete solution. It is therefore inevitable that, as a design is developed, previous assumptions may be challenged or reversed. This can happen in both positive and negative situations. Many times a better solution is developed, but the multiple implications following from it are not. Thus the perceived benefits are eroded by impacts in other areas.

The key elements of any strategy and plan are costs, time, resources and liability risk, either technical or commercial. The verification of changes must follow the benchmarks, then a specific strategy must be established to optimize the benefit or limit the risks if implementation is necessary.

Understanding the risk of change and balancing time to evaluate against minimizing delays by proceeding are the judgements every project manager must make to keep the project on track.

> Reduce the hostile chiefs by inflicting damage on them; and make trouble for them, and keep them constantly engaged; hold out specious allurements, and make them rush to any given point.

There is always the attraction of increasing project recovery by exploiting the cost benefits of change. As said previously, this has been seen as a key tactic used by many organizations. It takes its power from the risk to the customer of protracted delays and often therefore the high cost of change is accepted under pressure. This approach can in the end be detrimental, and while attractive when the opportunity is presented should not be used without careful consideration.

When dealing in certain parts of the world, the local infrastructure and regulations often detach commercial management from the operational drive. So, for example, while the operations side of the business is desperate to move forward, the bureaucracy may be ready to stand its ground indefinitely. Eventually, what was viewed initially as a golden opportunity to increase profit, becomes a millstone holding back project completion. The net results are that not only is it not possible to gain the additional income, but the original margins can also be eroded.

The application of an ethos of cost–benefit analysis must be instilled throughout the project team and often at a senior management level as well. All business is run for profit and shareholders external to the project will support the exploitation of opportunities to increase that profit. The project manager must be supported to resist exploitation at the risk of long-term objectives. To do this, there needs to be factual analysis and clear objectivity in relation to the critical path of the project.

More often than not, change becomes a trading exercise of pluses and minuses, which at some point are balanced and offset. When this is the strategy, the accurate monitoring of the impacts of cost and time is crucial to avoid simple bartering. Therefore, even when a change is implemented without debate the evaluation process still needs to be established.

> The art of war teaches us to rely not on the likelihood of the enemy's not coming, but on our own readiness to receive him; not on the chance of his not attacking, but rather on the fact that we have made our position unassailable.

Project managers who ignore the potential for change put their project's success at risk. To assume that there will be no changes is foolish and to adopt the negative attitude that change will not be accepted is misguided. To avoid the creation of a structure to handle change effectively will leave the project team in confusion. Unless there is a proactive and composite process to handle change, then risks will build up and only come to the surface when it will be too late for corrective action.

Change, when assessed, must be documented and recorded. The project manager must ensure appropriate control of implementation. Where applicable, any external parties need to be notified of the potential impacts, and given the opportunity to decline to proceed. This process must be swift to avoid creating even greater impacts by delaying activities pending resolution.

Where change is customer-driven, then understanding customers' key drivers is essential to having a workable strategy for handling variations. Often, when a change is requested it is evaluated and presented at high cost in the hope that the customer will decline. If, however, the driver for the customer is delivery, you will lose on two fronts: first, you may be instructed to implement a change where delivery impacts were not assessed, thus creating risk; and second, the relationship with the customers is damaged as they may consider your costs to be opportunist.

Change can be the benefit of all parties, or it can become a platform for dispute and conflict. It is the strategy of the project that will dictate which of these applies, and careful implementation of the strategy that will underpin success.

> There are five dangerous faults which may affect a general:
>   Recklessness, which leads to destruction;
>   Cowardice, which lead to capture;
>   A hasty temper, which can be provoked by insults;
>   A delicacy of honour, which is sensitive to shame;
>   Over-solicitude for his men, which exposes him to worry and trouble.
> These are the five besetting sins of a general, ruinous to the conduct of war.
> When an army is overthrown and its leader slain, the cause will surely be found among these five dangerous faults. Let them be a subject of meditation.

If success is to be founded on establishing sound relationships between the various parties, then the approach to change will probably be the most volatile of issues these relationships have to absorb. Understanding how the process could have an impact on these relationships is a crucial part of the project manager's role. Having a measured approach to evaluating the issues and implications is critical.

Those who ignore change will be forced to accept potential negative interference in their projects. Those who seek to use change as an avenue for speculative profit improvement will probably achieve a short-term gain but will certainly damage long-term relationships. This has been one of the traditional approaches to commercial relationships in the construction world, where profit has come not from the original commitment but rather from the pirating of opportunities for change once the contract was in operation.

Those adopting an approach that seeks to compromise previous commitments and liabilities without reason will be forced to retrench. Similarly, those who resist change without sound judgement will find their programme affected by indecision.

Relationships are a valuable asset for any project manager, and often these can only be built up over time; but they can also be damaged very quickly. To this end it is not simply direct impacts of change but also indirect impacts that can be detrimental to the overall project.

The impacts of change can be far-reaching and can totally change the progress profile. Thus, as part of any execution strategy, change management must be defined clearly, integrated and respected throughout the project's life cycle. Failure to recognize this will almost certainly result in the failure of the project.

The management must ensure that the project team understands every implication of any change and looks to exploit the benefits as well as to protect the core needs that may have an influence on progress. Since change will come about, whether as a result of internal developments or external influences, the planning and reporting programmes must be focused to identify quickly the implications and options available. For many in the business world who have worked within stable environments, the prospect of change is hard to assimilate and may often inadvertently hold back development. The reality is that, in the main, the only constant is change and this is particularly true within the context of project management.

Building a culture that accepts change is a difficult task in any business environment but it is particularly reflective of the business landscape that has little stability. In projects that have a development cycle, the challenge is increased where the implications of change can cause problems to both cost and time schedules.

CHAPTER 10

The army on the march

We come now to the question of encamping the army, and observing signs of the enemy. Pass quickly over mountains, and keep in the neighbourhood of valleys.

Probably the area of most potential conflict in any business environment is the world of negotiations. It is the point at which all operations tend to marshal their forces and attack the opposition. It is the one true contest of skill, experience and power. To most people it is the point of glory and recognition within their business area where typically there are champions and losers. It is generally the fulcrum upon which the future success or failure of a venture will be decided. Yet in many organizations the true nature of negotiation is misunderstood.

In the project world negotiation may be with both customers and suppliers and is seldom a single event but rather an extended process. In fact, those who consider it to be an event have probably already lost the advantage and failed to capitalize on their position. Negotiation strategy is complex and in general terms should be viewed as starting with the idea of what is desired to buy or sell and ending when all liabilities are complete on both sides.

The period between these two points is the true battlefield and should be approached only by those with the necessary experience and skills. Certainly, while many think authority and power make them good negotiators it is more likely that they will be losers in real terms. Negotiation is probably the closest thing to simulated martial arts than any other activity in business. The winner is the side that can use its skill to achieve its ends, irrespective of what the opponent believes to be the case.

All successful negotiations must start with understanding your opponent and be focused towards manoeuvring them into the position you need. As that is the outcome you require, you will ensure success by controlling the battlefield in every respect. The key difference is that, in most cases, you want your opponents to think they have won so that you will be able to work with them again.

> Camp in high places, facing the sun. Do not heights in order to fight. So much for mountain warfare.

The essence of any conflict is to bring the fight to you and ensure that you structure every approach and contact to build a profile of the opposition's position, while ensuring they have little or no idea of your true needs and breaking points. First to last, contacts must be carefully orchestrated, watched and understood, since it will not in fact be the actual meetings for negotiation that define the outcome, but rather the preparations and strategy you deploy that wins the day.

The project environment is a hostile one and the terrain often complex and unpredictable. The project team will often be faced with challenges that seem insurmountable, but each has a solution if it can be identified and exploited. Whatever the landscape, a strategy can be developed that will eventually draw the opponent into the most favourable position for you to succeed.

Negotiations often involve many people and multiple interfaces. Each of these can be used to your advantage or, if mishandled, can undermine your position. A single word or ill-thought-out question can change the balance and give away the high ground to your opposition. Successful negotiations must therefore be a controlled team effort.

Many times, advantage is lost simply by individuals trying to carry out their own tasks, but without an understanding of the implications of their comments or actions. In the engineering world, the problem is often amplified, as many clarifications may be necessary. Each of these contacts offers an opportunity for the opposition to gain knowledge and turn this to their advantage.

Project managers have a difficult task in maintaining the required relationship when there are many interfaces. Therefore they must ensure that all the players understand the rules of engagement.

> After crossing a river, you should get far away from it.
> When an invading force crosses a river in its onward march, do not advance to meet it in mid-stream. It will be best to let half the army get across, and then deliver your attack.

In all negotiations, time is the enemy, since if you do not control the timing you will inevitably lose control of the pace and structure. Planning has a major role to play in the effective exploitation of your position. Very often the assumption is made that negotiations will need to take place, but these can be condensed into whatever time is available. This will lead to loss of opportunity.

The phase leading up to negotiations and contract closure, during which tenders and evaluations have to be completed, can be extensive. The longer these actions take, the shorter the time available to manage the market. If negotiations are to be successful, one needs to ensure that as much time as possible is available to play the game. Failure to recognize this will create pressure to reach a conclusion, with the result that compromises will have to be made in order to maintain the overall project schedule.

Again, the crux of these timing issues is that most organizations fail to appreciate that real negotiations are is often concluded long before any official gathering. The project manager must consider, when establishing an execution plan, the creation of windows of opportunity within which to be able to play with time on his/her side.

If the opposition can identify a time constraint they will surely work towards limiting your options by prevarication and thus force you to select options or make agreements that do not fully realize the overall best options for you.

The aim should always be to work towards the opponent making the first significant move, then adjust the timing to your best advantage. To be able to move first you need be very sure of your position, or extremely adept at making changes on the run.

> If you are anxious to fight, you should not go to meet the invader near a river which he has to cross.
>   Moor your craft higher up than the enemy, and facing the sun. Do not move up-stream to meet the enemy. So much for river warfare.

There is often a lot of confusion around what should be negotiated and how to assess the structure of your approach. In many organizations, the infrastructure and policy is so well defined that the essence of making a deal is forgotten in favour of ensuring compliance with a series of rules. These may relate to contracting terms or perceived cost targets.

When approaching negotiations, the outcome should first look at the needs of the project. If these needs are not satisfied then whatever follows, the net result will not provide the project with a success platform. The absolutes must be established early, often long before the market has been approached, and these should be made clear to everyone involved.

It is also necessary to understand the way the market is currently performing. For example, in a seller's market the strength of the buyer may be significantly reduced and thus battling against the trend will simply exhaust those charged with finding a solution. It is better in these cases to structure your approach to exploit other options such as long-term relationships.

In a buyer's market, the focus would perhaps be better aimed at ensuring that, if you push the relationship to the most competitive outcome, you can still rely on support. Very often inexperienced negotiations will push too far in the short term and find further down the track that they are, for example, unable to match delivery or quality needs.

When the current stream of business is not in your favour, you must certainly not be seen to be weakened by this, but at the same time consider how to bring key players towards your goal. Alliances made at an early stage can provide such a platform.

> In crossing salt-marshes, your sole concern should be to get over them quickly, without any delay.
>
> If forced to fight in a salt-marsh, you should have water and grass near you, and get your back to a clump of trees. So much for operations in salt-marshes.

Most organizations have a tendency to focus on the strength of their position and therefore concentrate on the detail of minor issues, with an emphasis on compliance. Developing an agenda that can be used as the baseline for negotiations requires that one looks first at the issues that will be of significance to one's opponent.

There may be many issues that, while they are of little importance to your own drivers, can be traded during discussions. These straw issues should not be ignored, as they will later enable one to control the flow of any agreement.

The skill in developing negotiations is to ensure that minor issues do not become major topics of debate. While they may be important to the opposition they will consume time and effort, therefore they should be monitored and recorded for future agreement. Consideration given to not conceding issues early in order to clear the agenda. The straw issues can be used to control debate and given as concessions when appropriate.

The important factor in any negotiation programme should be to maintain the flow and timing to suit your needs, and not those of the opposition. The key driver must always be towards those items that are of the greatest importance to your objectives and plans.

In many parts of the world, negotiation is a way of life and it will therefore be seen as the main focus for those in positions of responsibility. These environments are very risky for those who have not experienced them previously, and should be approached with care, particularly where time is not seen as a priority and time will be used against you. In these cases, patience will be the key ingredient.

> In dry, level country, take up an easily accessible position with rising ground to your right and on your rear, so that the danger may be in front, and safety lie behind. So much for campaigning in flat country.

There are many factors to successful negotiations and in the front line will be the selection of the location. Often you have no choice when a customer calls you to a meeting, and in these cases you will have to develop a counter-strategy. The normal desire is always to hold discussions on your own territory, since this provides a comfort zone and ensures that you have your full resources behind you.

But if being on your own 'patch' is good for you, then the opposition must be at a disadvantage. This could be beneficial, but could also be seen as a disadvantage, since you bring into play the issue of remote authority. The essence of negotiations is to structure the debate and focus it towards your desired outcome.

Therefore, if your opponent is not able to bring the decision-makers to the meeting, then the debate will falter while waiting for instruction or agreement from other parts. This will enable the opposition to regroup and develop counter-proposals, which will defuse any structure you try to create.

The option of selecting neutral ground is often favoured, but this has a major disadvantage in that it will immediately declare an intent to compromise. The choice obviously depends on the issue under debate and the relative strength of the parties involved. If one is looking for compromise, then it may well be the best choice, but even in these cases the position is weakened.

Taking the debate to the opponent's territory may be more difficult, in that your own strength and resources may be limited. The key here is to ensure that you have the authority and major resources you need to hold the ground.

> These are the four useful branches of military knowledge which enabled the Yellow Emperor to vanquish four several sovereigns.

The four principle parameters for any negotiation are focused around location, agenda, timing and approach. If these issues are handled well and the strategy developed around them, then the chances of success will be greatly improved.

Having established the approach to timing, location and agenda, then the fourth element needs very careful consideration. The diversity of the global marketplace means that one is faced with many differing cultures and styles. In many parts of the world the way things are presented can have greater impact than the actual content of the discussions. A style that is very effective in one region may have a completely opposite effect in another.

The project world will of necessity face many different cultures at the same time, and it is crucial that these alternative relationships are managed correctly. The project team may find themselves switching between many countries and organizations, with each of these requiring strategies applicable to the approaches that are the norm in the individual regions.

When entering into negotiations it is also useful to have a good understanding of the local environment. For example, in many parts of the world local income levels may be quite low and thus the perception of value will also be significantly lower. Thus when one debates around costs which one might consider to be small, the local view could be quite different.

The global market is extremely complex and the project team have to be sure that they match their style and strategy to local conditions. Meeting the opposition on their territory means having a sound understanding of that environment, then adopting an approach that will be acceptable to the local culture.

> All armies prefer high ground to low and sunny places to dark.

As stated earlier, the main skill in successful negotiations is to ensure that you remain in control. This means that you have to focus on where you think the opposition will be coming from. Too often the effort is placed by organizations on their own objectives and they fail to recognize the drivers coming from the opposition.

Negotiation strategies need to be developed both for handling, say, the customer's perspective, as well as those from key suppliers and partners. The relationships that develop in any contract will outlive the negotiations and should therefore be approached in consideration of where the relationship is desired to lead in the longer term. For example, while one may apply significant pressure during negotiations, this should be balanced against the degree of collaboration that may be required downstream.

It is often a strategy to paint a rosy picture of future gains your counterpart may get in consideration of concessions made in the early days to conclude an arrangement, but the future relationship may well be placed in jeopardy if those project gains do not materialize.

In many cases the challenge of the negotiations prompts the players to bend the truth and create false impressions. This again is a risk, since false impressions may ultimately present stumbling blocks at later critical stages of the project.

Often, while it may be easier to present a perception of a glowing future relationship, it is better for long-term collaboration to err on the side of caution and be more pessimistic. The negotiation strategy must take these issues into account and develop a concept where all parties have a good understanding of future challenges. In this case, all parties will consider they have won and will be more willing to accommodate late downturns.

> If you are careful of your men, and camp on hard ground, the army will be free from disease of every kind, and this will spell victory.

A difficulty in many organizations is the construction of negotiating teams that reflect the key issues of the day. This is particularly difficult in major engineering projects, where there are many players covering multiple functions within the team. When too many people are involved it becomes very complex in terms of maintaining a focus during discussions.

The more people involved, the greater the risk of independent dialogues arising. The optimum grouping for any negotiation is three: one person to talk, one to listen and one to record the discussions. When there is a need to involve individual specialists, they should join and leave the discussions on an *ad hoc* basis, which will ensure that no secondary debates can get started.

In some regions of the world the number of participants can be significant. This does not always add strength, but is the natural way of things here. In these cases, there has to be strong discipline within the negotiating team, since there is a tendency to break into smaller groups and often attack the same problem/issue from various angles.

If your team is not co-ordinated and focused it will be drawn apart progressively and any initiatives diluted. To this end the project manager needs to maintain a very structured approach and to ensure that a pre-meeting run-through is undertaken and all key objectives and strategies agreed.

In negotiations, a team that is not fully integrated in its objectives and strategy will be divided and a skilful opponent will take advantage of this opportunity. This possibility has to be a goal of the project manager when considering his/her own strategy.

> When you come to a hill or a bank, occupy the sunny side, with the slope on your right rear. Thus you will at once act for the benefit of your soldiers and utilize the natural advantages of the ground.

The key issue in any negotiation is to ensure that, when the strategy is put into play, the real decision-makers are present. The structured approach to negotiations may be sound but if the game cannot be played out in full then any strategy will be wasted.

Too often those who did not attend the final meeting will sit back and suggest what should or should not have been the outcome. There can only be one leader and he/she must have the power and authority to control the game through to the end.

The role of the project manager is to ensure that whoever goes into the negotiations has the power to conclude a deal. If the management is not prepared to delegate then the managers must take to the field themselves. It may be that strict 'no go' parameters can be set, but otherwise the players have to be in control of the debate. If a negotiator does not feel he or she has the power it will be noticed.

On the other hand, if a negotiator knows he/she can proceed, all issues will be approached from a very positive standpoint. Therefore, if the organization is behind the negotiators they will press forward with confidence and this commitment will demonstrate itself in their demeanour.

Where possible one must also try to ensure that those debated with have the power to make commitments. To close a deal then, one needs decision-makers at the table. In a supplier market this is generally done by the method, manner and style of invitation: when a supplier thinks this is the only chance they will get, they tend to respond with a committed team.

> When, in consequence of heavy rains up-country, a river which you wish to
> ford is swollen and flecked with foam, you must wait until it subsides.

The timing of any negotiation should be adapted as far as possible to
take into account market conditions. The choice of timing seldom meets the
aspirations of those scheduling negotiations, and often the driver in these
situations will use time pressure to force a conclusion in his/her favour.

The oldest trick in the book is to target meetings with limited time for
debate because of deadlines such as weekends, travel plans or public holi-
days. This ploy can be effective but may also present a serious risk. Playing
for time may create pressures, but often this can be counter-productive,
since when no conclusion is reached the various parties have an opportunity to regroup.

When faced with a time-constrained proposition, it must be the negotiators' strategy to avoid being ring-fenced. Negotiations that are clearly
focused on creating a time barrier need to be countered with an approach
that convinces the other party that one will take as long as necessary to
close the deal. Often, once this position is established, the ploy will become
void.

Frequently negotiations will reach either a highly pressurized position or
an impasse, and on these occasions a negotiator needs to be able to take
time out or walk away. The natural approach to negotiations is to build up
pressure so the other party eventually concedes. It should always be
remembered that, for most business dealings, these negotiations will be at
the start of a relationship, and such pressure in the short term may be
reverse later in the project.

Time can be both a tool and a threat, and it needs to be managed in
consideration of the drivers at the time. Thus planning for the project
should take this into account, since negotiations are about establishing the
parameters of a relationship and not simply about immediate gains.

> Country in which there are precipitous cliffs with torrents running between,
> deep natural hollows, confined places, tangled thickets, quagmires and
> crevasses, should be left with all speed and not approached.
>   While we keep away from such places, we should get the enemy to
> approach them; while we face them, we should let the enemy have them on his
> rear.

Every negotiation is a combination of agreements, which form an integrated deal. There should never be conclusions or acceptance at the individual level but only on a complete package agreement basis.

Experienced negotiators will look at all situations from a position both of what they require and what the opposition would probably aim for. The rationale for this approach is to ensure that, as discussions progress, one needs to be fully focused on the 'stop' and 'go' positions.

The intent in any agreement is to work towards a situation where both parties believe they have won, since this will create a platform for future dealings. It is therefore important to establish what is important to the other party, or at least to assess what is likely to be a significant issue. During the exchanges these assessments need to be analysed and validated.

When recognizing that the opposition has a totally negative approach, the skilful negotiator will work around those 'no go' issues from their perspective, or will address these as clear, non-negotiable items and look for conciliatory concessions elsewhere. The trading of issues may become very complex, and therefore maintaining a clear focus on the major issues is the key to formulating an acceptable package.

Balancing the desires of both parties must drive the development of a negotiation strategy. The greater effort should go towards trying to isolate the major roadblocks to an agreement at the same time as avoiding significant pitfalls.

> If in the neighbourhood of your camp there should be any hilly country, ponds surrounded by aquatic grass, hollow basins filled with reeds, or woods with thick undergrowth, they must be carefully routed out and searched; for these are places where men in ambush or insidious spies are likely to be lurking.

It should always be in the forefront of any negotiator's mind that the opposition probably also has a very structured strategy. When the number of issues being debated becomes large, the likelihood is that the strategy is to create a very complex arena. This approach can work, but requires careful handling and constant restating of the relative positions.

In this environment, the discipline of the negotiation team is crucial, since when the debate gets confused the probability is that hidden in the debate are some serious negative issues. It is in these cases in particular that the control of any discussion is kept very tight. One can see that in political circles, for example, where counter-proposals become interlinked to the point where the original issues become obscure. In most cases the only control then is to take time out from the debate and reassess the position.

It is also a useful tactic to stop the debate and consolidate the current position before moving forward. The experienced negotiator will see this position developing and may often take a completely different route in order to force all issues back into a controlled position.

The clever negotiator may well be able to plant advantageous options into an agreement by knowing what may be developing outside the arena. This could be change to the project needs, or when alternative selections become available. This approach does have a potential downside, though, since once again it is the long-term relationship that may be at risk. In most business situations, and particularly in the case of integrated projects, every clever deal has to last the duration of the interdependence.

> When the enemy is close at hand and remains quiet, he is relying on the natural strength of his position.
>
> When he keeps aloof and tries to provoke a battle, he is anxious for the other side to advance.
>
> If his place of encampment is easy to access, he is tendering to bait.

In any negotiation, if you understand the drivers from the other side it should also be possible to analyse any concessions. When something is conceded it is generally for one of two reasons. First, that the concession is of no importance to the other side, or that by accepting the agreement one is being drawn towards another conclusion which is clearly more advantageous to the opposition.

The negotiator must be able to distinguish between which are straw issues and which are laying down a platform for some later concession. This interaction is clearly where the strategy of only agreeing to the final package is most important. Since until a final deal is created, neither side will fully understand the ramifications of the package.

In some case one may find what could be described as attrition negotiators. These are very common in certain regions of the world where negotiations are seldom driven by the same time pressures as in more industrial regions. The strategy here is to offer a concession against some interim agreement and then defer the final agreement. The next series of discussions will start from your agreement but ignore the counter-balance concession.

Most business environments do not have the luxury of time to use this tactic, since in general both parties have targets to meet. Nevertheless, the gift of some concession from one party to another should be understood for what its true driver is.

If one appreciates what is important to the other party one will be able to evaluate any proposition that appears to be in one's favour and assess the impact to one's position.

> Movement amongst the trees of a forest shows that the enemy is advancing. The appearance of a number of screens in the midst of thick grass means that the enemy wants to make us suspicious.

A clever strategy is to create obvious issues that one knows will be considered unacceptable. These will engender a reaction and the opposition will spend time trying to remove them from any agreement. Their efforts may be time-consuming but as they succeed their level of satisfaction grows. The effort that is expended chasing these false targets allows one's own strategy to evolve.

When evaluating a potential partner one will inevitably establish many items of minor consequence to one's own targets and objectives. This arises from the basic principle that most organizations have their standard methodology. In the engineering world of projects these may be either technical preferences or commercial baselines. Either way, the issues may not be fundamental but will be part of the assessment of acceptability.

The creating and playing of the 'straw issues' is a key tactic for manoeuvring any opposition and controlling their focus. The skilled negotiator will use these to develop pressure and this is often the reverse of a conciliatory approach, for each concession, draws something from the other side. Therefore you trade what you do not need and conserve what is important to you.

There are many examples, but say in the case of a supplier your driver is delivery. In the evaluation you establish that the payment terms requested are more expensive than your standard but in overall cost terms are acceptable. Then much debate surrounds the payment terms and as you move forward these become linked to key delivery milestones. The supplier may be happy with the outcome but fail to recognize that in fact you may have paid more for the delivery security.

In any negotiation, what you see is not necessarily what is being traded and understanding the drivers is crucial. The background thinking is often difficult to interpret but the more adept one becomes at sensing the ground, the more successful one is likely to be. The value of instinct is often confused with the ability of the experienced player to absorb information, often without realizing it, and devising a strategy or tactical move almost without thinking about the issue.

> The rising of birds in their flight is the sign of an ambuscade. Startled beasts indicate that a sudden attack is coming.
>
> When there is dust rising in a high column, it is the sign of chariots advancing; when the dust is low but spread over a wide area, it betokens the approach of infantry. When it branches out in different directions, it shows that parties have been sent to collect firewood. A few clouds of dust moving to and fro signify that the army is encamping.

Knowing your opponent is fundamental to all strategy development and it is the cornerstone of all negotiation tactics. When you start to move towards a conclusion you really need to be aware of how the opposition is approaching the final debate and agreement. In the same way as every comment or action you make is an indicator for your opponent, so then the reverse also applies.

The experienced negotiator will be working always at two levels: the first is the direction and objectives that are required, while at the same time a profile of what is driving the opposition is being developed. The complexity of many negotiations make the linking and balancing of these two structures very difficult.

The true skill is to anticipate where the trail is leading, and to develop alternative approaches that bring the flow around towards the targeted conclusions. Every action has a reaction and the same applies in the world of negotiations, where every concession or stance is part of a wider picture. If one is not to be led then one must lead.

Each step towards progress in concluding a deal needs to be analysed in terms of its effect on the desired outcome. In the majority of cases one can divide all actions into four categories. First are those that are acceptable but should be viewed as concessions; second, those that are cosmetic and have no impact; and third, those that are clearly unacceptable. The fourth category is the area of most concern, since if it is not apparent why or where something fits, then generally it is a precursor to something else and should be viewed with caution.

Humble words and increased preparations are signs that the enemy is about to advance. Violent language and driving forward as if to the attack are signs that he will retreat.

Most commonly, the tactics for negotiations will be driven by the obscure rather than the obvious. If an opponent offers a simple and straight-forward approach there is likely to be some alternative linkage behind the scenes. This is particularly true when one is trying to balance the emotional stances of the various parties.

Reverse emotion is one of the experienced negotiators' most useful weapons, since it can be employed to stimulate activity or defuse conflict. Correctly employed, it serves to manage any relationship and can often make the difference between meeting the end-game successfully and forc-ing discussions into a stalemate.

Those who are confident of their position will in most cases demonstrate a very conciliatory style since, if they are sure to win, creating a conflict will have no value or contribution. An alternative should also be consid-ered: in that those who profess to be strong often are covering weaknesses.

In the course of most negotiations there will probably be many issues arising, and the emotional swing will be constant. It is the challenge for all negotiators to ensure that they control this pattern to their own advantage. Part of this will be dependent on how well one understands the real drivers on the part of the opposition.

Recognizing that both parties are representing their relative organiza-tions, the use of counter-emotion has to be handled with care, since when an individual is attacked he or she reacts as though they are addressed personally, and this will generally detract from the flow. Therefore good moves are accepted personally and aggressive moves should be countered against the organization and not the individual. This enables the negotiator to maintain the relationship interface.

When the light chariots come out first and take up a position on the wings, it is a sign that the enemy is forming for battle.

In presenting a negotiation team it is easy to create the right message, that one is serious, by putting forward a strong and authoritative team. When faced with what may clearly be seen as a junior team one can easily assume that there is either little interest on their part or that this approach is a preliminary. It is therefore important to establish the credentials of the opposition.

Power mapping of an opponent is a useful approach, both to understand the roles of those that one faces but also to form a sound perspective of where the real authority rests. In many parts of the world the organizational structure may not truly reflect where the command structure is really effective. For example, in the Far East one can see that educational background creates linkages that transcend the official organization. If this is not understood, one may find effort being wasted or opportunities lost.

These power chains can be based on cultural origins as well, and thus having reliable local support is crucial if playing the global market. Status may be seen as paramount – for example, in Japan, where the hierarchical authority is clear; however, one may find from experience that this is far from being the real decision-maker's structure.

One approach that is often used in certain parts of the world is to dissociate the decision-makers from any discussion or exchange. This ensures that the senior management cannot be compromised. At the same time there is often an insistence that those attending to ensure that decisions can be ratified hold powers of attorney.

The structure of the team can give certain strength to the approach or can be clearly interpreted as a level of commitment.

> Peace proposals unaccompanied by a sworn covenant indicate a plot.

There is a growing trend in the business world towards exploiting the benefits of alliance-type contracts. These have been shown to deliver significant advantages to both sides of the contracting arrangement. It is, however, an approach that needs to be considered with care and focused only where it adds real value.

The term 'partner' is used very commonly today and in most cases it is utilized simply as a sales tool with no real commitment or intent. Many industries will foster this approach in their marketing presentations and when it comes to negotiations it is used as a valuable icebreaker. The approach needs to be tested if it was not an aim that was originally considered. The first obstacle will be when the subject of risk-sharing is raised. This is usually when the pure sales approach fails.

Partnering may have a place in the project, and approaching negotiations with this in mind will require a very careful development of strategy. The hard-line focus may need to be tempered, since if this type of relationship is really being considered then the parties will move to a collaborative stance, which can only be built on a win–win basis.

To be effective, these alliance-type approaches will necessitate negotiations taking place much earlier. The concept is sound and many examples can be found where these have supported benefits to both buyer and seller. The challenge is that, to move in this direction, both parties need to create a more open dialogue, with the danger clearly being that once the lid is off the box it will be hard to return to the status quo.

There can be great cost advantages, but these savings will take time and effort to develop. When offered without a true defined objective they can in general be assumed to be a ploy that can be dangerous. In simple terms, those who offer deals without being asked generally do so for their own advantage.

> When there is much running about and the soldiers fall into rank, it means that the critical moment has come.
>
> When some are seen advancing and some retreating, it is a lure.

In any negotiations, the starting point for either side will be their own aspirations. These may be realistic or simply a wish list of what they would hope to attain. The key is to ensure that from the outset you work to reduce your opponent's expectations before engaging in a detailed debate.

Those who feel they have a strong position need to be weakened quickly, while those who advance a comfortable position will need to be less confident if one is to have a valid outcome.

The apparently stronger the team you face, the more likely they are to be vulnerable and are often waiting for additional strength to come from your relinquishing of positions. This concept needs to be tested and balanced against your own profile of the organization; again, the underlying strength is to interpret what you perceive is the knowledge you have and turn this to your advantage.

Those who come to the negotiating table with a limited team will probably be ready to call their base for additional support, and thus are only there to draw out your key issues. These will then be dissected and utilized by the stronger team that is likely to follow. The use of low-level players is common in many regions, and they will be constantly pushed forward to test your resolve. One initiative is to place senior players at the table, who then use underlings to carry out the negotiations.

These strategies need to be understood and countered. For example, to reduce the expectations much of the effective work is done not in formal discussions but by side discussions and exchanges. There is a tendency to use unofficial chats to lay the groundwork and apply pressure by informally establishing parameters. Senior managers should be kept away from the front line until one is sure you have deal to be clinched.

Negotiations are not single events; they are carefully constructed strategies where every member of the team is a player.

> When soldiers stand leaning on their spears, they are faint from want of food.
>
> If those who are sent to draw water begin by drinking themselves, the army is suffering from thirst.
>
> If the enemy sees an advantage to be gained and makes no effort to secure it, the soldiers are exhausted.

The playing-out of negotiation strategy is very much dependent on the skill of the negotiator to read and understand not simply what is being said but also the style, approach and body language. The way in which people behave can frequently say more than words. In fact, the way in which people hold themselves or respond is a certain indication of how they perceive their position.

This is particularly important in those parts of the world where discussions can only be held through interpreters. This situation will create a great strain on most traditionally trained negotiators, who work by force and by dominating discussions. A powerful orator can command only so long as those listening can be drawn along by the flow. Where the language barrier becomes a factor, then the dialogue becomes a level playing field.

When faced with having to work through interpreters the negotiator is only able to use the strength of logical argument and the perception of those watching. In most cases the interpreter will take emotion out of any exchange and thus those who use the power of persuasion will be hindered.

The use of body language can become a powerful tool when linked to the exchanged words. Any emotion can be reflected immediately to all concerned and it will surmount any neutrality of the interpretation. In the same way, if one observes it is easy to see when conditions are being assessed or becoming confrontational.

What people see is how you act, and not how you speak, therefore, for example, signs of fatigue will encourage others to increase the pressure.

Those who understand these powers will benefit in foreign cultures. Understanding even a few words may create an impression of knowledge.

> If birds gather on any spot, it is unoccupied. Clamour by night betokens nervousness.
> If there is disturbance in the camp, the general's authority is weak. If the banners and flags are shifted about, sedition is afoot. If the officers are angry, it means that the men are weary.

Every position has some value even if it is to be traded as part of a wider perspective or plan. When concessions come easily they are generally of limited, or nil value to the other side. These are issues not to be balanced but simply to be acknowledged and discounted immediately. It should always be considered that whatever strategy you may plan, or tactics you employ, your opponent will have a similar plan.

In assessing the strength and approach one should monitor the amount of debate between the parties. Every negotiating team needs to have someone whose role is to watch and observe. In this way, your team will be able to form a view of the proceedings and the relative strengths of the debate. The more there is internal discussion, the more uncertain the opposition's position, unless, of course, they are playing for effect.

Evaluation of the behaviour of the opposition, rather than of the points of debate, is a crucial part of the information that will refine tactics. In every contest, and negotiations are a contest, strategy and tactics must evolve as the play unfurls. Monitoring of the interaction can create a valuable understanding of pressure points and areas of concern.

Understanding how to use the knowledge gained is the skill of the negotiator. For example, knowing when to insert comfort breaks into the discussion enables the play to be controlled. The timing of recesses during long negotiations is crucial to ensure a focus on key points.

Those experienced in the world of global projects will have met many of these approaches, and suffered no doubt from their skilful implementation.

> When an army feeds its horses with grain and kills its cattle for food, and when the men do not hang their cooking-pots over camp-fires, showing that they will not return to their tents, you may know that they are determined to fight to the death.

When developing a negotiation strategy it is important to establish one's objectives and what an acceptable solution would be. This is the baseline that will focus both approach and tactics. These should be based on a realistic review of the market. The reactions when faced with, say, a supplier who immediately concedes major elements of your requirements must be assessed, since you have misread the market or there is a significant issue behind the scenes that needs to be understood.

In an established market, even on the global stage, the variations that could be expected in area of products and services should be reasonably predictable. Therefore, if one encounters significant swings there is certainly a potential danger and thus a risk being created. There can be a number of reasons for these swings, which may result from a misunderstanding of the requirements, or alternative solutions that have not been adequately evaluated.

The riskier elements come from two directions. First, the supplier wants to break into a new market or penetrate your organization, which has previously been closed to them. Alternatively, the company has an urgent need to fill under-utilized capacity on a short-term basis. These are legitimate business strategies, but you need to understand the potential risks that you may face if encouraged to take the bait.

In the case of market or company penetration, this is manageable provided you can compensate for their lack of experience. The issue of filling empty workshops is potentially of greater concern, since once the shortfall has been rectified and the pressure removed, the reduced value of your work may detract from the focus you need to complete your goals.

Opportunities should be explored but the risks should also be appreciated and built into the overall equation before committing to the approach. The outcome can be beneficial but the promise of benefit should not cloud the focus on initial objectives and needs.

> The sight of men whispering together in small knots or speaking in subdued tones points to disaffection amongst the rank and file.

The object of any negotiation is to take advantage of the market, but at the same time to create a relationship that will support the overall objectives of the project. The professional opponent understands this and will act in a manner that acknowledges their right to concede or walk away. This is the basis of good business and a fundamental part of building a successful network to benefit the project.

The key element is always to remember the goal, and to accept that once past the negotiation stage the parties will be to some extent interdependent, to the extent that one is able to judge these situations. The approach taken during negotiation will reflect the style and manner of later relationships. This should be accepted as part of the process.

Those who concede with a professional approach will probably attack challenges later with a similar degree of commitment. Those who take a position of acceptance but spend their time complaining at the result will probably maintain a similar position throughout all dealings.

During the execution phase of any project there will be problems, and this is inevitable in the complex world of projects. It is the manner in which such problems are handled that distinguishes the professional organization.

One should not, however, take this to be a global trait, as in some regions of the world the negotiation process is intended to continue during the time-span of the whole project. This is the nature of the local culture and must be understood. In these cases one must be aware that while the organization is acting perhaps counter to previous agreements, this is their way. Naturally, the culture of the project has also to adapt to this style of relationship.

> Too frequent rewards signify that the enemy is at the end of his resources; too many punishments betray a condition of dire distress.

When focused on the negotiations it is often tempting to push beyond the original principal objectives. This tends to happen when the opposition, for many different reasons, is inclined to accept more risk and offer greater concessions. This appetite for maximizing the benefits of negotiation must be understood and evaluated.

When you achieve more than you expect, then the motivation behind that success must be considered. Where a supplier concedes continually they obviously have a different agenda than the one that was envisaged. As expressed earlier the art of skilful negotiation is to aim for the maximum, but hold back from going over the limit of what is reasonable. Those who offer much more than the market conditions would suggest are probably hiding some secondary strategy.

The counter to this may also be true, in that as the opposition takes a more rigid stance the probability is that they have reached the end of their scope for concessions. This is the point at which the experienced negotiator will spot the change and begin to consolidate rather than to push.

In negotiations around potential alliances these two trends will be seen even more frequently, since the nature of the exchanges will be trying to find common and mutually beneficial ground. As such, the efforts of all parties will be focused on building a strong relationship that can deliver an integrated solution. The pressure increases as both parties try to maintain their own advantages while struggling to concede where necessary to ensure the integration.

Negotiations are based around people, and thus to manage them well requires an appreciation of both business issues and personal involvement. The exploitation of relationships is the foundation of business, and the development of trust a crucial factor in those relationships. Exploiting the personal challenge must also reflect implications for the future.

> To begin by bluster, but afterwards to take fright at the enemy's numbers, shows a supreme lack of intelligence.

People management is a key factor in negotiations, and the best exponents are generally those who have a natural interest in people, for while the business organization will set the targets and agendas it is the style and approach of the individual that will eventually deliver the results.

In general terms, people seek satisfaction and recognition. Therefore, not only during negotiations will they assess how they are managing against prescribed aims, but they will also evaluate how the progress may reflect on them personally. Thus, to achieve the best results, the skilled negotiator will try to ensure that at the individual level the results can support their position.

A negotiator who elects to use strength and aggression as an opening stance will be unlikely to achieve the best results. In fact, it is probable that such an approach, even if it results in a contract, will create frictions that others will have to handle. In the intricate and complex world of projects, the future relationship will be a significant factor in success. Thus whatever may be agreed at the initial point in time, the relationship will last for the duration of the project.

This is an important consideration and requires careful assessment as to whether the team that negotiates should also be the team that executes. This has two benefits: first, that with an eye on future relationships the agreement will be more balanced; and second, that during execution, issues cannot be laid at the feet of the negotiators.

The opposite view may also be applicable, in that if the agreement has been achieved through aggressive negotiation it may be more appropriate to disengage the conflict from future dealings.

Each approach has both merit and risk, and has to be considered as part of the negotiation strategy.

> When envoys are sent with compliments in their mouths, it is a sign that the enemy wishes for a truce.
>
> If the enemy's troops march up angrily and remain facing ours for a long time without either joining battle or taking themselves off again, the situation is one that demands great vigilance and circumspection.

Developing a strategy and tactics initially will only provide a platform. As the debate expands and develops, the judgement must be on how the opposition reacts. The approach and style they present may provide an insight into the strategy they are pursuing. Alternatively, it may be shielding some weakness that they do not want to have exposed.

A conciliatory approach may be appropriate in the case of post-contract negotiations during the execution phase. This is, however, unlikely to be applicable in the pre-contract stage. Therefore, if such a style is presented it needs to be assessed with great care. When a style is inappropriate to the circumstances it should be evaluated to understand the drivers involved.

The reserve position creates a similar field of concern, or at least it should. When one's opposition takes an aggressive stance but continues to try and advance their case this should be a warning sign to the negotiator. If one fails to recognize these traits and investigate or test the background, then it is likely that some risk or opportunity will be overlooked.

There may be many reasons behind the approach taken. For example, a customer may need to demonstrate that they have fought hard even if they wish to close the issue. They may be so set against your organization that by adopting an aggressive approach they hope you will retire from the race. Or it may simply be that they recognize that their position is weak and they therefore wish to dominate.

Whatever the driver, if it is not understood then the probability is that you will lose control of the negotiations and thus forgo some opportunity.

> If our troops are no more in number than the enemy, that is amply sufficient; it only means that no direct attack can be made. What we can do is simply to concentrate all our available strength, keep a close watch on the enemy, and obtain reinforcements.

The complexity of creating the correct negotiation strategy is clear, but the execution of that approach is greatly dependent on the team put forward. If one understands the opponent and has established a sound platform, then the team will be the weak link. Often the team is selected on the basis of seniority rather than skill or suitability. As with all things in the project environment, the focus should be on outcome and not on individual prestige.

Selecting the appropriate players is a crucial part of the strategy and must be considered with care, balancing the knowledge of the opposition, their background, relative speciality and the power structure of their organization. Acknowledging personal relationships against the particular issues involved, may also drive it. There is no substitute for exploiting long-term relationships, but in certain cases this may inhibit the approach taken.

In many industries with long associations between organizations, it is inevitable that individual relationships will be generated. These are the backbone of most industries, and in some parts of the world it will be the relationships that make things happen. The downside of these special associations is that in some positions they can be stretched or even broken because of the issues of the day.

All negotiation teams must be created from the best combination of required skills, knowledge and effectiveness. Often salesmen see themselves as the prime movers, but in some cases, depending on opposing styles, this could be detrimental to the outcome. Seniority may be required, but this poses the challenge that, for example, the CEO has nowhere to hide and can be manoeuvred into compliance where more junior players would not be.

> He who exercises no forethought but makes light of his opponents is sure to be captured by them.

Projects are strictly a team effort, and when it comes to negotiations the team concept must be even stronger. Many negotiations fail because those involved do not act in concert towards the agreed objectives.

Every negotiation must have a team leader, who is given the clear overall authority to drive the pace and structure. Participants must be under no illusion as to who is leading the play. While much preparatory work can be done, and tactics clearly defined, it is certain that changes in approach will be needed. This must be orchestrated carefully to ensure that there is no inadvertent slip by other members of the team.

The biggest risk area is the individual who, for whatever reason, elects to take a solo approach. In most cases this is a result of ego or inexperience, or believing that they alone have the winning hand. The rogue player will certainly undo any carefully laid initiative. Even worse, when they begin to exercise alternative styles they present an opening to be exploited by the opposition. The toughest barrier to breach is the one that is totally consistent.

Where many contributions may be required negotiation must always be done within a small group at any one time. If multiple side-discussions are initiated, the leader will not be able to control the action. The basic rule of a maximum of three players at a time should be maintained.

Any differences between the team must be resolved in private, and then a position decided with which all comply. This is often difficult when specialists are involved, or where more senior members have taken a backseat. The project manager must reinforce the discipline and ensure that the team is focused and in agreement.

> If soldiers are punished before they have grown attached to you, they will not prove submissive; and, unless submissive, then will be practically useless. If, when the soldiers have become attached to you, punishments are not enforced, they will be useless.

The personal aspirations of individuals are a constant challenge for any leadership. In the project world this becomes amplified tens of times as many different skills and talents are concentrated to forge the most effective team. Each member of the project team will, it is hoped, be giving their utmost and as such will expect both recognition and opportunity.

Strangely, the perceived glamour of negotiations brings out the strongest desires for recognition and status. Generally, negotiations are associated with successful outcomes: winning contracts or concluding a deal on favourable terms. In either case the organization will often tend to herald those who led the charge. So everyone wishes to be the leader, and clearly this is not an appropriate rationale for selection.

This is a significant issue for most project managers, who need to balance the interests and support of the individual alongside the most effective team to achieve the desired goals. This becomes exaggerated even further when these individuals have special knowledge and believe that only they can win the day. Even when they are part of a team they elect to take their own route through the negotiations.

In the worst case, it may even be necessary for the team leader to remove such individuals from the discussions. This often arises in the engineering world, where technical opinion may create a personal challenge that detracts from the overall plan.

Project managers must be aware of these issues, which commonly do not arise until too late to rectify and the damage is done.

> Therefore soldiers must be treated in the first instance with humanity, but kept under control by means of iron discipline. This is a certain road to victory.

As with any part of the project process, the negotiation environment needs a close team working towards an agreed set of objectives. Developing the strategy, selecting the right team and preparing the tactics are all crucial parts of the process. If negotiations are to be successful they must be orchestrated and implemented in a unified manner.

Building a team is not simply about bringing a group of specialists together, it requires the creation of a focused group. The team needs to accept that it must take maximum advantage of the knowledge and resources it has available, and these must be tuned to the specific challenge at hand and not linked to personal drivers.

When the strategy is in place, the team must be selected and the whole project group focused behind them, understanding that strength in any particular area may be less critical than the optimization of the objectives. This follows the basic principle that strength alone is not the only criteria, and often it is the skill of the players that wins the day.

The negotiation team should not concentrate only on their individual issues; they need to have a holistic view of the deal. This can be developed through preliminary meetings and even on occasion trial runs. This preparation gives the whole project team an opportunity to help refine their message. Sharing information and ideas will enable the team to face the challenge as prepared as they can be. Negotiations are a critical part of the process and their success will dictate the overall success of the project.

> If in training soldiers commands are habitually enforced, the army will be well-disciplined; if not, its discipline will be bad.
>
> If a general shows confidence in his men but always insists on his orders being obeyed, the gain will be mutual.

Negotiations are the business battleground and are a crucial part of the overall project strategy. If they are handled with care and focus they can underpin the efforts of the project team. Those who consider the process to be a simple one have generally failed to understand the complexity that can be involved.

Project managers need to be involved directly in setting out the pattern and strategy. They must also be ready to select the most appropriate players and then support them. Every negotiation is different, and the assessment of when, where, how, who and what is as important as the definition of the issues involved.

This element of the project world must be focused on what the project needs and drive towards that end. The negotiation team must be well prepared and given enough authority to take advantage of opportunities to deliver the objectives.

At every stage of the project and at every level of the team, some input to negotiations will be required, either directly or indirectly. The project manager must be sure that he has fielded the best team, and be ready to stand by their success. Those who stand outside the contest must accept the outcome, since it is easy to be wise after the event: only those directly involved can truly assess the ebb and flow and respond accordingly.

Negotiations are the battles, but the overall objective is to win the war for the whole team.

CHAPTER 11

Terrain

We may distinquish six kinds of terrain: accessible ground; entangling ground; temporizing ground; narrow passes; precipitous heights; positions at a great distance from the enemy.

Successful projects do not just happen; they are planned and managed to achieve their aims and objectives. In the world of global projects, the complexity of both the challenges and risks is very significant. The management of these in relation to the project and changing trends is crucial, and requires visibility to assess impacts.

However well a project is planned, though, there is little possibility of it maintaining the original projections. As variations come into play, the project management team must be able to respond with considered judgement to mitigate the problems.

Most projects need to be planned completely, but in fact it will be the true critical path that dictates success. Developing a project plan that takes into account market trends and changes is important, but what is more important is understanding where the pinch points will come, where there is no alternative route or solution.

Critical path analysis is the main tool for managing a project's pace and probability. It will also be the driving factor behind most of the risk management strategies that will be needed to keep the project on track.

The other balancing factor will be the development of a close-out programme. The many facets of politics, culture and economics complicate major projects, particularly those in the more remote parts of the world. The challenge for the project manager is not only to win the contract and execute it, but also to ensure that the intricate arrangements can be closed out effectively. Establishing a close-out programme is something that should be initiated on day one of the project and developed alongside the critical path.

Ground which can be freely traversed by both sides is called Accessible.

With regard to ground of this nature, be before the enemy in occupying the raised and sunny spots, and carefully guard your line of supplies. Then you will be able to fight with advantage.

Ground which can be abandoned but is hard to re-occupy is called Entangling.

From a position of this sort, if the enemy is unprepared, you may sally forth and defeat him. But if the enemy is prepared for your coming, and you fail to defeat him, then, return being impossible, disaster will ensue.

Every step or action in the project must be linked to impacts on the critical path and close-out programme. These linkages must be understood by all concerned, and no action taken without due consideration for the impact it might have. Changes and variations to the base programme must be reviewed and analysed to ensure that while performing one action, risk is not being created.

As changes occur, the key stages or steps may also be affected and thus corrective actions or the exploiting of opportunities can obscure the true impact. Bottlenecks or delays can arise for many different reasons, and each of these may, even inadvertently, cause a domino effect that could change the whole profile of the project.

The integrated nature of engineering projects, particularly those on a fast track, will create the need for parallel development. This approach can be planned and controlled, but the moment there is any cause to change the sequence will have a serious impact on the original logic.

Projects must be reviewed on a regular basis, and the impacts of change impacts or alternatives to maintain the programme must be fully analysed. The ongoing creation of the close-out plan must also be modified to accommodate the changes.

Progress may be swift, but the net result may be delay, and the focus must be on what makes the difference. Often this is missed on the deployment of strategies for closing out the programme.

When the position is such that neither side will gain by making the first move, it is called Temporizing ground.

In a position of this sort, even though the enemy should offer us an attractive bait, it will be advisable not to stir forth, but rather to retreat, thus enticing the enemy in his turn; then, when part of his army has come out, we may deliver our attack with advantage.

The project plan is about the effective utilization of resources towards the project completion. The critical path is focused on the final goal and outcome. These may on occasion be in conflict despite every attempt to maintain commonality. The project manager must control this situation and ensure that the true needs are identified and addressed.

Many times, the conflict may be in establishing a strategy with regard to customer interfaces and commercial issues. A clear and simple approach is that, if the customer does not agree to a change, work stops. This is a problem in certain parts of the world where, as discussed above, the commercial and operations organization may be separate. Deciding when to fight and when to concede may not simply be a question of right and wrong: it may be an issue of which option has the least impact.

This conflict of drivers can easily be seen in examples such as change or detailed preferences. The contract may be in your favour, but the impact of an extended dispute might in fact be detrimental to your end-game. To assess the best option, one has to have a clear and concise perspective on the implications.

A similar consideration must be made when dealing with suppliers; one's position may be clear but it depends who must stand the greatest loss if the prevarication is protracted.

Understanding when to fight and when to be magnanimous is an important issue, and in a complex world like that of projects it is not one decided on intuition but on fact. There is always an option to proceed in secret for some time in order to maintain the fight but still protect the programme.

> With regard to Narrow passes, if you can occupy them first, let them be strongly garrisoned and await the advent of the enemy.
>
> Should the enemy forestall you in occupying a pass, do not go after him if the pass is fully garrisoned, but only if it is weakly garrisoned.

When the project team understands what is critical, it is able to anticipate in a practical way the most effective course of action. The art of good project management is in anticipation, not reaction. Focusing on the key issues draws the team to consider the fastest and most economic routes to the planned objective, both short- and long-term.

Understanding the opposition's critical path also enables the project to maintain the lead in any obstacles that may be encountered. This is an advantage in projects where, for example, the customer has part of the project under his/her control. This can happen when, say, others are responsible for its execution. Their progress, though not directly your responsibility, will clearly have an impact on your ability to complete tasks within planned expectations.

As in all cases, the more you know, the more influence you can have on the outcome. The output of others may have either a direct or indirect impact on your programme. Thus if you can anticipate their progress and challenges while not your responsibility, it may still be of ultimate benefit to you. It is also possible that, given this knowledge, you are able to benefit by creating opportunities to present options that favour others as well as yourself.

In complex projects where many parties may be involved, it is essential to understand their plans and critical steps. Where these can be assimilated into your own programme with little impact you can ensure that you drive towards your goals and are not forced to accept the problems of others.

> With regard to Precipitous heights, if you are beforehand with your adversary, you should occupy the raised and sunny spots, and there wait for him to come up.
>
> If the enemy has occupied them before you, do not follow him, but retreat and try to entice him away.

The most successful projects are those that devote time to considering alternative approaches or 'thinking outside the box'. The danger with any plan is that obedience to the rule stifles opportunity. Therefore, when obstacles are encountered either directly or indirectly, the traditional straight-line thinking stops. The eventual result will certainly at some point have an impact on your organization, even if the problem is not 'home-grown'.

There is seldom only one solution to a problem, but experience shows when obscure alternatives can be presented. These, if they relate to the issues of others, can then be turned to your advantage by exploiting the position. Most challenges can be overcome if the drive is there to find the answer, and the knowledge is there to consider the multiple variations. Understanding these opportunities and responding in a proactive manner can only be done when the implications are clear.

When faced with an impasse, the project manager needs to evaluate all the options available to the project and assess the impact. Effective risk assessment must be based on considering the full spectrum of changes that may be required, and not simply the initial issue.

Furthermore, the impacts of assessments on the critical path are those related to the steps necessary to pursue the effective project close-out, since this may be beyond the actual physical completion of the project, where long-term performance guarantees and bonds may be affected by failure to address key issues even though these did not impinge on start-up progress.

> If you are situated at a great distance from the enemy, and the strength of the two armies is equal, it is not easy to provoke a battle, and fighting will be to your disadvantage.

Most projects, however well planned, will at some point reach a constriction in terms of resources. This is likely to occur because of many different factors, such as delays or changes. These bottlenecks, if not dealt with, are likely to generate confusion, overlap and waste. The net result will be an impact on the project schedule and certain compounded delays to the overall project.

The management of resources and their effective disposition when faced with conflicts has to be decided against a background of understanding the most expeditious route forward. For what may be assumed to be the most important needs might in fact be the least important, and vice versa. Since no project should ever be over-staffed and the parachuting-in of additional resources is seldom effective in the short term, the project manager needs to decide as to where to focus the effort.

Similarly, when there is a need to take action it should always be positively focused, and not simply use to build progress that is not contributing directly to the end-game.

Developing the close-out programme alongside the critical path also ensures that where special tasked teams are required to prepare the ground, they are not taken away from key activities. It may be that, given the analysis of the impacts, the project manager can undertake a cost–benefit analysis to involve additional teams or resources.

The fine-tuning of projects is a constant process that must be managed carefully and monitored to ensure the most cost-effective outcome. Knowing when to inject extra resources and when to hold back is only possible when the effect can be measured.

> These six are the principles connected with Earth. The general who has attained a responsible post must be careful to study them.

The experienced project manager will recognize the benefits of both long-term planning and critical path analysis as crucial tools in the effective control and direction of project teams. Developing strategies to handle both the predictable and unpredictable events that the project will face is only possible if one has a clear idea of the way forward.

The sole objective of the project team is to achieve the initial goals, and where possible take advantage of the opportunities that present themselves along the way. Each stage or phase of the project must constantly be adjusted to maintain the momentum to meet the end-game. In some cases this may even require that opportunities are specifically passed over in favour of maintaining the ultimate goal.

Recognizing when bottlenecks and obstacles will impinge on progress is the key to adapting the team focus. At the same time, understanding when it makes sense to move forward and when to hold back will support the economic utilization of resources. Balancing the distribution of effort towards those hurdles that will make a difference as opposed to playing the whole field will retain potential resources for when they are truly needed.

Understanding the value of integrating a strategy to close a project alongside completing the necessary functions and tasks will bring the critical path into prominence at all stages of the activity.

Project managers who appreciate how to use these tools will create a stable platform on which to succeed. Those who charge forward without a focus will probably fail in their tasks.

> Now an army is exposed to six several calamities, not arising from natural causes, but from faults for which the general is responsible. These are: flight; insubordination; collapse; ruin; disorganization; rout.

The failure of most projects can be attributed not to external influences but to the failure of the project manager and his/her team to maintain a focus on what really matters. The major problem generally stems from not getting the balance right in the early phases between adequate resources and flooding the project without appropriate direction. Developing a project strategy must concentrate on the maximum value added from all assets.

The targeting of activities is crucial to ensure a smooth flow throughout a project's life-cycle. If the attention is on volume of progress rather than on what is critical, there will inevitably be budget overruns and delays. The resource profile must be matched to the real demands and requirements.

Maintaining the discipline of this approach is the task of the project manager. While individualism and innovation should be exploited, it is essential that the team functions in a cohesive way. Focused tasking will also help to prevent individuals being overloaded and ensures that the team maintains continuity.

There should also be a monitor of all tasks and a clear strategy regarding those that are non-critical; while it may be possible to delay specific tasks, the long-term impact may be to generate a bottleneck in the future.

To ensure that a project has every chance of success, the project manager must focus on pinpointing the key issues and maintaining overall pressure. When problems arise generally they result not from error but from a failure of the business processes employed and a lack of clear direction.

> Other conditions being equal, if one force is hurled against another ten times its size, the result will be the flight of the former.
>
> When the common soldiers are too strong and their officers too weak, the result is insubordination.
>
> When officers are too strong and the common soldiers too weak, the result is collapse.
>
> When the higher officers are angry and insubordinate, and on meeting the enemy give battle on their own account from a feeling of resentment, before the commander-in-chief can tell whether or no he is in a position to fight, the result is ruin.

Complex projects are difficult to undertake and in the global market this complexity is amplified by multiple factors that can influence the outcome.

The physical tasks involved to reach a practical conclusion is only one aspect of this complexity; the more difficult concern is to close down the activity in a controlled manner. In the final stages of a project, planning and control tend to be overlooked in the pressure to finish. It is following this intense period that projects will generally start to bleed resources and funds.

Project managers need to establish close-out strategies to ensure, first, the physical completion and then the effective rundown of resources consistent with the contract's requirements. It is seldom the planned activities that cause delays in closure; the real pain comes from concluding commercial arrangements and paperwork.

Failure to recognize these issues will inevitably lead to extended operations, with the associated impact on the bottom line. The focus of the team must be maintained in both aspects, and all the key players have to operate in unison. The danger is that individuals will try to finalize their own responsibilities without considering the implications for others in the team.

The project manager has to maintain an integrated approach from start to finish. The strategy of the project must be developed not simply to meet the physical requirements, but all aspects that will eventually allow the project to be closed.

> When the general is weak and without authority; when his orders are not clear and distinct; when there are no fixed duties assigned to officers and men, and the ranks are formed in a slovenly haphazard manner, the result is utter disorganization.
>
> When a general, unable to estimate the enemy's strength, allows an inferior force to engage a larger one, or hurls a weak detachment against a powerful one, and neglects to place picked soldiers in the front rank, the result must be a rout.

The key role for the project manager is to assemble the appropriate team and then ensure that the team members are directed carefully. If large teams working on complex projects are not focused well, the project will probably fail. Understanding what is critical to the project's aims is major issue, and creating the project strategy and making sure it is implemented properly is a significant challenge.

Leadership is not generally given, it is *taken*, and the project manager who can maximize the utilization of his/her team will surely be followed. When direction is unclear and the goals not sufficiently defined, the team will lose momentum and the project will suffer.

Independent thought is valuable, but it should not be allowed to move forward unless within a structured programme of activity. Constant reference to the critical path and the analysis of intermittent changes is crucial if the direction of the team is to be maintained.

Project managers need to watch the key elements of the operation and create a uniform ethos across their team. It is not possible to have every decision made at the top. The project manager must create the framework but the team must operate consistently within the established boundaries.

The skill in managing of these large teams is to capitalize on one's knowledge of the business landscape, then convert this to an effective strategy that is always concentrated on the key issues for immediate action as well as the long-term goals.

These are six ways of courting defeat, which must be carefully noted by the general who has attained a responsible post.

In most projects there will be only a few people who have an overview of the whole programme, since the range of issues and their complexity will not be clear to all. Appreciating the multiple elements that contribute to success is the primary duty of the project manager. If the focus is maintained on what is really important and records kept ensuring that all tasks are eventually dealt with, the project has a solid platform on which to move forward.

The decision process must be flexible enough to satisfy the individual contributions, but rigidly disciplined to ensure that rogue actions do not compromise the whole strategy. When people understand that their effort is being properly utilized they will tend to follow willingly. If they fail to recognize that there is clear direction from above, they will operate independently and thus be less efficient.

Every action needs to lead to the ultimate objective, and constant analysis of the implications of change is an essential part of maintaining this dictum. The combination of need and resource is a careful balance between effectiveness and cost benefit. If work is not critical it can be deferred, but it must not be ignored.

The challenge of enabling both progress and consistency is a task for the project team management. The merging of parallel trains of activity can only be done effectively by making clear what is crucial at any given time, blending physical needs for completion with commercial demands and risk mitigation.

The team's aim is to meet the objectives and every process or action must be channelled towards this target. Even negative situations may be considered acceptable if they improve the overall probability of success.

The natural formation of the country is the soldier's best ally; but a power of estimating the adversary, of controlling the forces of victory, and of shrewdly calculating difficulties, dangers and distances, constitutes the test of a great general.

He who knows these things, and in fighting puts his knowledge into practice, will win his battles. He who knows them not, nor practices them, will surely be defeated.

The management of risk in any project is clearly an integral part of the project team's responsibility. Measuring the approach to be taken against the changing landscape of the market and the impact on the overall outcome must be directed by the project manager. Failure to take a consider approach may well end in a loss of opportunity or failure.

Maintaining the critical path and focus on completion are part of the project manager's checklist for judging how the project is going. Appreciating the lie of the land and centring the resources on the optimized route is crucial to success. This is particularly important in projects where risk and reward are linked to overall profitability. Where other partners are involved it is of great importance to ensure they too have visibility with respect to their operations.

The growing trend towards alliance-type contracts places a responsibility on all participants not only to protect their own activities but also to recognize the impact on others. Since the eventual outcome of these types of project is dependent on everyone being successful. These alliance contracts place a further dimension of pressure on the project manager and the team, for what may not be critical to your area may have significant effects on others.

Focusing on integrated projects may add considerably to the value proposition, and the benefits should not be ignored. The downside is that the project team has to consider a multidimensional effect on their individual operations.

> If fighting is sure to result in victory, then you must fight, even though the ruler forbid it; if fighting will not result in victory, then you must not fight even at the ruler's bidding.
>
> The general who advances without coveting fame and retreats without fearing disgrace, whose only thought is to protect his country and do good service for his sovereign, is the jewel of the kingdom.

Most major projects, and particularly those in the global marketplace will be circled by very complex and rigid contracts. The project team will also be encased within the limitations of estimates, budgets and corporate expectations. These may to some extent create a straitjacket for the project manager, who then has to walk a fine line between what is written in the plan and what is necessary.

On many occasions, the project manager may be faced with decisions that certainly conflict with one or more restrictions. For example, conceding to requirements that are clearly outside the existing scope, in order to ensure the overall programme being maintained, or the expending of resources that had never been envisaged. To support being able to take the appropriate action, and where necessary defend that action, the project manager must be able to assess the pros and cons of the impact.

Success will only be measured at the end of a project, by which time many of the intermediate issues will have been long forgotten. Project managers with experience will take up the challenge and succeed; and those who are less confident will falter and probably fail.

The essence of winning is to adjust to the flow and take proactive decisions that will keep the programme on track. This can only be done if one understands what is needed and when.

> Regard your soldiers as your children, and they will follow you into the deepest valleys; look upon them as your own beloved sons, and they will stand by you even unto death.
>
> If, however, you are indulgent, but unable to make your authority felt; kindhearted, but unable to enforce your commands; and incapable, moreover, of quelling disorder: then your soldiers must be likened to spoilt children; they are useless for any practical purpose.

The project manager's greatest asset is the project team he or she leads. If the team is focused and understands what they need to do, they will follow the manager's direction. If the direction is unclear they will wander, creating more confusion and risk. Maintaining the attention to the key activities is the surest way of keeping the team targeting the right issues. Understanding which issues these are is the role of the project manager.

One of the principal factors in maintaining order, discipline and focus is to ensure that there is clarity of purpose. People want to be valued and believe their efforts to be worthwhile. Without this they will not gain any satisfaction from their commitment to a project. Therefore, clear direction and tasking is essential, and making the individual contributions valuable means understanding where to apply that effort.

In most cases, if people are treated with kid gloves they will become progressively less focused and less committed. The manager must pay attention to making their efforts both valuable and rewarding. Expending their effort to no advantage will quickly result in a deflated attitude that will further erode the programme.

The full contribution of the team members and the interaction with external partners needs to be driven proactively towards the critical requirements of the project – the eventual close-out. In all cases, balance must be maintained to ensure that all members of the team are recognized for their efforts.

> If we know that our own men are in a condition to attack, but are unaware that the enemy is not open to attack, we have gone only halfway towards victory.
>
> If we know that the enemy is open to attack, but are unaware that our own men are not in a condition to attack, we have only gone halfway towards victory.
>
> If we know that the enemy is open to attack, and also know that our men are in a condition to attack, but are unaware that the nature of the ground makes fighting impracticable, we have still gone only halfway towards victory.

Knowledge and strategy of the project must be filtered down through the whole team to ensure that everyone understands his/her role, in both the short term and the end-game. Projects cannot be 'half successful': they either meet their goals or are considered as failures. Whether in terms of time, performance or cost, the ultimate and only acceptable outcome is success, not only for the organization but also for every member of the team.

The focus that is needed to create an effective project team and platform to execute a project will be invalidated if the delivery is late or the close-out protracted. The information flow and development of strategy and tactics when the critical path is interrupted must be adjusted. The team must be able to react quickly to logical counter-measures that will correct any lost of drive or direction.

The regular analysis progress and the end-game should produce input to the critical path of the project. This can be factored into the future activities of the team and the strategies for handling the multiple influences from outside the project.

> Hence the experienced soldier, once in motion, is never bewildered; once he has broken camp, he is never at a loss.
>
> Hence the saying: if you know the enemy and know yourself, your victory will not stand in doubt; if you know Heaven and know Earth, you may make your victory complete.

If the strategy is sound, and if all is known, the successful execution of a project rests on implementation. The magnitude of the challenge should not be considered an obstacle but an opportunity. If the team is confident in its capabilities and has clear direction and focus, then only the unexpected can affect the results.

When unplanned factors arise, the project manager and the team must be able to appreciate the implications, then consider and evaluate potential alternative solutions, always recognizing the overall objectives. This visibility in complex projects comes from effective planning of the critical path and a clear identification of the key issues that will demonstrably affect the final outcome.

The effective close-out of a project and the focusing of resources and commitments towards this must be linked to the efforts and activities necessary to achieve both plant and contractual liabilities. When this is effective, the chances of success are greatly improved. Without this focus, the risk and probability of failure will be apparent to all.

Understanding the needs and recognizing the balance required to achieve the objectives for the project is the responsibility of the whole project team. The project manager must promote and foster commitment at all times. Recognizing that strength alone will not be a solution, the battle must be defined before the team is pushed forward and resources stretched or wasted. Closing-out a project is not just something that happens; it must be engineered.

CHAPTER 12

The nine situations

The art of war recognizes nine varieties of ground: dispersive ground; facile ground; contentious ground; open ground; ground of intersecting highways; serious ground; difficult ground; hemmed in ground; desperate ground.

The globalization of the marketplace has become a common feature of today's business world. It is no longer novel, but accepted as the future battleground of all ventures, not the least of which is the major project arena. Thus, in developing any project strategy, these external influences and drivers must be assessed and taken into account.

Even those opportunities in one's established markets have become greatly influenced by the implications of global accessibility. This is certainly true for the major development project, since even established customers and suppliers will expect to compete with, or combine, offerings from low-cost providers around the world.

In the majority of industries the emphasis for future business opportunities is outward-looking to the developing world. Communications has expanded now to such an extent that no real hindrance or advantage can be exploited by distance.

Investment strategy is now centred primarily on the economic drivers of low-cost manufacture, labour and resources. The environmental pressures and demands of established industrial markets have moved the focus to those regions where greater flexibility can be enjoyed.

Developing project strategies for this disillusioned landscape requires a careful analysis of its pressures. For while the expectation will be there to benefit from all the global market has to offer, there will be still the presumption that traditional relationships and performance will prevail. These contradictory aspirations lead to conflict and a breakdown of past affiliations. This can be seen in many industries, at every level. The world of projects is no different, and is perhaps in some respects even more vulnerable.

> When a chieftain is fighting in his own territory, it is dispersive ground.
>   When he has penetrated into hostile territory, but to no great distance, it is facile ground.

The temptation therefore is to venture into new territories and exploit the expertise that has been created in the past. Many have gone in search of the valuable prizes that have been identified, and failed because they did not commit themselves to understand the nature of the marketplace they faced.

To build a new capability outside one's comfort zone is not an approach that can be taken lightly. There is a need for positive investment to understand the rules of engagement. A cursory analysis of the potential benefits may soon be challenged when tested against an approach that has not been tested in that environment. Many major projects have failed based on the assumption that what worked at home will work anywhere.

The exploitation of low-cost labour and resources is quickly tested when it is realized that the infrastructure and skills base is not what had been imagined. The strategy that assumes that a single model of organization can be transported to distant parts without adjustment is certain to come under tremendous pressure. Even worse is the perspective that such exploratory ventures can be executed from the home base.

Many have learned this lesson the hard way, and others will perish as they ignore the fate of those who have gone before and push forward, disregarding the business landscape and approach they will meet.

The project world has seen many such expeditions fail, and projects which should have been the cornerstone of future investment becoming millstones for those involved.

Moving the complex project environment into new territory must be done with consideration and strategies that recognize the full extent of the challenge being faced.

> Ground the possession of which imports great advantage to either side, is contentious ground.

The most significant factor in all new global business activities is the appreciation of the cultural differences that can exist even a short way from one's established terrain. These under-developed or relatively poor areas can provide the backdrop for international investment funding, which may present great opportunities, but the structure and style of business may be diametrically opposed in business approach.

The conflicts that arise are not based on commercial or technical debate, but rather on the fundamental differences in the culture of those dealt with. In many parts of the world, the trading tradition dates back to the beginning of civilized development. The process for business and the interpretation of events is often coloured by a viewpoint that is incomprehensible. However obscure the approach, the reasoning is based on cultural differences that may take many years to appreciate and will perhaps never be understood.

These are markets where the ability to exploit the available competition is a natural way of life; where loyalty may be solid at a personal level but in a business context it does not exist. These cultural barriers to business and simple slips of protocol can turn opportunity into failure in a moment. These are regions where competition is always in contention, generally manipulated by skilled traders and the frequent and relatively readily availability of information, at a price.

Venturing into these arenas without a firm understanding of how they operate and without local knowledge to lead one through the maze will tax the most efficient of organizations. Trying to operate complex projects in this type of territory will certainly drain the most committed of project teams.

> Ground on which each side has liberty of movement is open ground.

The global market and freedom of communication have created the opportunity for a new breed of entrepreneur to emerge. The relative freedom that has come to many parts of the world in recent times has opened up possibilities to develop private ventures, which previously would not have been possible. The individuals, however, lack much of the background skill or knowledge that is required to exploit the ideas and resources they have.

These new ventures can be great opportunities, but they need a different style of approach to the conventional corporate organizations one may traditionally have served. In many respects they present an interesting challenge, but at the same time they can be confusing and frustrating, since they fail to recognize the more established structures of business and look for innovation and speed of decision-making that does not come easily to many organizations.

They project a very personal approach to business and expect even major developments to be initiated without the traditional appreciation of risk. They view their focus and commitment to be all that is needed and look to others to fill the gaps, often ignoring the very basics of good practice. Many established operations look at a potential venture and say, 'Why should we?' while the entrepreneur says 'Why not?'

To the established project organization, these ventures are complex and difficult to master. Many prospects will be trafficked between possible sponsors and many will eventually fail. Some, however, will find the right combination of partners and flourish.

For the project organization, they also need to adapt and become more innovative if they believe the potential should be exploited. Alternatively, they should walk away and find other grounds to develop.

> Ground which forms the key to three contiguous states, so that he who occupies it first has most of the Empire at his command, is a ground of intersecting highways.

All business is dependent on market demand, and even more on the implications of economic changes. The advent of global communications means that ever major marketplaces are both assessable and vulnerable to the swings of economic variables. For the major project development, this is a significant factor both in terms of potential ventures being viable and the impacts of changes during execution.

Favourable conditions can turn overnight towards the benefit of competitors. The baselines established perhaps as little as two years previously can suddenly become invalid and risky. The fluctuations of stock markets can make a once-valuable and financially sound organization impoverished within days.

The impact of economic change can occur in any territory or be an influence in any venture. The intersection of economic impacts across any defined strategy can turn it from a relatively safe proposition into a potential nightmare.

The globalization of investment strategies can now be influenced by factors that may seem inconsequential and distant. The linkage between market values and financial institutions is now a feature of daily life. Thus projects in some parts of the world that may be viable and progressing well are suddenly at risk and potentially defunct.

A change in policy or scandal in one part of the globe may suddenly erupt into a major economic storm. The development of projects must understand these pressures and establish strategies that will protect the venture and investment. This is now the nature of such major developments, and organizations that have enjoyed a stable economic environment must be prepared to respond.

> When an army has penetrated into the heart of a hostile country, leaving a number of fortified cities in its rear, it is serious ground.

Major projects are often the desire and requirement of governments, and this is one area where every project organization needs to take great care. The capability of government organizations to both complicate and protract any business dealings is almost unmatched anywhere in the business world.

This is in general a common problem for any state-sponsored project. The capability of bureaucracy to complicate even the simplest of business issues is limitless. The internal frictions between departments, ministries and politicians can generate pressures on a project even when business measurement and logic is screaming for solutions.

The problem arises basically from a question of accountability, where multiple organizations within government have different tasks, which are not always aligned to those of the project. When the role of each group is clear, but the interrelationship is not there, then the decision-making process loses touch with the overall objective.

This can be seen, for example, in the speedy processing of changes. A commercial group will press to achieve the lowest possible impact irrespective of the delays that may result. There is no normal balancing that would be part of the business consideration, thus the single-minded approach ignores the overall picture. Individuals become focused on their image and risk rather than on the operation of an effective project.

Again, when many decisions reflect on political considerations, obvious business actions will become secondary to the solution. The problem can be further complicated when, as in certain countries, the national banking system is also part of the bureaucratic chain.

Projects that are either for a government organization or under the supervision of a government department will provide a labyrinth of red tape that often defies business logic.

> Mountain forests, rugged steeps, marshes and fens, all country that is hard to traverse: this is difficult ground.

The global market is also very susceptible to the machinations of political change. The implications of parliamentary elections is only the tip of the iceberg, but these can at least be anticipated and often managed. Occasionally this may lead to projects being stopped or deferred. It may also lead to uncertainty in the decision-making process.

The wider implications of international upheavals in alliances or political acceptability can overnight change the profile of a project. It may also add seemingly impossible restrictions on project execution time frames. As governments have been declared out of favour, the whole project strategy can be turned on its head. This may involve relocation of activities, changes in management or a need to readdress the sourcing profile completely.

In some parts of the world the decisions made by governments can put severe strain on relationships at the working level. It is even possible in some circumstances that the project site may need to be evacuated. These are considerations the project team, and management in particular must build them into their project strategy.

Major terrorist activities (or even small, isolated incidents) can cause significant damage to the flow of a project. At the bottom of the scale, restrictions on individuals travelling may have to be considered. In the more global context, these events can disrupt the complete business agenda.

There may be financial insurance that can be taken out to cover political risk, but the biggest impact is on the whole viability of the operation. Delays which cannot be directly attributed, will still have to be accommodated. The political landscape is a bad and unpredictable arena to operate within, but often it is a common challenge for many global projects.

> Ground which is reached through narrow gorges, and from which we can only retire by tortuous paths, so that a small number of the enemy would suffice to crush a large body of our men: this is hemmed in ground.

Advances in technology have added new dimensions to the project profile, both in terms of communications but also in the areas of technology generally. These enhanced capabilities can offer a great opportunity, but at the same time can be a serious risk to market potential.

From a communications standpoint, the ability to reach almost any part of the world instantly has set an expectation that 'follow the sun' operations should be the normal baseline, but as we all understand, this can be restricted by time differences. Thus, when a message is sent, the impression is that it will be answered immediately. Unfortunately, when both time changes and cultural working programmes in, say, in the Middle East are considered, the actual operating window is quite small.

The advent of the Internet has provided a platform for many businesses as well as the capability for even small organizations to create the impression of being global players. Similarly, access is provided to information is extensive, thus making even the most remote businesses very knowledgeable. Technology can surround a project but not always add value.

Technology has also to be balanced against the local capability to support and operate. As the more industrialized regions expand the use of modern technology, so they promote solutions, which may be inappropriate to the actual application. Simply when looking at the advent of remote monitoring capabilities and consider these in a country where external communication is controlled by strict government regulations, may cause one to consider alternative approaches.

Technology is also something that, if it provides a competitive edge, will be actively sought by local markets to improve their own position globally.

> Ground on which we can only be saved from destruction by fighting without delay, is desperate ground.

Operating projects in a global marketplace introduces the need to utilize local markets. For those who have never ventured into these disparate locations, the implications can be very risky, and many who made a first attempt ended up failing, with projects that overran and suffered delays. This resulted from not understanding the implications of local business methods, together with customs and practices.

The temptation of low-cost markets or the pressure to maximize local content for political reasons often seems to good to miss. The reality is that these local markets can be minefields of risk that need to be navigated carefully. It is easy to assume when, for example, looking at manufacturing skills locally, that these can satisfy one's requirements. The problem is that unless you invest in the training and development of these skills you will find the real output very different.

Very seldom has any organization taken its first step without some pain being absorbed along the way. It is likely that the true benefits will not be seen for a period of time. Therefore, assuming an immediate transfer and return is likely to end by being very disappointing. Many organizations have tried and failed.

Similarly trying to compete with local organizations exposes one to many factors that are often only appreciated after the risk has materialized. Thus, attempting to break into new markets requires not only investment but also local partners who can smooth the way and guide one past some of the many obstacles.

Finally, one needs to be aware that in many parts of the world a partner you create today will be your competitor tomorrow. In fact, in some parts of the world technology transfer is a government objective.

> On dispersive ground, therefore, fight not. On facile ground, halt not. On contentious ground, attack not.
> On open ground, do not try to block the enemy's way. On ground of inter-secting highways, join hands with your allies.
> On serious ground, gather in plunder. On difficult ground, keep steadily on the march.
> On hemmed-in ground, resort to stratagem. On desperate ground, fight.

The development of a project strategy needs to consider these very different market situations and the implications for risk management. The issue needs very careful thought, since in today's world these are not exclusive conditions. The likelihood is that most projects will encounter combinations of these issues. In the global marketplace a project will almost certainly want not only to utilize traditional relationships and markets but also to remain competitive, there will be a need to harness low costs and local markets as well.

There is never going to be a 'one size fits all' solution and the project strategy must identify the various challenges and establish an integrated approach that addresses all complications. Often, in military terms, there may be options of not going into battle, but in the project business world these options are limited. If, however, the risks can be identified and miti-gation plans put in place they can be managed.

In the complex world of global business the risks can be increased expo-nentially by not understanding the individual issues as well as the interac-tion of these various problem arenas. When projects run into to trouble it is seldom the impact of one particular focus but rather the lack of integrated thinking. On large projects, because many specialists will be involved and often located around the world, their individual actions may satisfy one of the challenges but inadvertently create problems elsewhere.

The role of the project manager is first to identify what variables there are, create a focus and then ensure that the whole project team maintains a joined-up approach to the solution.

> Those who were called skilful leaders of old knew how to drive a wedge between the enemy's front and rear; to prevent co-operation between large and small divisions; to hinder the good troops from rescuing the bad, the officers from rallying their men.
>
> When the enemy's men were united, they managed to keep them in disorder.
>
> When it was to their advantage, they made a forward move; when otherwise, they stopped still.

The skill in project management is not simply to address a strategy to contend with a variety of market conditions and challenges, it is also to exploit the opportunities that these arenas create. Few business ventures will survive on a strategy of defensiveness; there will always be someone ready to take a lower price or a greater risk. Therefore, when developing a strategy it is not a case of merely circling the wagons; one must consider mounting the horses and attacking the Indians.

In establishing your own proposed course of action, you have to in parallel create a picture of how your competition will be positioned in these various areas of operation. In fact, the more you focus on exploiting the gaps in the competition's approach, the more likely you will be to find effective solutions for yourself.

Thus. where competition is strong. the approach must be to exploit the options in which they are clearly weaker. Where the competition is weak, the focus must be on finding a solution they do not have and build around that. The target of a sound strategy is to exploit the terrain, the competition's weaknesses and those strengths where you feel superior.

The project team's effort should not be wasted on trying to match the market: it must be challenged to outpace the market. Selecting a team and alliance partners must not be done on the basis of availability, but directed towards fitting the battleground and a counter-strategy towards the competition.

If asked how to cope with a great host of the enemy in orderly array and on the point of marching to the attack, I should say 'Begin by seizing something which your opponent holds dear, then he will be amenable to your will.'

Many times in this book we have viewed the project from a position of establishing alternatives strategies. Clearly, when faced with multiple combinations of market conditions and conflicts, this adaptability must be exploited to the full. The assessment of which options and what the impacts will be is crucial to ensuring one has a sound strategy in place.

As discussed earlier, when faced with a major project, competitor or customer, there has to be a clear and integrated approach which is focused on the objectives. In cases where these major challenges are encountered, there is a need to understand which options to put forward and which to pull back from.

This type of situation can, for example be seen in the buyer–supplier relationship, where at the end of the day there are generally three basic evaluation criteria: price, quality and delivery. Seldom, if ever, are these three fully satisfied, and as a result, an understanding of which to present versus what you wish to achieve are important facets of managing a strong opposition.

If a customer is driven by any of these three key drivers they will be prepared to sacrifice part of their strength in the other areas. So if delivery is the number one criteria, then offer long delivery periods. As one is pressed to bring that down to acceptable levels, price and quality will be relaxed. Where quality and reliability is most prominent, then propose low cost but emphasize the use of cheaper, but perhaps less secure, markets. The counter will be to consider higher cost.

Understanding what are the drivers enables one to remove the strength of the most able competitor.

Rapidity is the essence of war: take advantage of the enemy's unreadiness, make your way by unexpected routes, and attack unguarded spots.

In the most difficult of business environments where one is faced with multiple conditions, the appropriate selection of a project team is crucial. The building of the team must also consider where the specialist resources will come from, either internally or as alliances with those who can add specific value to the strategy.

What must be clear to all is that, to be successful in these complex cases of global projects, there is a dependency on innovative approaches, to contend with the challenges but also, more importantly, to exploit the gaps quickly and effectively. Working with a solid understanding of the opposing strength and capability that one faces.

The team must also be ready to adapt to changes in the business environment, for while one may experience many of these influencing conditions, they may not all be apparent at the outset. As a project develops, the initial strategy will have been based on certain assumptions. When these change, one faces a new combination that must be evaluated and addressed.

Essentially, project teams must maintain visibility at all times, and as far as possible be in a position to predict what is ahead. These individual grounds for business can be like shifting sand, movement of which is hard to anticipate except by watching the direction of the wind. Thus to be effective, the team (and particularly the project manager) must always know the position of the project and be able to develop alternative strategies and tactics.

The opportunities within these variable markets can also become significant vulnerabilities if not watched and matched by the project team.

> The following are the principles to be observed by an invading force: the further you penetrate into a country, the greater will be the solidarity of your troops, and thus the defenders will not prevail against you.

When you move into new territory you will inevitably be more focused on what the local business landscape is like, and how best to position yourself in it. The experienced project manager will be able to combine tried and tested methods with the influences of the local culture. The most successful military empires recognized that, to be successful in a distant land, they needed to absorb local forces into their campaigns.

Therefore, when developing projects in distant parts, one must consider how to merge the efficiency of establish methods with the flexibility and knowledge of local players. This can often be a real challenge for Western organizations moving into foreign parts, because translating methods to fit the local business culture is not something that happens by order: it requires both investment and training, but in many cases has been shown to be very successful.

When you take the best of the local capability and combine it with established skills from outside organizations can be created that are both effective and superior to the challenges from the local competition.

In major development projects, the utilization of local sourcing and technology is increasingly becoming a feature of business drivers, particularly if these are government sponsored projects, with an additional desire in the longer term to raise local competency levels. Therefore, recognizing that one needs to incorporate this into the strategy of a project is important both for immediate and for long-term needs.

The project manager must be sensitive to these business grounds and present the approach that takes these multiple factors into account.

> Make forays in fertile country in order to supply your army with food.
>   Carefully study the well-being of your men, and do not overtax them. Concentrate your energy and hoard your strength. Keep your army continually on the move, and devise unfathomable plans.

The global market offers many opportunities, and if handled well can provide many benefits to the eventual outcome of the project, and satisfaction for the project team. These same regions also hold many risks, and these must be a balance against what in the short term are seen as significant gains.

The development of a project team must be structured both to exploit these opportunities and to manage the inherent risks. Over-stretching the capability of the team may ultimately create unnecessary demands that will drag the team down, and lead to the eventual failure to meet the project objectives. The effective project team must be focused on the varying demands of the multiple business landscapes that have to be mastered to be successful.

The right blend of skills is not simply about moving a successful team into a new domain; it must be structured around the true needs, then properly managed to ensure that these skills and resources are not expended against short-term opportunities.

The optimum use of the project team requires effective and targeted planning which has been developed to achieve the end-game. Resources must be conserved, in terms of numbers and cost as well as effort.

The strategies employed must be adaptable to the changing face of the market and the business terrain. Dedicated focus is good if this ignores the possibility of variations in demand, when it may well be burned out without gain. This is the challenge for the project manager to exploit opportunities and manage the impacts on the team and the project.

Throw your soldiers into positions whence there is no escape, and they will prefer death to flight. If they will face death, there is nothing they may not achieve. Officers and men alike will put forth their uttermost strength.

Soldiers when in desperate straits lose the sense of fear. If there is no place of refuge, they will stand firm. If they are in hostile country, they will show a stubborn front. If there is no help for it, they will fight hard.

Development of a successful team and the exploitation of innovative thinking come from pitching the team against significant challenges. When there is no challenge, there is no incentive to develop new thinking. This is a difficult task for any manager, to balance the pressure of failure with the stimulus that comes from meeting the challenge. In the complex world of projects, which brings teams together for relatively short periods, the task is doubly difficult.

The hardest task is to create sufficient pressure to force imaginative thinking while it is not so great as to become self-defeating. The key factor in this is individual and collective commitment to the project objectives, since there is a natural tendency for people to push harder if they feel that lack of effort will reflect on the team. Thus creating a strong team spirit is one of the tasks a project manager must consider within the management style adopted.

The majority of people, while they appreciate strong leadership, will ultimately lose drive if they do not see any focused recognition of their effort. It may also be that, in demanding a single focus and continued pressure without consideration for individual creativeness and recognition, that they will not give of their best.

Commitment to the challenge comes from having sound knowledge of the goals and an appreciation of risk-management strategies. Risk will create innovation and the right degree of pressure will cement commitment.

Thus, without waiting to be marshalled, the soldiers will be constantly on the qui vive; without waiting to be asked, they will do your will; without restrictions, they will be faithful; without giving orders, they can be trusted.

When a sound project team is brought together, if they see a challenge and a good structure and strategy they will focus on the task at hand. When they see a successful project manager in the driving seat they will come forward to be part of a successful team. When the project team is empowered to be creative they will generally exceed any demands laid upon them. The role of the project manager is to exploit these traits and focus them towards the true needs of the project.

In the complex world of projects it is never possible to scrutinize every single detail and tactic. The individuals who are best suited to a particular task must be allowed to utilize their full skills potential. When faced with many and varied market roles in a single project, the team must be driven by objectives and allowed to exert their potential.

The complexity of the markets creates a need for specialized skills in many different disciplines. Each has a role to play, and having selected a team that meets the challenge they must then be encouraged to be creative. Thus, to meet the demands in these markets, the skilful project manager will set the goals and stand back, while maintaining overall visibility.

There is a distinct difference between command and control, and leadership. The more complex and diverse the markets being addressed, the greater the need to take maximum advantage of the skills available.

Once a team is assembled to suit the task the team members must be encouraged to use their skills and be trusted to meet the project goals. Few, if any, project managers can handle every issue in a complex project, and failure to recognize and utilize the appropriate knowledge and talents will ultimately lead to missed opportunities and failure.

> Prohibit the taking of omens, and do away with superstitious doubts. Then, until death itself comes, no calamity need be feared.
>
> If your soldiers are not overburdened with money, it is not because they have a distaste for riches; if their lives are not unduly long, it is not because they are disinclined to longevity.
>
> On the day they are ordered out to battle, your soldiers may weep, those sitting up bedewing their garments, and those lying down letting the tears run down their cheeks. But let them once be brought to bay, and they will display the courage of a Chu or a Kuei.

As we have seen, global projects have many variations and can create complexities through combinations of these. The traditional organization will often flounder in these environments, because their strategies and methodology are fixed on a historical platform. The impact of this establishment perspective will be to engender doubt among those being asked to undertake tasks in a new market place.

There is no doubt that tradition creates a solid base against which people can measure themselves and those they follow. Thus, when faced with new challenges, they are sceptical of the potential for success and may well fail to optimize their skills. Since the global market by its very nature will provide multiple challenges that have to be addressed, there must be a basic belief in the potential for success.

It is the role of the project leaders to demonstrate that they both understand the risks that lie ahead are understood, and strategies to handle those issues have been assessed. There must be confidence at every level that success is not only possible, but also achievable. Those who doubt the potential for success will not meet the challenges with enthusiasm, and thus will probably fail.

This is a problem for many organizations venturing outside their traditional comfort zone and looking to exploit the opportunities that are available. This can be seen, for example, in many established manufacturing-based companies where the only hope for the future is to build new, low-cost capabilities. The traditionalists will ask why this is necessary. The futurist will say, 'Why not?' So for the project world the challenge is even greater because there is a multitude of options that must be exploited.

> The skilful tactician may be likened to the shuai-jan. Now the shuai-jan is a snake that is found in the Chung mountains. Strike at its head, and you will be attacked by its tail; strike at its tail, and you will be attacked by its head; strike at its middle, and you will be attacked by head and tail both.

In this global environment, the project must move quickly and effectively to take maximum advantage of the opportunities, while managing the risks that are inherent in such ventures. The strategies deployed must address every possible combination of risk, and retain the flexibility to react to change.

The project team must understand their individual and collective roles and be ready to respond to change, which will certainly come in one or many forms. As we have seen already, the global landscape for business can be very diverse and the project that tries to take advantage must be able to react to the many twists and turns that it confronts.

Building up the skills base to take the risk out of this complexity is the biggest task any organization will face, since it will be recognized that what works in one theatre will not necessarily be effective in another. Project teams have the added dimension that they are not fixed organizations and thus must quickly adapt to form a cohesive operation that is able to take maximum advantage of the marketplace.

Training for this level of diversity is not easy, and those organizations that see their future in a global context must be prepared to invest. Projects in this complex world are ideal nurturing grounds for the future because they offer multiple opportunities. Sadly, many organizations have failed to recognize this need and have thus simply pushed their traditionalist thinking into a new arena, with the obvious outcome.

Project managers should take the mentoring part of their role seriously, because they have the platform for this ongoing development in real time.

> Asked if an army can be made to imitate the shuai-jan, I should answer, Yes. For the men of Wu and the men of Yueh are enemies; yet if they are crossing a river in the same boat and are caught by a storm, they will come to each other's assistance just as the left hand helps the right.
>
> Hence it is not enough to put one's trust in the tethering of horses, and the burying of chariot wheels in the ground.

Those who do not recognize the potential future development of business will generally fall back on historical rhetoric and proffer only gloom and doom. What should be appreciated is that every day the world is changing and the pace of change is getting faster. This can be seen in the post-Second World War period let alone the movement since the Industrial Revolution. The project world see this change even faster since the expectations of the marketplace perceives opportunity even if has not been tested.

The task for the project manager is to create an effective team quickly and get it focused on the challenge of the day. This can be complicated by the nature of individual team members. We are all different, and when forced together it is inevitable that we do not always agree on everything.

The development of a team spirit within the project is an essential part of building an effective organization. Project managers who experienced the many facets of major projects will understand the importance of having the team focused on common objectives. This lifts the team above personal issues and creates the impetus for success.

At the same time, if the team is hemmed about with rules and commands it may get bogged down in minutiae that can only hinder progress. The team needs lateral vision and the confidence that, while not every idea will be accepted, they will all get a fair hearing.

It must be the goal of the project manager to engender the right ethos within the team to exploit the full capabilities of the individuals under direction.

The principle on which to manage an army is to set up one standard of courage which all must reach.

How to make the best of both strong and weak, that is a question involving the proper use of ground.

The strategy of a project must be developed both to exploit the potential of the various marketplaces it interacts with and to guard against the risks this contains. Each of the outlined nine grounds (or business landscapes) has its own special features, and as we can easily see, a project may encounter many if not all of these during execution.

The global market is both complex and demanding, with the ability to bring forth new and varied challenges at every turn. Effective project management must be able to build the right combination of skills to meet these opportunities and to respond with effective solutions.

The development of effective strategies is the first stage in mastering the environments faced, then to move forward with tactics that can be successful. The leadership of projects under these conditions requires mastery of both discipline and mentoring, often used in tandem.

For any strategy to be effective it must be deployed with the appropriate level of uniformity. At the same time, the taxing environment requires the need for innovation and adaptability. These two often-conflicting traits must be fostered simultaneously.

The business battlefield will inevitably change and so must the deployment of strategy, within given parameters, which are focused on the overall objective. The skill of the project manager is to identify the specialist talents needed, and then ensure that they are utilized to maximum advantage, recognizing that some may be capable of tackling a variety of situations while other may need to be kept for specific roles and tasks.

Thus the skilful general conducts his army just as though he were leading a single man, willy-nilly, by the hand.

It is the business of a general to be quiet and thus ensure secrecy; upright and just, and thus maintain order.

The more experienced project manager will understand that success comes not from a single individual talent or skill but from a combination of perhaps conflicting capabilities. The project team must, however, be focused on a common objective and be able to respond as one, recognizing that each has a task to fulfil. The project objective has to be the bonding factor, otherwise the team will start to pull in different directions and thus fail.

The importance of effective leadership in these complex projects cannot be understated, since only through clear vision can players understand their individual roles. The project manager must create confidence in the team, and ensure there is adequate direction at every level.

The more complex and challenging the task, the greater the dependence on effective open communication to ensure success. The whole team must always understand the objectives and be informed of current and future strategy. This becomes even more necessary given today's communications capability, as the team may be based in many different locations.

There must be a uniform and structured approach to which the whole team can relate, and within which each clearly appreciates his or her individual role. This structure must at the same time be flexible enough to meet the changing face of the market. This is the dilemma of the global environment within which most organizations now have to operate.

For the project manager, developing and managing such a task is far from the traditional single-location concept of past business cultures.

> He must be able to mystify his officers and men by false reports and appearances, and thus keep them in total ignorance.
>
> By altering his arrangements and changing his plans, he keeps the enemy without definite knowledge. By shifting his camp and taking circuitous routes, he prevents the enemy from anticipating his purpose.

There is clearly a conflict in the need to maintain effective communication, but at the same time not to disclose too readily the many options that may lie ahead. Since the majority of people can only assimilate a certain amount of change in their life at any one time before becoming confused, there is always the danger that when a team perceives many potential changes afoot before any particular one has been selected, they will back away from their current task.

It also possible that, if the perceived approach is only one option but gives a clue to the next stage that some will try to forge ahead in anticipation, with the net result that, if change is required, they may need to backtrack.

One vital talent that any project manager needs is to have multiple options arranged within the overall strategy. The problem with this is that, with many different ways of moving forward, the team may sense a lack of direction and therefore not move at all.

The project manager must balance adaptability and information with so many options that create confusion. The need for confidence and credibility is absolute, since when change occurs it must always be seen in a positive light.

Major projects are complex machines to drive forward, and by virtue of needing skilful players with open minds, the variety of choices may encourage indecision. These issues must be balanced adequately to ensure that overall objectives are not lost because too many options are being considered at one time. Thus, when a change is made, it must be communicated clearly and explained so as to maintain confidence at every level.

> At the critical moment, the leader of an army acts like one who has climbed up a height and then kicks away the ladder behind him. He carries his men deep into hostile territory before he shows his hand.
>
> He burns his boats and breaks his cooking-pots; like a shepherd driving a flock of sheep, he drives his men this way and that, and nothing knows whither he is going.

The challenges of a major project should not be underestimated, particularly when these have to be executed in new and untested regions. The biggest lesson for any project manager or organization is to appreciate what they do not know, rather than exploit what they do know.

Project teams need careful managing, and where new ground is being broken they must not be allowed to rest on past success. Removing the comfort zone is a task the project manager must undertake. This has to be handled with caution to ensure that the commitment and focus of the team is not lost. Creating a true understanding of the need for facing new markets and risks has to be done to ensure there is clear direction and effort towards the tasks ahead.

It is interesting to see how different organizations react when faced with a drive towards uncharted territory. There is a fine balance between excitement and fear. The former will energize those with a thirst for adventure, while demotivating those who look for traditional security, and the latter is a very dangerous management style, since fear is a short-lived emotion and will quickly deflate people's drive.

Maintaining a balance when taking on new challenges has to be recognized and managed. The team must take courage from having a common objective, and appreciate that change is necessary for sustainable growth in a global market place.

> To muster his host and bring it into danger: this may be termed the business of the general.
> The different measures suited to the nine varieties of ground; the expediency of aggressive or defensive tactics; and the fundamental laws of human nature: these are things that must most certainly be studied.

The most exciting part of project life is that change is an everyday event. The wider the scope within global markets, the greater the opportunity for change, and thus variety. It must, however, be recognized that not everyone will react at the same or a similar pace. The assessment and development of effective project strategies not only provides a road map for the project execution, it also provides a level of confidence for the whole team.

New and different regions and markets offer opportunities and challenge, and each needs a different approach. The project team needs to be structured around these varying demands and to some extent forced into accepting the way forward. This is the task of the project manager for when people have no choice and are under pressure they generally respond best, although one also needs to take into account cultural differences as these can in some communities become defensive under pressure rather than proactive.

As the project moves forward into these new markets, the project manager will have to adapt strategies and tactics to meet the day-to-day challenges. This creates additional pressure and stress for those who started the journey without experience, or perhaps even enthusiasm. These factors must be part of the management style.

The difficulty in today's global market is that time and distance have taken away traditional safety nets leaving most businesses with little choice. One either takes up the gauntlet or goes out of business. For the project world this is a daily challenge.

> When invading hostile territory, the general principle is, that penetrating deeply brings cohesion; penetrating but a short way means dispersion.
> When you leave your own country behind, and take your army across neighbourhood territory, you find yourself on critical ground. When there are means of communication on all four sides, the ground is one of intersecting highways.

When you penetrate deeply into a country, it is serious ground. When you penetrate but a little way, it is facile ground.

When you have the enemy's strongholds on your rear, and narrow passes in front, it is hemmed-in ground. When there is no place of refuge at all, it is desperate ground.

Therefore on dispersive ground, I would inspire my men with unity of purpose.

On facile ground, I would see that there is close connection between all parts of my army.

On contentious ground, I would hurry up my rear.

On open ground, I would keep a vigilant eye on my defences.

On ground of intersecting highways, I would consolidate my alliances.

On serious ground, I would try to ensure a continuous stream of supplies.

On difficult ground, I would keep pushing on along the road.

On hemmed-in ground, I would block any way of retreat.

On desperate ground, I would proclaim to my soldiers the hopelessness of saving their lives.

For it is the soldier's disposition to offer an obstinate resistance when surrounded, to fight hard when he cannot help himself, and to obey promptly when he has fallen into danger.

Therefore, for the project managers there is a need to control the strategy and communication of change based on the overall objectives. The goals have to be structured around a sound understanding of the challenges, ensuring that objectives at every level are tough but achievable. The project team must be tuned to change and project managers must be ready with alternative strategies that can meet the demands of the day. The business landscape is varied and difficult, and to exploit the opportunities one must also be ready to manage the risks.

We cannot enter into alliances with neighbouring princes until we are acquainted with their designs. We are not fit to lead an army on the march unless we are familiar with the face of the country – its mountains and forests, its pitfalls and precipices, its marshes and swamps. We shall be unable to turn natural advantages to account unless we make use of local guides.

To be ignored of any one of the following four or five principles does not befit a warlike prince.

When a warlike prince attacks a powerful State, his generalship shows itself in preventing the concentration of the enemy's forces. He overawes his opponents, and their allies are prevented from joining against him.

Understanding the business environment for each region or ground to be exploited is the key to setting down a meaningful project plan. When the strengths and weaknesses of the opponents are appreciated then strategies can be put in place that will be successful. Without these two ingredients, the chances of success are slim.

Understanding the local culture, custom and practice is crucial to being able to exploit the potential. Each locale has its own special drivers, and not appreciating the differences need to master these landscapes may well end in failure.

The approach must always be to find local partners and guides who can lead your team through what in many parts of the world can only be viewed as a maze, whether this is the regulatory environment or simply language difficulties. Strategy and execution plans must be developed and structured to ensure that the appropriate resources are in place at the right time and deployed to best effect.

The creation of alliances should be a major consideration as these enable the project team to utilize a much wider skill and knowledge base. Selecting the right partners and binding them to your plans will also prohibit them from becomes an asset to your opponents.

> Hence he does not strive to ally himself with all and sundry, nor does he foster the power of other States. He carries out his own secret designs, keeping his antagonists in awe. Thus he is able to capture their cities and overthrow their kingdom.

The difficulty with any new venture is to be credible, not simply with potential customers but also with supply chains, the competition, and more often than not the financial institutions. Most major development projects today rely more on the route to funding than the technical skills of those who propose to execute the development.

In most regions of the world, relationships and history count for more than size. These trading environments need to see both capability and sustainability being developed. Alliances cannot be formed overnight, and thus, when trying to exploit the potential opportunities for these markets, a lot of investment is needed, sometimes over long periods.

When developing new supply sources, local personnel will not react well to a 'fly-in-fly-out' approach. Therefore to establish oneself in these areas needs time, effort and commitment. When eventually one is established in the market, one needs well-grounded relationships, and often partners.

Those who will partner on first contact will generally not be considering a relationship for the long haul, and are thus unlikely to be of much benefit.

The creation of effective project networks needs careful and deliberate development over time. Often, when focusing overseas, one can exploit home ground relationships that have already established communication lines and alliances of their own.

Thus, when addressing the markets one starts from and established position and creates a degree of confidence among customers and suppliers, while establishing a significant challenge to the competition and presenting a valid proposition. This will be hard for others to undermine.

> Bestow rewards without regard to rule, issue orders without regard to previous arrangements; and you will be able to handle a whole army as though you had to do with but a single man.
>
> Confront your soldiers with the deed itself; never let them know your design. When the outlook is bright, bring it before their eyes, but tell them nothing when the situation is gloomy.

Managing a diverse project team and at the same time moving forward to exploit new opportunities is a major challenge for project managers. The project team may often comprise several different organizations, depending on the skills required. To be successful, all members must have the same objectives and act as a single focused unit. This is hard enough to arrange within a single large organization, and in the wider, global context it can be daunting.

There must be incentives for all, and in the development of alliances this is particularly true. There have been many examples of alliances failing because the leaders did not share the benefits appropriately, while distributing the risks liberally. These relationships have to be based on trust, and this does not grow instantly. Trust is based on emotion, not words, and thus can only be built through real experience, and taking the sometimes small, steps that demonstrate a true sharing of risk and reward.

Teams need to be created with a clear single focus, and motivated to maintain common goals. Enthusiasm comes from seeing that effort is recognized at every level. There must be clear communication that does not exclude peripheral parties. This is often difficult in a multi-company environment, but if the team is to work as one, all must be treated equally.

Confidence is an essential factor, and this will only be generated if those involved understand the strategy being deployed, which on occasion may look to be less than to their advantage.

Place your army in deadly peril, and it will survive; plunge it into desperate straits, and it will come off in safety.

For it is precisely when a force has fallen into harm's way that it is capable of striking a blow for victory.

Given the complexity of the global market and the need to take a positive position in developing it, is a significant task for project managers to create enthusiasm and focus within their teams, since many from more traditional backgrounds or who are risk averse will falter unless their safety blanket is removed.

The world is in a constant state of flux, and world economies generate daily variables that must be addressed. Those who take tentative steps will probably not be successful, so the drive towards the project's objectives must be firm and consistent. When there is no choice, the only outcome must be to become creative and use lateral thinking in all aspects.

Project developers and project managers must recognize these potentially negative impacts and develop strategies that demonstrate that the risks can be managed, not simply for the team tasked with the project's execution, but also for the senior management who will need to support the strategy.

The business world is built on risk and the greater the risk the greater the potential reward, provided the risk is managed carefully. When future business is more evident outside the comfort zone, there is little choice but to follow opportunities. Calculated risks must be part of the business profile, and the recognition within project teams must be that there is only way forward, and thus effort will be focused on the management of risk.

The creation of proactive project teams will only come if there is confident leadership and support. A leader must be chosen who can provide meaningful and succinct strategies that the team can believe in and follow.

Success in warfare is gained by carefully accommodating ourselves to the enemy's purpose.

By persistently hanging on the enemy's flank, we shall succeed in the long run in killing the commander-in-chief.

This is called ability to accomplish a thing by sheer cunning.

On the day that you take up your command, block the frontier passes, destroy the official tallies, and stop the passage of all emissaries.

Be stern in the council-chamber, so that you may control the situation.

The efforts of the project team must be properly directed towards specific tasks. The team must be selected to provide the capability that matches the varied business landscapes to be addressed. The integrated strategies must recognize the milestones that need to be achieved, then the full force of the capability and drive must be towards the challenges ahead.

Wherever the challenge or opportunity may be, the project must centre its efforts solely in the direction of a solution. The total focus of the team, whether in a single location or networked around the globe, must be towards success. There must be no looking backward or challenging of the tasks. The organizations that placed them in the project must commit to a common objective and must not distract team members with extraneous issues.

There must be clear lines of communication and direction built into the execution plan, and the strategies and tactics to be deployed fully understood by all who must undertake them. There can be only one direction in which to go, and that is towards the overall objective.

The role of the project manager must be well defined and established, with full authority to deliver the objectives. There must be a centralized leadership with defined delegation through a single channel. The complexity of these major global projects cannot be compromised by indifferent guidance. Selecting project managers and training them for this ever-changing battlefield is a commitment organizations must undertake.

If the enemy leaves a door open, you must rush in.

Forestall your opponent by seizing what he holds dear, and subtly contrive to time his arrival on the ground.

Walk in the path defined by rule, and accommodate yourself to the enemy until you can fight a decisive battle

At first, then, exhibit the coyness of a maiden, until the enemy gives you an opening; afterwards emulate the rapidity of a running hare, and it will be too late for the enemy to oppose you.

The world of global projects is complicated by the multiple markets (or battlegrounds) within which it must operate. These markets present opportunities if exploited properly, and appropriate attention is given to risk management. There are many ways forward and strategies must be developed that are specific to the task at hand. They must be based on having a sound understanding of the business environment and the local cultures that may be encountered.

The project teams must have both discipline and flexibility, relying on the careful selection of team members and partners. Strategies must take into account potential changes, and the project manager must be ready to adapt and seize every opportunity once the risk has been assessed.

In a world of change and increasing competition, the future will always contain a high degree of uncertainty that must be recognized. Confidence and success will not come simply from tradition; it must come from an ever-evolving skill base.

The mark of a good leader with a sound strategy is that the opposition cannot ascertain the tactics being deployed until it is too late. The project team must be responsive to change and ready to reflect adaptations. A unified project group that can move swiftly and surely, will be successful even against stronger opposition, if given the right direction and support. The battlegrounds may change but the central focus must be consistent.

CHAPTER 13

The attack by fire

There are five ways of attacking with fire. The first is to burn soldiers in their camp; the second is to burn stores; the third is to burn baggage trains; the fourth is to burn arsenals and magazines; the fifth is to hurl dropping fire amongst the enemy.

In order to carry out an attack, we must have means available. The material for raising fire should always be kept in readiness.

There is a proper season for making attacks with fire, and special days for starting a conflagration.

The proper season is when the weather is very dry; the special days are those when the moon is in the constellations of the Sieve, the Wall, the Wing or the Cross-bar, for these four are all days of rising wind.

The basic driver for all business is profit, and therefore, as in all business, the financial aspects of a project operation must be to give a return on investment. There is much in common between finance and fire. While fire can create heat and energy, it also has a great destructive capability. Similarly in the life of a project, the financial aspects of the business can be destructive if not taken on carefully and managed correctly.

Projects on a global platform have a greater exposure to financial risk than many other business ventures. Using these five themes, one can see similarities – for example, in the burning of people or resources without gain. There is also the exposure that can be created through using global supplies or from pre-defining selection of equipment or supplies. Most projects have contingencies or reserves that can easily be 'burnt up'.

Finally, one needs to look at the tools or weapons available to manage the whole aspect of project financial control, ranging from the project's funding options through currency, cash flow and planning, bonds and liabilities, and profit-taking. These are complex issues, but they must be considered in the overall strategic assessment of how the project is to be developed and operated.

In attacking with fire, one should be prepared to meet five possible developments:

when fire breaks out inside the enemy's camp, respond at once with an attack from without;

if there is an outbreak of fire, but the enemy's soldiers remain quiet, bide your time and do not attack;

when the force of the flames has reached its height, follow it up with an attack, if that is practicable; if not, stay where you are;

if it is possible to make an assault with fire from without, do not wait for it to break out within, but deliver your attack at a favourable moment.

Sound financial management is not something that just happens; it has to be an integrated feature of the project execution plan. If it is left to evolve, then the likelihood is that ultimately it will turn back on the project and create failure. This major issue needs to be out in the open from day one and reflected in adjustments to the project plan in order to maximize the opportunities that exist.

The measure of a successful project in general terms will not be viewed only as a 'happy customer and on-time completion'. These are certainly key aspects of overall success, but failure to deliver the projected profit will overshadow all other issues. The project manager will be expected to deliver all these external pluses, but must meet financial goals as well.

This aspect of the project requires careful planning and strategies that recognize the areas of risk and opportunities for mitigating these risks. Too often, particularly in technically-based organizations, financial issues are deemed to be secondary to the best product and satisfactory completion.

When products are to be incorporated into a project they are often developed with a focus on excellence rather than suitability. Estimations of cost are generally conservative in a competitive situation and are put at risk when their application drives towards the best possible solution.

Every project must therefore be planned to monitor cost versus performance need, and with sufficient time to manage any disparity. Many projects fail because the time allocated to evaluate and correct imbalances is too short.

At the same time, effort to make progress forces expenditure ahead of need, with a direct impact on cash flow. Since all issues within a project have a cost, this must be recognized during the planning stages.

When you start a fire, be to windward of it. Do not attack from the leeward.

When a project plan is laid down there will be many assumptions, particularly in respect of currency, which is a highly volatile aspect of the global marketplace. This can be most evident in long-term projects spanning several years. Earlier gains or expectations of gains can slowly be eroded without day-to-day activities being alerted or affected.

Currency hedging is a specialized skill and not one found in many project teams, thus the experience project manager will try to limit exposure by working in the currency of the contract. This may create false impressions where national accounting rules are in a different currency.

In the development of supply chains, the issue gets even more complex if the impacts of currency are not properly managed and visibility maintained. For example, a great contract can be made with savings, but over time currency variations can turn the savings into deficit while the assumption persists that success is secured.

The currency of a contract can be sound, but the rules of supply may drive one into a corner relative to unanticipated exchange rate changes. This is certainly a problem in some part of the world where, for example, one is paid in dollars but restricted to local purchase without any linkage to the contract currency.

There are hedging deals that can be made, but if a project is extended the security becomes a millstone. Since many projects rest on high proportions of external supply, the management of procurement within a global marketplace is crucial.

Projects that today have to trade in multiple currencies must ensure they have adequate management in place to identify both opportunities and risks as they unfold over time.

A wind that rises in the daytime lasts long, but a night breeze soon falls.

There has probably never been a project that was so well defined on its first day that it never needed some reserves in place. There will always be something that changes, or is missed. It may be that issues arise that had never been anticipated. Projects are risky ventures, and thus there must be some form of financial safety net to bridge the gap.

The difficulty in many organizations is that reserves and contingency can be viewed from outside the project as potential additional profit, while inside the project they may be viewed as just a pot to dip into when things get difficult. If a project is estimated well and proceeds exactly to plan there should never be a need to draw on reserves, but this is an unlikely situation.

When reserves are used up early in the project, the end result will almost certainly be an overall loss. The challenge for the project manager is to understand when and where to start using reserves, and in the early stages forcing the development of alternative solutions that are more cost-effective.

For the management of organizations there should be clear policies establishing that contingency is not extra profit: it is there to maintain the original projections. If not used it is a bonus.

There should also be a strategy within the project that early savings, however achieved, are placed in reserve and not simply released as profit. In the global project business there are so many potential risks that no estimate could remain competitive and be risk free. Thus whatever can be accumulated should be held, and released only after adequate risk assessments have been made. For the project team, there should be a painful interrogation when contingencies are required to be released, to prompt more innovative thinking.

> In every army, the five developments connected with fire must be known, the movements of the stars calculated, and a watch kept for the proper days.

Successful projects are ones where the whole team takes ownership of the budget and works to improve the financial out-turn. The five key drivers must be fully appreciated even though specialists may be, and should be, part of the team.

Strategies need to be adaptable as far as is possible, and changes in the market or the project plan evaluated to consider the financial implications of every adaptation that comes along. Failure to structure the project in this way will inevitably lead to waste and possibly cost overruns.

Cash flow is often viewed as the domain of accountants, but what is misunderstood is that their role is merely to report: it is the responsibility of every member of the project team to consider the cost implications of their actions. Paying early or late can also have positive or negative effects; expending cash early must make some positive contribution to the overall project.

When the strategy and planning of the project is set, then the financial benchmarks can be established. These are not simply to provide progress reporting; they may well define opportunities or risks. If changes occur in the plan these need to be analysed for their financial effects as well as impacts on the schedule. Often this is considered to be secondary and thus overlooks a key part of project measurement.

Adaptability has to extend into financial structures and control, since any change in direction or plan will have a cost effect. Changing supply sources, for example, may appear on paper to be rewarding, but in financial terms could have a negative effect, particularly where, in low-cost regions, proactive funding may be required. Efficient cash management can often add substantial benefits to the bottom line of a project.

> Hence those who use fire as an aid to the attack show intelligence; those who use water as an aid to attack gain an accession of strength.
>
> By means of water, an enemy may be intercepted, but not robbed of all his belongings.

Project funding is a major factor in all developments. It often appears that the source of capital has more influence on the selection of organizations to execute than capability. The direction and political constraints that funding can bring is also a major factor in the development of a project execution strategy. It may even at times define the alliance partners that can be mobilized. In effect, who brings the cash wins.

For many funding arrangements the spending rules can be very specific in terms of sourcing strategies. For example, the limitations placed by ECAs or government-backed projects are often linked to future local development. This in turn will dictate where and what can be procured to meet the challenges of the projects. Frequently, these rules will also demand additional controls, which can cause significant impacts on the programme.

In many cases the rules of the lenders can be influenced by environmental considerations, thus adding further demands on the project team. World Bank investments, for example, have demands related to environmental and local industrial development plans, to such a degree that often customers using WB funds have little control over the final selection process.

The financial sponsoring body has great influence, but often little detailed knowledge, which may add yet another complication. Therefore the development strategy not only has to comply with the challenges of the project, but also the many restrictions that have no material bearing on the outcome.

The rules of funding need to be very well understood and incorporated into the strategy to ensure that everyone on the team appreciates what has to be done to comply, while still meeting the objectives of the project.

Unhappy is the fate of one who tries to win his battles and succeed in his attacks without cultivating the spirit of enterprise; for the result is waste of time and general stagnation.

Hence the saying: the enlightened ruler lays his plans well ahead; the good general cultivates his resources.

Move not unless you see an advantage; use not your troops unless there is something to be gained; fight not unless the position is critical.

The control of the project costs is a crucial factor for project managers, since this is one area that can easily overrun, and where waste is hard to prevent. The main cause of this is the desire to make progress, and thus effort is expended without producing any real effect. Clearly, every task must be done to satisfy the total picture, but the sequence is often driven by availability rather than immediate need.

Manpower is a costly commodity, whether in a engineering or a construction environment. Spending profiles must always be linked to progress that is contributing in real terms. To use resources without real benefit will generally result in overruns and cash flow problems. This is sometimes difficult to manage, when key resources have to be held and kept gainfully employed. One of the key challenges for project managers is to ensure that they maintain the right levels of resources and gain effective output.

The major impact in the area of project control comes in two key areas. The first is obvious: excessive delays to the project schedule. Once significant delays start to occur the resource pattern and productivity drops, resulting in long exposure and less output. The second is less obvious, and that is the discipline the project manager needs to avoid maintaining his/her comfort zone. They retain key resources for their continued knowledge when realistically these individuals are no longer effectively contributing.

Project controls are a key function, and project managers who try to avoid this discipline will eventually pay the price.

No ruler should put troops into the field merely to gratify his own spleen; no general should fight a battle simply out of pique.

If it is to your advantage, make a forward move; if not, stay where you are.

Anger may in time change to gladness; vexation may be succeeded by content.

But a kingdom that has once been destroyed can never come again into being; nor can the dead ever be brought back to life.

Hence the enlightened ruler is heedful, and the good general full of caution. This is the way to keep a country at peace and an army intact.

The major area within projects that must be properly organized and controlled is that of profit-taking. There are many acceptable methods for calculating profitability, but when projects have failed the biggest single cause is the desire to take profits early. Many times, what should have been successful ventures have found themselves in the closing stages struggling to meet deadlines and to conserve what is left of the margin.

The project strategy must develop a clear focus for assessing appropriate milestones, where the risks can be balanced against completion. For major development projects concise guidelines should be established recognizing both profit and contingency release.

Experienced project managers will know that, in general terms, the last few percentage points of progress can take a disproportional amount of time to reach. Resources become stretched, but still the final hurdles have not been reached. It is at this point that failing to have sufficient reserves in place to fund the 'final mile' will more than likely extend the programme even further.

Many projects with great potential for success have been deemed failures in the end, not because they did not achieve their physical goals, but because the financial goals did not meet their aspirations. On the other hand, projects that perhaps were considered marginal have been deemed great successes, not from the completion point of view, but because of effective financial strategies and project management.

CHAPTER 14

The use of spies

Raising a host of a hundred thousand men and marching them great distances entails heavy loss on the people and a drain on the resources of the State. The daily expenditure will amount to a thousand ounces of silver. There will be commotion at home and abroad, and men will drop down exhausted on the highways. As many as seven hundred thousand families will be impeded in their labour.

Hostile armies may face each other for years, striving for victory which is decided in a single day. This being so, to remain in ignorance of the enemy's condition simply because one grudges the outlay of a hundred ounces of silver in honours and emoluments, is the height of inhumanity.

One who act thus is no leader of men, no present help to his sovereign, no master of victory.

Thus, what enables the wise sovereign and the good general to strike and conquer, and achieve things beyond the reach of ordinary men is foreknowledge.

In a business environment the use of the term 'spies' would be considered emotive. However, what we hope is apparent by this stage is that development of an effective strategy relies on knowledge and how it is interpreted and used. In a military context, it would be impossible not to consider the crucial importance of intelligence gathering. It should be no different in a commercial environment; however, one should acknowledge that the methods that might be acceptable to the military would not be appropriate for business.

The creation of alternative business propositions and innovative approaches requires an appropriate combination of skills, resources and information, in understanding what is being offered by others in the market, and more importantly what is really required by customers. Knowledge is power, and today the focus on knowledge management is recognizing that the intellectual capital of organizations, both in terms of acquiring that knowledge and then retaining what is created internally.

There are many routes to acquiring this knowledge and each can provide valuable insight into the power structures and cultural boundaries that must be overcome to be successful. Tapping into these various streams of data is crucial to being able to achieve goals and exploit potential, whether in buying or selling. In the complex world of projects that span the globe, such knowledge will define both winners and losers.

> Now this foreknowledge cannot be elicited from spirits; it cannot be obtained inductively from experience, nor by any deductive calculation.
> Knowledge of the enemy's dispositions can only be obtained from other men.

Very often, the basis of many decisions is founded on what we think is a situation rather than its reality. Even simple cases of assessing pricing levels there is a significant difference between ability to pay and willingness to pay. Many organizations build up data banks of historical knowledge and then use this to develop their own assessment of the marketplace. This can be valid in terms of commercial movements in the market, but the more complex implications of technical requirements are driven more often than not by internal assumptions and self-interest.

For whatever action the organization has to take, there should be some attempt to validate the approach externally. This may range through technology, time-scales, manufacturing preferences, and equipment and component supply. Too often, organizations focus on what they believe to be their most important features and capabilities, and fail to recognize the requirements of the customer.

> Hence the use of spies, of whom there are five classes: local spies; inward spies; converted spies; doomed spies; surviving spies.
> When these five kinds of spy are all at work, none can discover the secret system. This is called 'divine manipulation of the threads'. It the sovereign's most precious faculty.

Developing a strategic approach means building on the capabilities of the organization to meet the challenges of a particular market opportunity. The information network is crucial to this process, and adopting a multiple approach provides the ability to test information and validate it.

A local representative or agent is clearly one route that is commonly employed, but these must be managed carefully since in many parts of the world such agents may have many masters. They can often be helpful, but may also be a liability in areas where their interests are well known. The insider information flow is not one that should be promoted, but it would be unrealistic to ignore that they often do exist. The reverse approach can be very effective, by outwardly promoting an approach that is not the real strategy. The transmitting of false information can create opportunities, particularly during negotiations.

All these options provide a pool of information, but experience has shown that seeing for oneself aids the interpretation and refining of the application of the data collected.

It should also never be ignored that, while you may be building your network of information, so is the opposition. Therefore, in understanding the potential benefits of the various approaches to gaining information, it should also kept in mind that you have to protect against the outflow of information that could undermine your position.

> Having local spies means employing the services of the inhabitants of a district.
> Having inward spies, making use of officials of the enemy.
> Having converted spies, getting hold of the enemy's spies and using them for our own purposes.
> Having doomed spies, doing certain things openly for purposes of deception, and allowing our spies to know of them and report them to the enemy.
> Surviving spies, finally, are those who bring back news from the enemy's camp.

Developing a business network is a crucial part of building effective operations. As part of the overall process of establishing a business strategy it provides a platform of information that will be used to validate ideas. Many organizations adopt a process of replicating their standard approaches, which while providing a consistent process may often miss the changes that the market in question requires.

The network may be developed in various ways, which are not focused solely on employing external sources. Trade associations and conferences often provide valuable insights as the current drivers in the market. Much information is available in the public domain regarding government investment programmes. The supplier base is one of the most effective networking platforms, since many suppliers work with both with competitors and customers, therefore their activities and manufacturing programmes can often provide an insight into developments.

> Hence it is that which none in the whole army are more intimate relations to be maintained than with spies. None should be more liberally rewarded. In no other business should greater secrecy be preserved.

The value of reliable market information is markedly beyond the value it may take to acquire it. The principle avenues of this data will be sales-people, local representatives, agents, suppliers, networking and basic market research. Individually, these may provide only part of the overall picture, but collectively, if properly analysed, they can provide insight to the project developer that outlines both the landscape and safe courses to follow.

The cost of any campaign is high, and the risks perhaps even higher, so to proceed without collecting a truly reliable contour map of the terrain is simply to compound the risk element. In many cases the information is readily available but difficult to interpret by those who do not fully appreciate the local environment. The cost of capturing reliable market knowledge often outweighs the potential impact of not understanding the strengths and weaknesses of the opposition.

A difficult task for any organization is to evaluate the true strength and reliability of information being offered. This assessment comes partly from experience and partly from the aggregation of many inputs. As with the dissemination of any information, it is not individual elements that matter, but the bench-marking and validation from multiple sources.

The strongest of organizations may be hamstrung by not appreciating the terrain or the true decision markers in any given structure. Thus a focused, flexible group with the best intelligence can outstrip much stronger competition.

Projects in the global market must be able to draw on effective information to make maximum use of their resources and create winning strategies. The biggest danger to any organization is to assume that strength and market position alone can win the day.

> Spies cannot be usefully employed without a certain intuitive sagacity.
> They cannot be properly managed without benevolence and straight-forwardness.

> Without subtle ingenuity of mind, one cannot make certain of the truth of their reports.
> Be subtle! and use your spies for every kind of business.

There are many options and sources from which to collect information, and all of these should be recognized and exploited. Many organizations ignore what is readily available to them simply by drawing on their own supply chains. Salespeople from external organizations often deal with both your customers and those of your competitors. In their daily work they meet many people and collect information which means little to them, but which can be vital to you.

Representatives who initially support you in one market, meet and collect information from both customers and competitors in other regions. The knowledge they accrue again may be of little value directly to them, but it can offer insights into other issues; for example, the strength and investments of the competition. Where your competitors are investing their efforts can tell you much about their future plans.

Networking at neutral events can give you information about recruitment or restructuring plans that will support impressions of other strategic moves being made. Even simple information on travel plans can indicate where the next focus might be.

Understanding local cultural connections through agents can start to build power maps. For example, ethnic or education connections may provide valuable insight as to which decision-makers can really influence events.

At a more basic level, simple market research covering investment trends can heighten focus on project viability or probable success in funding needs. All information is valuable and should be analysed.

> If a secret piece of news is divulged by a spy before the time is ripe, he must be put to death together with the man to whom the secret was told.

The successful exploitation of information must be based on establishing 'early warning radar'. What is in the public domain may underpin what is really useful, but in general terms if it is readily available then it is history, and not valuable.

Strategies, to be effective, have to be able to create innovation and be adaptable to exploit change or opportunity. What everyone knows is of no advantage. Return on investment must be structured to reflect the value of the information, and thus consideration should be design to respond to results.

In many parts of the world, the culture has been based for centuries on local influence in all trading arrangements. Those who say they have insider knowledge seldom actually do. However, those who offer to share rewards are more likely to have influence or knowledge.

Information must be tested or validated in some way, and this is a challenge since often the real knowledge that can truly aid strategies to be proactive and anticipate change is well protected. Reliable information networks can make a difference between success and failure.

In developing major projects, the costs are high, and often information that simply advises against following particular investments can be very valuable. Deciding which projects to pursue is a tough task, so even negative intelligence can create value.

The skill in using this information chain is being able to distinguish the wheat from the chaff, ensuring that efforts are projected towards potential success.

> Whether the object be to crush an army, to storm a city, or to assassinate an individual, it is always necessary to begin by finding out the names of the attendants, the aides-de-camp, and door-keepers and sentries of the general in command. Our spies must be commissioned to ascertain these.

The true value of information is to allow a real focus for your efforts and an understanding of where and when to make strategic moves. We have already seen the extended capability that alliances, for example, can bring to a project operation. When looking to build and alliance it is import to ensure that those who become your partners do not in turn create an obstacle to your success.

The skills they bring may be valid but if, for example, they have a negative profile in certain arenas then these skills are of no use, since by association you endanger your own power. Establishing potential allies' track record in the marketplace may be a crucial factor in the overall viability of your proposition.

Appreciating the influences and focus of individuals is also a key factor. If you understand and appreciate the drivers of those you have to deal with, this can ensure that what you present or pursue will be accepted. Simple aspects such as their education or business background will largely define the approach you should take.

Building confidence through indirect sources can also be constructive. For example the way you are perceived by your suppliers will often create a good image among other customers. It should always be remembered that, as you collect data, so do others.

Even the style and loyalty of your staff can reflect an impression of the manner in which you approach business. Since most commercial activities are based on relationships, these key indicators will often set the standard by which you will be judged.

> The enemy's spies who have come to spy on us must be sought out, tempted with bribes, led away and comfortably housed. Thus they will become converted spies and available for our service.
>
> It is through the information brought by the converted spy that we are able to acquire and employ local and inward spies.
>
> It is owing to this information, again, that we can cause the doomed spy to carry false tidings to the enemy.
>
> Lastly, it is by his information that the surviving spy can be used on appointed occasions.

A successful strategy is largely built on surprise and adaptation. Thus, when you seek to understand the aims and approach of others, so they will be watching you, and their propositions will be affected by how they perceive your progress. It is therefore crucial that as you develop your plans, the impression that is given externally must not reflect your actual intent.

When your competitors see a certain indicator they will use this in their own strategy and aim to exploit what they see as your weak points. Therefore, misinformation or even complete silence can be very effective in establishing an advantage.

This can be as simple as avoiding suppliers during key negotiations, so as to confuse those who are watching. As in any negotiation, what is most valuable is often what is not said rather than what is voiced publicly.

The crucial element to any strategy being truly effective is that one understands what the paramount factors are for the opposition. With the knowledge of this driver, the proposition presented may initially suggest a different direction to that being taken in reality and thus gain an advantage.

Information is both a boon and a liability if one does not appreciate what is true or false. Costly strategic errors may follow if a proper analysis is not undertaken.

The end and aim of spying in all its five varieties is knowledge of the enemy; and this knowledge can only be derived, in the first instance, from the converted spy. Hence it is essential that the converted spy be treated with the utmost liberality.

Understanding how to disseminate information and how to collect it must be a focus for the project developer. Since not only will the project be looking to create the right proposition with a potential customer, it will also need to maximize the benefits of the supplier base, thus both exploiting and misdirecting the market simultaneously.

Local connections must be established in every potential market under consideration. These intelligence networks will feed the strategy and, if handled correctly, can also confuse the market. Insiders are a more difficult proposition, and may range from those who can guide on local protocol to those who may offer strategic information. It must be for each individual to decide if, and how, to use such connections.

The appropriate use of reverse information flow has to be carefully managed, since to be effective it must be credible, or it will be seen as misinformation and interpreted negatively. This will have the opposite effect to that sought, and those who divulge the information will be identified as 'dead spies' by one's opposition. The final option is the targeted approach that looks to validate all the known information by establishing key elements.

Information is power, and power can be exploited where traditional strength may on the surface appear to be weak. In this way the project strategy becomes the cornerstone of success. Without reliable information on the business landscape and the terrain, even the most well-established organization may fail.

Those who recognize the power of knowledge will create an environment for success and build strategies that have a greatly increased chance of meeting the objectives and overcoming variable market swings, anticipating change to exploit opportunity.

Of old, the rise of the Yin dynasty was due to I Chih who had served under the Hsia. Likewise, the rise of the Chou dynasty was due to Lu Ya, who had served under the Yin.

Hence it is only the enlightened ruler and the wise general who will use the highest intelligence of the army for purposes of spying and thereby they achieve great results.

Spies are the most important asset, because on them depends an army's ability to march.

In the business environment there are few circumstances where the conventional application of battle strategies would be appropriate. Today's business battles are fought around knowledge, resources and influence; and among these, the greater the level of knowledge the more opportunity to develop successful strategies and risk-management programmes. It is important not only to have the right skills and processes, but also to understand which battles to focus those assets towards.

Postscript

Sun Tzu advocated a philosophy that has many parallels today, and this book has been our attempt to couple his thinking with our own experiences. It was not intended to be the definitive work on business strategy but rather a starting point to raise awareness of the importance of strategic thinking. To be successful does not necessarily mean being the strongest, but we hope that through this work you can begin to appreciate that adaptability, skills and resourcefulness can prevail.

Understanding the five key facets as defined by Master Sun and reflecting them in the development of business strategy provides a valuable framework that aids appreciation for the multiplicity of issues that need to be considered. The objectives (the Moral Law) of the organization provide the basic drivers for any strategy. The economic environment (Heaven) influences market demand, while the political regulatory influences physical constraints on logistics (Earth) are crucial to building effective operations. Management (the Commander), as always, has a major impact on the way strategy is developed and deployed. Finally, the business processes (Method and discipline) and application forms the fifth element of successful strategy.

The global business battlefield is a complex and volatile arena for commercial ventures. It is an exciting environment filled with risk and opportunity, which must be managed to achieve the aims of the organization together with the rewards and satisfaction of individuals or the project team. The business culture globally can offer many challenges, and the commercial terrain is extremely varied, providing a trading landscape that must be mapped, evaluated and understood in order to promote success.

The development of a sound strategy has to be the fundamental building block of any execution plan. The greater the knowledge accumulated, the stronger the chances of success. This strategic viewpoint should be the cornerstone on which a project is undertaken and must guide the leadership or project manager throughout the life cycle of the programme, recognizing the four key stages of any venture (concept, contracting, construction and closure).

The initial concept is formulated around the objectives of the organization, but for the strategy to be effective it must consider the further stages of development. The contracting relationship will in many ways define how the parties will work together, since the greater the degree of integration and the longer the duration of the proposition, the more attention needs to be paid to building a contracting approach that facilitates the development.

It is also crucial when developing the contracting approach to consider the execution of the commitment. Committing to deliver a programme must reflect the ability to meet the objectives. The construction approach will probably have a major impact on the contracting process, which will be driven by a strategy that recognizes the overall plan, not to mention the implications for developing a negotiation strategy that identifies the risks and opportunities to be addressed during the contracting process.

The greater the attention to a strategic approach, the higher the probability of success. Creating a foundation of knowledge of the terrain, the strengths and weaknesses of the opposition, recognizing those tendencies in one's own organization, and combining the best possible skills and tools to deploy appropriate tactics – together with developing the right combinations of alliances to strengthen the business proposition and underpin success. The right alliances can provide valuable support in establishing appropriate influences with customers, and confidence in seeing a strong team to perform the work.

The construction phase of a programme or venture will clearly involve more detailed planning that should be developed pre-contract and then expanded in the execution stage. At the same time, the initial strategy will also expand and, one hopes, cascade down through the individual tasks and team activities. What is equally important in the execution is to identify those actions and impacts that have an effect on the close-out programme, which may in some ventures be many years off, but can be influenced by actions in the early stages.

The capability of anticipating the changing face of the market and the variety of options, which must be analysed to ensure maximum advantage at all times, is essential. This is the task of sound leadership, who can direct and focus a team to deliver not simply what is expected but also to exploit the potential of every opening that is presented, providing a flexible and reactive capability to adapt and manoeuvre within often complex and culturally varied landscapes.

The foundation of the strategic thinking process is to develop high-level approaches that recognize the needs of the end-to-end process or programme being developed. This must be conveyed effectively to those who need to implement key aspects, to allow them to build complimentary strategies supporting the overall end-game. Appreciating the integrated nature of strategy will ensure that the approach is not constrained in the long term by actions taken in the short term or at a local level.

Experience has shown that many organizations fail to recognize the integration that must underpin an effective strategy. This is reflected most commonly in the breakdown of communications between sales and execution. The impact goes further, however, where management fails to recognize the limitations of its resources and the lack of cultural commonality between the various elements of the wider organization, particularly in terms of alliance partners. Strategic development needs to encompass all stages of the programme, and consider the impact on every level of the organization.

It is important to consider the many pinch points across the organization, whether internal divisions or wider alliances partnerships, that will create strategic stress, causing a drain on the operation's capabilities, focus and energy. This will by default build weaknesses into the programme that can be exploited by the opposition. It must always be remembered that business ventures are not one-sided, and whatever careful plans you may put in place, the opposition is taking similar steps.

There is balance in every aspect of life and this extends through the business environment. The impact of creating an imbalance will be to introduce additional complications to what many would consider to be a difficult enough strategic arena. Understanding these forces, where the negativity generally emerges from failing to recognize the counter-pressures within the project and then exploiting the positive forces, is a challenge for the leadership. The more holistic the focus for developing strategy, the greater the probability that it will encompass both internal and external influences and exploit the balance for success.

The strategic thinker looks not only towards their own capability, but also balances this against the capabilities of the opposition. This is then reflected on to a background of the environment within which the contest, contract or challenge is to be played out.

Those who recognize these basic and timeless strategic needs will place themselves in a winning position long before there is ever a need to join a conflict. The organization with the best strategy has the greatest potential for success, and if the strategy is clearly the most superior it is likely that success will come through others not wishing to enter the battleground. Winning without fighting the battle is the ultimate accreditation of a successful strategy. Using the opposition's strength against themselves is the fundamental ethos of martial arts and is the foundation to every aspect of the art of war.

This is the philosophy that Sun Tzu offered over 2,500 years ago and which we, through our own experiences, believe is equally valid in the project battleground of today.

Index